History Hikes
OF THE SMOKIES

History Hikes

OF THE SMOKIES

Text by
Michal Strutin

GREAT SMOKY MOUNTAINS ASSOCIATION

© 2003, 2012 Great Smoky Mountains Association

Edited by Kent Cave and Steve Kemp

Designed by Christina Watkins

Production by Amanda Summers

Photographs courtesy of the National Park Service
  & the Duane Oliver Collection

Photographic research assistance by Joey Heath & Annette Hartigan

Cartography by University of Tennessee Cartography

Editorial Assistance by Shelly Burnell, Elise LeQuire & Cari Ramsden

Printed in the USA on recycled paper by Jones Solutions Company LLC.

5 6 7 8 9

ISBN 0-937207-40-3

Great Smoky Mountains Association is a nonprofit organization which
supports the educational, scientific, and historical programs of Great
Smoky Mountains National Park. Our publications are an educational
service intended to enhance the public's understanding and enjoyment
of the national park. If you would like to know more about our publications, memberships, and projects, please contact:

Great Smoky Mountains Association, P.O. Box 130, Gatlinburg, TN
37738 (865) 436-7318.

www.SmokiesInformation.org

To Blossom and Irving, my mother and father,
and their own remarkable histories

ACKNOWLEDGMENTS:

If it were not for Steve Kemp, editor of the Great Smoky Mountains Association, this book would not be. My thanks to a fine editor and his unflappable good humor all along the way.

This book required a great deal of research, both on my feet and poring over the voluminous archives at Great Smoky Mountains National Park. Park Librarian Annette Hartigan provided access and invaluable assistance in sorting through the archive's rich trove of historical material.

Park historians, too, gave me guidance and checked my facts, most especially Park Historian David Chapman, Kent Cave, and Tom Robbins. A number of other park personnel were helpful with advice, stories, and historical information. Jacqueline Lott was a terrific and terrifically informative hiking companion. Thanks also to George Minnigh, Walt West, Joe Ashley, Keny Slay, Steve Kloster, John Garrison, and Jody Fleming. A particular note of appreciation to Glenn Cardwell, generous with his time, and generous with his memories of his Smokies' boyhood and his many years as a park district supervisor. We saw one huge, gorgeous timber rattler on our hike together.

For providing background on Smokies history, I appreciate the help of Herschel Caldwell, Raymond Caldwell, Beatrice Monteith Douthit, Lance Holland, Eugene and Willa Lowe, David Monteith, Bob and Mary Alice Owensby, Bob Palmer, Floyd Sutton, and Helen Vance.

A number of people provided pleasant company on my hikes. Thanks to all of them: Mike Faith, Nancy Seymour, Lou Ernst Fonberg and Ignacy Fonberg, and Tom Huang, who helped me out of a rather wet spot on—or should I say in—Forney Creek.

Last but certainly not least, Michael Sinensky, my husband and primary hiking companion, provided lots of support and good Sherlock skills in helping me track the remnants of Smokies' cultural history.

CONTENTS

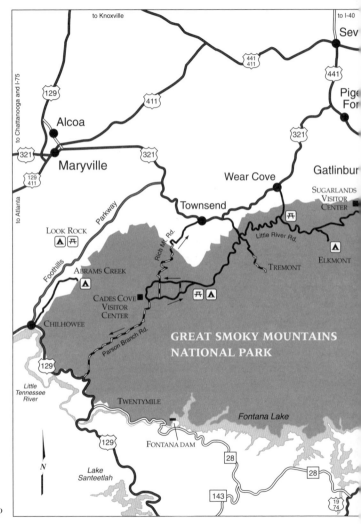

to Knoxville

to I-40

Sev

441
411

441

Pige
For

to Chattanooga and I-75

129

411

Alcoa

321

129
411

Maryville

321

321

Wear Cove

Gatlinbur

to Atlanta

Parkway

Townsend

SUGARLANDS
VISITOR
CENTER

LOOK ROCK

Little River Rd.

Foothills

Rich Mt. Rd.

TREMONT

ELKMONT

ABRAMS CREEK

CADES COVE
VISITOR
CENTER

CHILHOWEE

Parson Branch Rd.

129

GREAT SMOKY MOUNTAINS
NATIONAL PARK

Little
Tennessee
River

TWENTYMILE

Fontana Lake

N

129

FONTANA DAM

28

Lake
Santeetlah

28

143

19
74

8

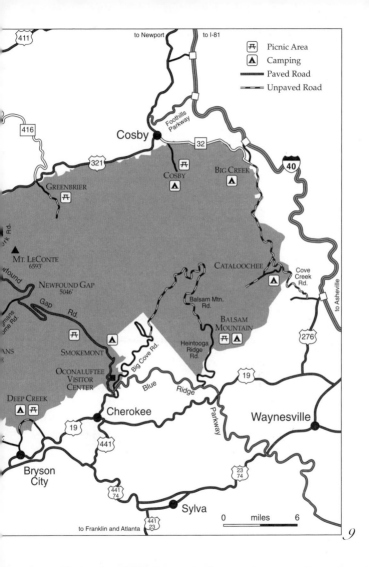

INTRODUCTION

*T*wo hundred years ago the Great Smoky Mountains looked much as they look now. Yes, the trees were bigger, the forests deeper, and the native species—from brook trout and turkey, elk and wolf, fir and chestnut—were all in more or less healthy balance then. But a long view would have looked the same.

Between 1800 and 1934, however, an arc of human history changed the look of the Smokies quickly and dramatically. Of course people traversed, hunted and fished in, even lived in the Smokies before the late 1700s. Evidence of prehistoric peoples dates to more than 10,000 years ago.

For centuries, the Cherokees farmed and lived in villages at the foot of the Smokies along rivers fed by myriad mountain streams. The mountains, too, were important to their lives. Cherokees hunted in the Smokies, fished in its streams, and gathered berries, nuts, and wild plants among the great forests. Some even lived in small settlements tucked into mountain valleys.

It was not until settlers of European descent began to arrive in the last years of the 1700s and in the early 1800s that the Smokies became a different place. As the coastal plain and piedmont filled up with farms, people wanting their own plot of land to make their own destiny had to move west, into the Appalachian Mountains, or on into the Ohio Valley.

Those who moved into the Appalachians eked out a living much as Cherokee mountain dwellers had: by subsistence farming and hunting and gathering. At the same time, the U.S. government was moving the Cherokees out, treaty by treaty. In

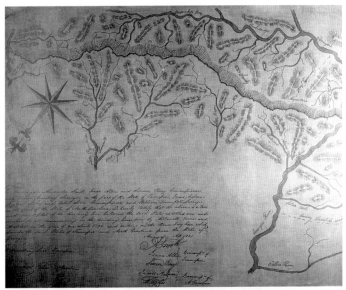

Cherokee Indian lands.

1838, orders came from Washington to move all Cherokees west to Oklahoma, initiating the infamous Trail of Tears. Only the Qualla band of Cherokees, now centered on the Cherokee Reservation in and around Cherokee, North Carolina, remained. Some attained legal land ownership; others managed to hide out, thus escaping the Trail of Tears.

The numbers of whites settling in the Smokies increased each decade of the 1800s. They cleared the stream valleys and the lower slopes of the mountains, tree by tree, rock by rock. The first generation or two built log cabins, log churches and schools, and small tub mills on the streams. Their children spread farther through the Smokies, clearing more land, building larger log homes. They went beyond subsistence, planting apple orchards and other commercial crops, raising cattle and hogs, trading and selling what they produced in general stores in their own communities as well as building roads to take their goods to larger towns.

The Steve Woody farm in Cataloochee Valley. The house and spring house stand to this day.

In the 1880s, however, this simple and often harsh life based on a modest farm economy changed irrevocably. Lumber companies, having taken what they could from the Northeast and upper Midwest, moved west...and south, into the Smokies. Mill towns sprang up to support the network of narrow-gauge railroad tracks and logging trains that began to crisscross the mountains. The idyllic look of cornfields enclosed by neat rock walls was soon overwhelmed by acres of ugly stumps and piles of brush debris as a dozen or more lumber companies reaped the wealth of the mountains—its trees.

The logging era, which lasted from the late 1880s through the 1920s, also brought changes in the mountain economy. Farmers who obtained a bit of money by selling surplus produce at market began supplementing their income by working part of the year as loggers. With more cash came store-bought clothes, kerosene lamps, and many other amenities via "wish books," such as the Sears and Roebuck catalog, and the general stores that had popped up in each mountain community. Lumber mills and cash allowed mountain dwellers to build new frame houses that might include two stories, gables, broad porches, hardwood floors, and paneled walls. Along with architectural amenities came a parallel blossoming of the social structure. From a collection of scattered folk in rough cabins rose functioning communities, with schools and churches, post offices and stores, barbershops and social halls.

The logging era and the sheer numbers of people living in this fragile mountain environment eventually devastated the Smokies. At the same time, vacationers began discovering the mountains as a get-away for fishing, hiking, and scenery. Local business interests saw the economic value in preserving the Smokies. Others saw the inherent value in preserving the Smokies. The national park movement grew. In 1934, this movement culminated when Congress established Great Smoky Mountains National Park.

The Depression coincided with the creation of the park. The Civilian Conservation Corps (CCC), created to provide jobs during that grim period, constructed 22 camps throughout the Smokies. The young men who lived in these camps built trails, bridges, fire towers, roads, and other structures for the newly established park.

With the coming of the park came the end of an incredibly rich, if short, historical era in the Smokies. The logging companies had taken what they could and moved on. The move was far more painful for the farmers who had put down a few generations of roots. All were paid for their land and houses. Some were allowed to live out their lives in the Smokies. The rest moved on, many only a few miles beyond park borders.

WHAT HISTORICAL SITES REMAIN

The National Park Service has reinvigorated and continues to preserve the natural history of the Smokies, from plants and animals to streams and geological formations. As the park's human history fades, however, park visitors have become increasingly interested in the people who settled here and how they lived. Many, too, find the logging era fascinating, with its sawmills and mill towns, its tough little Shay engines, squealing wheels switchbacking down impossible pitches, and flatcars full of logs.

Great Smoky Mountains National Park preserves more than 100 historical structures, including one of the largest collections of historical log buildings in the East. In addition, the park contains over 200 cemeteries, from large fenced areas with hundreds of graves to rough places with just a handful of graves.

The park's historic buildings include a representative selection of log homes as well as schools, churches, mills, barns, and other characteristic structures of settler life in the Smokies. In the mid-1900s, frame houses did not seem historical—the majority of Americans lived in similar dwellings—so most were removed from the park. Missing, too, are representative stores and post offices that formed the center of community life. Yet, a sense of the Smokies human history remains.

The national park's most concentrated collections of historic structures can be found in Cades Cove, Cataloochee, the Mountain Farm Museum near the Oconaluftee Visitor Center, and along Roaring Fork Motor Nature Trail. An even better way to get a feel for mountain life in the Smokies is to walk the history-rich trails that traverse every sector of the park.

The park's human history reveals itself along its trails, and this guide puts these cabins, schoolhouses, mills, and ruins into context. In addition to explaining each historical remnant, *History Hikes of the Smokies* endeavors to present the broader picture of each community found along the park's historical trails.

Many of the historical trails wind along the lower slopes of the mountains because this is where most settlers lived. Fire lookouts and logging-era camps lie high in the mountains, and so do the trails that reveal this type of history. The national park's 20 most historically evocative trails provide a rich taste of the past. They include the following:

Little Cataloochee Trail, with its church, log homes, and applehouse, is a relatively easy step into a wealth of history.

Grapeyard Ridge Trail dips into a lovely little valley once filled with farms, then rises to the headwaters of Injun Creek with its astonishing sight: a wrecked engine.

Forney Creek Trail winds down from Clingmans Dome, a journey through the Smokies logging and railroad past.

Old Sugarlands provides a picture of CCC life in the park.

Mount Cammerer is capped by a handsome and evocative historical fire lookout.

Hazel Creek Trail affords a look at Proctor, the ultimate mill town, which still retains the ruins of a huge old sawmill, as well as many other historical sights.

Jakes Creek Trail shows off the Avent Cabin, the summer home of a nationally known artist.

Old Settlers Trail is so full of cabins, barns, rock walls, and chimneys it is impossible to forget that this was once one of the most populated part of the Smokies.

HOW TO SEE WHAT REMAINS

Discovering the past in the Smokies by means of the park's historical trails can be an incredibly exciting exercise in discovery. Once you understand how early settlers lived, you learn where to look for, say, the springhouse or the family cemetery. Part of the pleasure is using Sherlock Holmes detective sense to spy out Smokies history.

A good imagination is a great companion on history hikes. Let your eyes learn to push back the forests so that you can imagine the sunny corn and potato fields enclosed by rock walls; the dog-trot cabin decorated with daffodils and rose-bushes; mills full of cornmeal, flour, and energy; lumberyards full of stacked boards; CCC camps with barracks, neat path-

ways, and parade grounds where young men marched and
played baseball.

A FEW TIPS:

Because the Smokies are among the most luxuriant
forests on earth, foliage can obscure the less obvious historic
remains. Often the best time to hike historical trails is between
late autumn and early spring, when trees, shrubs, and vines
have lost their leaves, exposing low rock walls, foundations,
and other subtle remnants.

Give yourself plenty of time to observe historical remains.
Exploring a historical site adds time—and pleasure—to any hike.

Snakes sometimes curl up in rock wall crevices; just be
aware of their preferences when approaching such structures.
During cooler times of year snakes hibernate, so are of little
concern.

It is best to hike with a companion. A twisted ankle is a
problem when hiking with a companion, but a dangerous situation when hiking alone.

Take only photographs; leave only footprints. Everything
within the national park, from rocks, plants, and animals to
historical remains, is protected by law. Please do not leave litter; it degrades the park and the experience of other visitors.

Wear adequate footwear and bring along a hat for protection against sun or cold. Because weather in the Smokies is so
variable, it is a good idea to carry rain gear and dress in layers.

❦ Always carry plenty of water, and remember to drink it.

❦ If camping, be sure to observe all regulations, including obtaining the mandatory permit and hanging your food to avoid tempting bears. Please remember to pack out everything you packed in.

❦ Some hikes are best done using two-car shuttles. Another option is to leave your car at the end of the trail and hire a taxi to drop you off at the trailhead. The Gatlinburg Chamber of Commerce (800-568-4748; 865-436-4178) and the Swain County Chamber of Commerce (800-867-9246; 828-488-3681) can provide numbers of companies that provide such services.

❦ A wealth of information is available at Great Smoky Mountain National Park's websites: www.nps.gov/grsm and www.SmokiesStore.org

❦ The national park's general telephone number is 865-436-1200; backcountry planning is 865-436-1297; and backcountry reservations is 865-436-1231.

The people who settled the Smokies were stalwart folk. Their motto was "make do or do without." Hiking through history on trails in Great Smoky Mountains National Park provides a glimpse of their lives, and how they changed over time. To the end, Smokies residents displayed the kind of resourcefulness and self-reliance that is bred in the bone.

History Hikes

OF THE SMOKIES

NORTH CAROLINA

BONE VALLEY TRAIL

DIRECTIONS: The easiest access to Bone Valley via Lakeshore and Hazel Creek trails is by boat. From the town of Cherokee, NC, travel west on U.S. 74. Then take Route 28 west, winding along the south side of Fontana Lake toward Fontana Village. Or, from the western edge of the park, take the western Foothills Parkway to Routes 129 and 28 and travel east to Fontana Village.

Two miles east of Fontana Village, take the spur road north. Almost immediately the road will fork. Take the right fork to the Fontana Village Marina (the left fork goes to Fontana Dam). To arrange boat transportation, call the Fontana Village Marina at 800-849-2258. Shuttle service and boat rentals are available year-round. The boat ride across Fontana Lake takes about 30 minutes.

LENGTH: 1.8 miles one way. This hike goes from the Bone Valley trailhead, where it meets Hazel Creek Trail, to the trail's end and back. Although the Bone Valley hike is short—only 1.8 miles, one way—getting there is long. Starting from the Fontana Lake boat dock near Campsite 86, it is 6.0 miles, one way, to reach the Bone Valley trailhead via Lakeshore and Hazel Creek trails. (From dock to Campsite 86, 0.5 mile on Lakeshore Trail. From Campsite 86 you are on Hazel Creek Trail.) Round-trip it's 15.6 miles, from the dock to the end of Bone Valley Trail and back.

Because the trail is broad and the grade gentle, it can be done in a day, with boat transport. Those who prefer to take more time to explore both Bone Valley and the Hazel Creek watershed can obtain a permit to camp at one of the Lakeshore or Hazel Creek trail campsites.

PHYSICAL PROFILE: Once a roadbed, the Bone Valley Trail is broad until the last few hundred feet. The trail crosses Bone Valley Creek four times and Mill Creek once. Although it can run hip high—and dangerously fast—during and after wet weather, Bone Valley Creek is usually knee-deep. It can be even shallower in dry weather.

CULTURAL PROFILE: Part of the historically populous Hazel Creek community, Bone Valley now exhibits one of the most picturesque and the most remote of the log cabins maintained by the park. Nearby are a cemetery and the remains of the Kress hunting lodge.

*B*one Valley was part of the larger Hazel Creek community, as were all the homes and farms that dotted tributaries of Hazel Creek. (For an overview of the Hazel Creek community and its rich history, see Hazel Creek Trail.) In fact, the Bone Valley community actually starts on the Hazel Creek Trail, where two mainstay institutions were located, the church and the school.

0.0 Near Campsite 83, just before the junction of Bone Valley Trail with Hazel Creek Trail, stood the Bone Valley Baptist Church. Directly across from the church, a path leads up to Bone Valley Cemetery. The cemetery's 82 graves make it the second largest in the Hazel Creek area. (See Hazel Creek Trail for both Bone Valley church and cemetery.)

The knoll that overlooks Campsite 83 held both the first

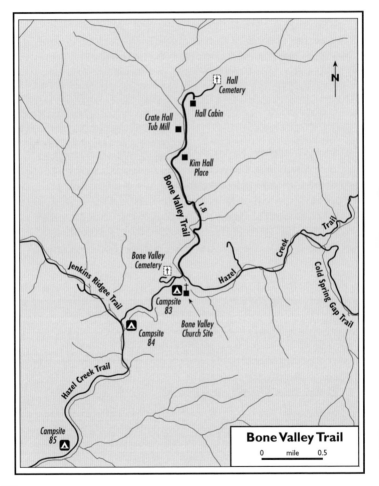

Hall Cemetery

Crate Hall
Tub Mill

Hall Cabin

Kim Hall
Place

Bone Valley Trail

1.8

Jenkins Ridgee Trail

Bone Valley
Cemetery

Hazel

Creek

Trail

Cold Spring Gap Trail

Campsite
83

Bone Valley
Church Site

Campsite
84

Hazel Creek Trail

Campsite
85

N

Bone Valley Trail

0   mile   0.5

and second Bone Valley churches. The first church was built around 1880. Like most early churches in the Smokies, it was a one-room log building that also served as a schoolhouse.

Joshua Calhoun, one of Hazel Creek's earliest and most influential settlers, organized building of school and church. He farmed for a living, but served as an itinerant preacher at the Bone Valley church and as far away as Cades Cove.

Calhoun Place, 1938.

In those days, it was a rarity for mountain communities to see an officially trained preacher. When towns such as Bryson City, Waynesville, and Newport became more established, they became centers from which ordained ministers went into the mountains, riding the circuit of communities from Sunday to Sunday.

Until professionals became more common, mountain preachers were usually accomplished, or simply enthusiastic, lay leaders who rose to the calling. And call they did. Reverend George Britt, who grew up in the Hazel Creek community, remembered visiting lay preachers praying loudly enough to be heard great distances.

When Ritter Lumber came into Hazel Creek in 1902, the company transformed the area with railroads, the Ritter-built town of Proctor, a full-time doctor, and many other improvements. Bone Valley benefited, too. About 1914, the old dual-duty log church and school was torn down to make way for a frame church with store-bought pews and a pump organ.

The foundations of this church are still visible on the knoll above Campsite 83.

Mary Walker Proctor was born in 1904 at the mouth of Bone Valley where it meets Hazel Creek. She wrote in the North Shore Historical Society Newsletter that her father, John Walker, who helped build the town of Proctor, also built the new church. He made coffins for the deceased, and Mary's mother, Ellen Parton Walker, lined the caskets with cambric or sateen. They may have done so for John Newman, a Civil War veteran who was the first person buried in Bone Valley Cemetery.

Horace Kephart was an avid hunter and outdoorsman. Photo circa 1907.

When the National Park Service started buying land for the park, much of Bone Valley—in fact, much of Hazel Creek—was owned by Jack Coburn. In the 1890s, Coburn had come from the lumber camps of Michigan to work for Taylor and Crate, the first logging company on Hazel Creek. He stayed and eventually became important in Ritter Lumber, buying and selling land, amassing hundreds of acres in the process. He built his home at what is now Campsite 83 and, somewhere beneath the site, his horse Button is buried.

Coburn also befriended Horace Kephart, who had fled family and a settled academic life in St. Louis to live on Hazel Creek. Kephart became the first chronicler of Hazel Creek and a popular chronicler of the southern Appalachians in general. Coburn had a skill that intrigued Kephart. "Pugilism," Kephart wrote in his book, *Our Southern Highlanders,* "was an unknown art in the mountains until Jack introduced it." Kephart may have remembered Coburn as a pugilist (boxer), but the land records of that time reveal an affluent mountain businessman.

In the 1880s, before Coburn arrived, the Laney family lived in the first house up Bone Valley. After the Civil War, three Laney brothers, war veterans all, moved to Hazel Creek. Pete and Nan Laney built a cabin on Sugar Fork. (For more on Pete and Nan Laney, see the Bone Valley Cemetery stop on Hazel Creek Trail.)

James and Ruthy Jane Laney settled at the mouth of Bone Valley and there raised seven children. In 1895, James Laney was ordained in the original Bone Valley Baptist Church. For years, when visiting preachers came to Bone Valley, they stayed with the Laneys.

The trail was once a road into Bone Valley and still serves National Park Service staff when they drive up to Hall Cabin to perform regular maintenance on this remote historical structure. The trail also approximates Ritter's spur railroad line up Bone Valley from the days when narrow-gauge Shay engines hauled flatcars loaded with big logs.

The grade is gentle, the edges of the trail grassy, and occasional pink roses reveal that people lived along here, planting roses and other shrubs that gave them pleasure. But, just when you are getting comfortable, this pleasant, rural walk is punctuated by a stream crossing.

0.5 First creek crossing. Just before the first creek crossing, the remains of a road lead upward on the right to what was once an old homesite, now reclaimed by the forest. Bone Valley Creek is about 15 feet wide at this and the subsequent three crossings. Usually the water is near knee-deep. In wet weather it can run a foot or more higher than that. And in dry weather it may be little more than ankle-deep.

0.7 Second creek crossing.

1.2 Third creek crossing. During Horace Kephart's day, Kim Hall's place and a store stood near the third crossing. Small stores came and went, and changed hands, as did homes and property. Although the Hall and Laney families are especially associated with Bone Valley, life in the mountains was not as settled as the stones of history would sometimes have us believe. Especially during the logging era, people moved with the job.

The first logging company in the valley was Taylor and Crate, who came in the 1890s to log selectively: tuliptree (yellow poplar), cucumber tree, and ash. Homes and farms lined Bone Valley, and one woman remembered seeing logs snaked past her family's place by teams and drivers.

Farther up, toward the head of Bone Valley, where the Hall cabin still stands, Taylor and Crate built a splash dam. They let a head of water build up behind the dam, then, coordinating the timing with other splash dams on Hazel Creek, they opened the broad wooden gates in the middle of the dam. Water surged out with a roar, sweeping huge logs down to the Little Tennessee River, where they would be rounded up in giant log booms and floated downriver to mills in Chattanooga.

W.C. Heiser of Michigan and Mountain Timber Company followed, but it was Ritter Lumber, with its railroad efficiency that really cut these forests. Ritter came in 1902, taking eight years to prepare its operations, building a railroad, mills, and the town of Proctor. The company began cutting in 1910 and, by the 1920s, had concentrated its operations on Bone Valley and Sugar Fork. It took mostly chestnut, but also high-quality maple and northern red oak. Hemlock was shipped to Champion Fibre Company's mill at Canton to be pulped.

Despite Taylor and Crate's search for the best tuliptrees, a few giants remained in Ritter's time. It is said that the largest tuliptree taken from the Hazel Creek area was cut in 1919 in Bone Valley's Horse Cove, a cove or two above the Hall place. In his book *Hazel Creek From Then Till Now,* Duane Oliver says, "the tree was six or seven feet in diameter, 190 feet high, and 54 feet to the first limb."

It took four men pulling a ten-foot saw, alternately in teams of two, 15 hours to cut the enormous tree, which was then cut into logs and dragged to the railroad by teams of Percheron horses. This one tree produced 18,000 board feet of lumber, some boards 54 inches wide.

Although Ritter left in 1928, that was not the end of logging in Bone Valley. Stikeleather bought up much of Ritter's land and logged the upper portions of Hazel Creek and Bone Valley for a few years.

1.4 Mill Creek crossing. About half as wide as Bone Valley Creek, Mill Creek comes in from the left. Just a few yards upstream, an open area along Mill Creek and a pile of stones on the creek bank hint at the remains of Crate Hall's tub mill, which once stood here.

Tub mills dotted the banks of streams throughout the Smokies; Bone Valley was no different. Tub mills were usually rough log structures no bigger than an outhouse, set at the side of a creek, often with two feet set in the creek. The grindstones, two to three feet in diameter, were driven by a horizontal water wheel about the size of a large washtub. They could grind about a bushel of corn a day, just enough to serve a family and its immediate neighbors.

The restored Hall cabin in Bone Valley in 1944.

1.6 Fourth creek crossing. Just before this last crossing of Bone Valley Creek, look for earth berms paralleling the road on the left. These are probably from the days of road-building in the late 1920s and 1930s, when cars first came into Hazel Creek and Bone Valley. Today, beavers have been busy behind the berms.

A series of ponds, canals, and beaver dams are open to the sun. This level area has been open to the sun since the late 1800s, when the Halls cleared the land for fields.

1.8 Hall cabin. The broad trail tapers to a path. A narrow boardwalk passes a copse of trees before ending at a small clearing where the historical Hall cabin stands. Nearby lie the remains of Kress lodge. Just up the hill, Hall Cemetery holds the graves of the people who once lived here.

One of the most pleasant places in the Smokies, the Hall cabin has a view of Locust Ridge and, beyond, Welch Ridge. Before the cabin spreads a grassy "front yard" full of daisies, blue sage, and other wildflowers. In Crate and Polly Hall's day more of the area surrounding the cabin was cleared. A vegetable garden would have been nearby, full of sweet potatoes, beans, and other vegetables. Apple trees probably shaded some part of the yard.

This, the second of the Halls' cabins, is about 16′ x 22′, with a covered front porch running the length of the building. It has been restored, so the stone supports are relatively new, and it is missing the fireplace and chimney that were once a central feature of any mountain home. A staircase leading up to the loft divides the bottom room in two. In smaller cabins, such as the Halls' first home, a simple ladder would have led to the loft where children slept. The broad siding is notched for half dovetails at the corners, somewhat easier to fit than full dovetail notching. And the cracks between the timbers would have been chinked with mud.

About 1877 Jesse Craten ("Crate") Hall, his wife Mary

("Polly") Talitha Dills, and their four young children moved here from Jackson County, North Carolina. They brought everything they had with them in a horse-drawn sled. In mountains where roads were rough to nonexistent, sleds often made better transport than wheeled wagons.

In his book, Duane Oliver lists the things the Halls brought with them: axe, plowshare, hoe blades (handles would be cut from wood on site), seed corn, Dutch oven, skillet, frying pan, clothing, blankets, quilts, bed ticks (filled first with dry grass, later with shucks from their first corn harvest), pothooks, broadax and froe, plates, cups, forks, knives, spoons—all of tin. A small spinning wheel and a large pot, which was used for cooking, washing clothes, soap-making, and hog-butchering, rounded out the necessities.

The Halls built their first cabin, cleared land, and planted fields. In summer, they ran hogs and cattle on the grassy balds. They put together a solid life and, in 1892, when their first cabin became too small, built another with the help of their neighbors. When they first moved to Bone Valley, their closest neighbors were six miles away, but the intervening years had brought more people, and the valley filled up with other families.

During the Ritter logging era, Bone Valley was an open place full of fields and homes belonging to Halls, Laneys, Woodards, and others. Families who came for logging jobs lived here, too. There were enough children in Bone Valley for Ritter to bring in a temporary school building.

The company off-loaded the school next to the spur line of railroad tracks that ran up Bone Valley. The school was one of the red boxcar homes that lumber companies in the Smokies used as portable housing for loggers. The houses were rectangles that fit on a flatcar and could be hoisted on and off, depending on where the lumber company was logging.

For the Bone Valley school, Ritter fitted one of these "boxcars" with desks. In those days, schoolteachers were supported by subscription. So Ritter deducted $2.50 each month from the paychecks of the families who sent their children to the Bone Valley school.

Kress Lodge in 1944. It stood adjacent to the Hall cabin and was a wilderness haven for hunters and anglers.

Kress Lodge. Less than a stone's throw from the Hall cabin, the ruins of Kress lodge lie hidden among the trees. If you are facing the cabin steps, walk right (southeast) about 20 feet to the edge of the trees. If the grass is high, it is not a bad idea to swing a stick through the grass as you enter, to make sure you and a snake do not surprise each other. A small path enters the young trees and you will see the 25-foot-high chimney of the Kress lodge.

The chimney was centered in the middle of the lodge, with fireplaces on either side. A two-foot-high foundation, now covered with moss, outlines the dimensions of the building, which was about 50 feet long and about half that in width.

In the early 1900s, after Ritter opened up Hazel Creek to the larger world and Horace Kephart and other writers intrigued readers with stories about this Eden in the mountains, people began filtering in to the Smokies to vacation. Hazel Creek, especially, became known for good fishing. In the 1920s, J.H. Kress of New York, who gained a fortune from his chain of five-and-dime stores, built a luxurious hunting and fishing lodge. In addition, they leased the Hall cabin as a guest lodge. In the 1960s, a fire demolished the Kress lodge—all but the stonework.

Hall Cemetery. At the back of the Hall cabin, near the hitching post, a path tracks up the hill 0.2 mile to Hall Cemetery. Crested dwarf iris and wild geraniums carpet a forest floor canopied by maples, oaks, and tuliptrees.

The cemetery holds at least 18 graves, all Halls or Hall relatives. The tallest gravestone belongs to Craten Hall, the first of the family to settle in Bone Valley:

1849-1903
"Although he sleeps, his memory doth live.
Cheering comfort to his mourners give."

The Bone Valley trail ends at the Hall cabin, but not Bone Valley history. At the end of the 1800s, Crate Hall built a herders cabin atop the grassy balds where many Smokies farmers grazed their cattle in summer. After fattening the cattle, herders drove them down to a railhead and, from there, to eastern markets.

Granville Calhoun, a son of Joshua Calhoun, one of Bone Valley's first settlers, was one of those multi-talented, hard-working individuals who rose to prominence in Hazel Creek. At one point, he was asked to do an official census of the Hazel Creek population. By asking around, he even did a rough survey of cattle-grazing on the balds. Oliver says Calhoun estimated that, in the summer of 1918, 1,600 cattle grazed on the balds of the Smokies.

Bone Valley got its name from a cattle-grazing incident that occurred in 1888, a year of bad snowstorms. Some farmer had taken his herd toward the balds early in spring—a little too early. The cattle were caught in an unexpected snowstorm and froze to death. For years their bleaching bones were found scattered over the head of what became known as Bone Valley.

Just beyond Horse Cove, but on the other side of the creek, Little John Cable had a cabin. This was around 1907, when Horace Kephart spent time with Cable, who was known as one of the best bear hunters in the Smokies. Little John was a grandson of Samuel Cable, who came into Hazel Creek from Cades Cove around 1835, another of the creek's first settlers.

"Little" John—so called to distinguish him from his father, John senior—was respected in the Hazel Creek community. With his rifle, which he crafted himself, and his dogs, Little

John Cable helped farmers clear out bears, mountain lions, and wolves that threatened livestock, crops, and sometimes farm families. He also liked bear hunting for pleasure.

Kephart went out with Cable, Granville Calhoun, and a couple of others one dreadfully cold day. For the most part, Kephart saw what he wanted to see in the mountains—mainly a moonshining, ripsnorting, out-of-bounds way of life. He paid scant attention to community and the almost unrelieved hard work required to keep a family together in the mountains. But Kephart's description of this particular bear hunt is dramatic, visceral, and probably fairly accurate. The group of hunters started from Little John's cabin up Bone Valley:

"A powerful gust struck the cabin," Kephart wrote in *Our Southern Highlanders.* "...a great roaring surged up from the gulf of Defeat, from Desolation, and from the other forks of Bone Valley—clamor of ten thousand trees struggling with the blast."

He was speaking of two streams near the headwaters of Bone Creek where, in the 1880s, hunters met bad weather and worse luck, so named the creeks after their experience. After their unsuccessful day bear hunting in upper Bone Valley, Kephart quotes Little John:

"The pup Coaly chased off atter a wildcat," blurted John. "We held the old dogs together and let him rip. Then Dred started a deer. It was that old buck that everybody's shot at, and missed, this three year back. I'd believe he's a hant if 't wasn't for his tracks—they're the biggest I ever seen. He must weigh two hunderd and fifty. But he's a foxy cuss. Tuk right down the bed o' Desolation, up the left prong of Roaring Fork, right through the Devil's Race-path (how a deer can git through thar I don't see!), crossed at the Meadow Gap, went down Eagle Creek, and by now he's in the Little Tennessee. That buck, shorely to God, has wings!"

Despite losing a bear and following a buck on a wild goose chase, Kephart said Little John ate a small slice of fried pork, a chunk of johnny-cake, drank a pint of coffee, and was ready to go again.

The vales and balds above Bone Valley Trail were made for stories. It seems that one day, while taking his cattle up on one of the balds, Granville Calhoun did see a flying deer. It was such an astonishing sight that it took Calhoun a while to realize that what he saw was a large eagle carrying a half-grown deer in its claws. Whether or not such a feat is aerodynamically possible, it makes a good tale.

In a found-and-lost situation in the 1920s, Fidelia "Dilly" Welch may have found a vein of silver up Bone Valley. But Dilly kept the location to himself and died before he had a chance to pass along the information to his son.

BOOGERMAN TRAIL

DIRECTIONS: From Interstate 40, take Exit 20 (U.S. 276) and, almost immediately, turn right onto Cove Creek Road, which leads 10 miles over Cove Creek Gap and down into the national park. About three of these miles are on gravel road.

Where the paved park road begins, follow it into Cataloochee Valley, and pass the large campground on the left. Just beyond the campground, on the same side of the road, and just before the ranger station, lies Caldwell Fork trailhead. Because Boogerman Trail is a semicircular loop off Caldwell Fork Trail, the hike goes in and out on Caldwell Fork Trail.

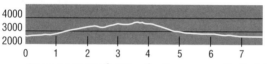

LENGTH: 7.7 miles. Caldwell Fork Trail to Boogerman Trail, 0.8 mile; Boogerman Trail, 4.1 miles; return to trailhead via Caldwell Fork Trail, 2.8 miles.

PHYSICAL PROFILE: Boogerman Trail rises from Caldwell Fork to Sag Gap with a couple of easy rock-hops over streams. Then it descends to Caldwell Fork and its many stream crossings via footlogs on the return. Much of the land traversed by Boogerman Trail is old-growth forest with many stately trees.

CULTURAL PROFILE: "Boogerman" Robert Palmer and only a few others lived in this section of Cataloochee, a forest primeval protected by Palmer. Rock walls, old fields, and remnant homesites are the primary signs of human habitation.

Caldwell Fork Trail.

0.0 Begin by crossing Cataloochee Creek near its junction with Caldwell Fork. The 25-foot-long railed bridge may be the longest footlog in the park. The trail then parallels Caldwell Fork for 0.8 mile to the Boogerman trailhead. Caldwell Fork was one of the three large settlements in Cataloochee Valley. The other two were Big Cataloochee Valley itself, now bisected by the park road, and Little Cataloochee, which lies over Noland Mountain off Pretty Hollow Gap Trail.

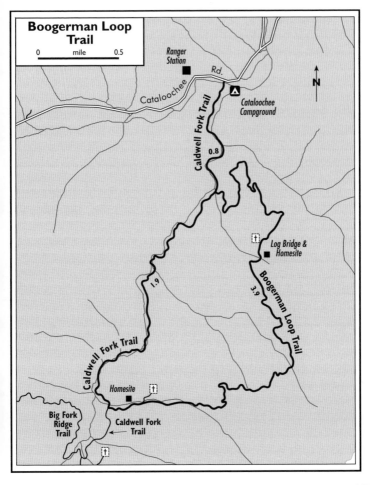

Boogerman Loop Trail

0   mile   0.5

Ranger Station

Cataloochee Rd.

Caldwell Fork Trail

Cataloochee Campground

N

0.8

Log Bridge & Homesite

1.9

Boogerman Loop Trail

3.9

Caldwell Fork Trail

Homesite

Big Fork Ridge Trail

Caldwell Fork Trail

37

This beginning section of Caldwell Fork, however, was not the populated area. The broad trail is often muddy and choppy from horse traffic, and footlogs cross the stream a number of times before reaching the Boogerman Trail. The first 0.8 mile stays low and fairly level along Caldwell Fork, winding between thick patches of dog-hobble under the shade of tall hemlocks.

Boogerman Trail junction.
0.8/0.0 From Caldwell Fork Trail, Boogerman Trail veers off to the left where a yellow birch marks the entry to the trail. Climbing gently but steadily up the flank of Den Ridge, the hikers-only trail passes rhododendron, mountain laurel, and hemlock. As the trail climbs higher and the sun reaches through, oaks, especially northern red oaks, mix with white pine and Fraser magnolia. Rectangular holes in a large downed log and raucous birdcalls signal the presence of Pileated Woodpeckers, birds that flourish in old-growth forests.

The forest is tall and thick through this first mile or so of Boogerman Trail, but ahead lie even larger trees. For this we have "Boogerman" Robert Palmer to thank. More than 250 acres of this land was his. Robert Palmer was a character, like his brother "Turkey" George, but definitely less gregarious. He was sitting at a desk on his first day at school and, when the teacher asked him his name, the shy boy buried his head in his arms. Flustered, he blurted out, "Boogerman." "Blind" Sam Sutton told the story another way. He said that when asked in school what he wanted to be, Robert Palmer said, "the Boogerman."

Either way, the name was somewhat self-fulfilling. The

Boogerman was known as a loner who chose to live at a remove from the already rather isolated Cataloochee community. His full beard and gruff appearance scared children—he did not mind fitting the role of boogerman.

Palmer had no use for government or for the large logging company that tried to buy his land. Logging companies bought and cut much of the Smokies between the late 1800s and early 1900s, but Palmer was a holdout. He did not even allow neighbors to cut wood from his property. We are the fortunate beneficiaries of his stubbornness. The old-

In 1935 this footbridge spanned Palmer Creek in the vicinity of Turkey George's home.

growth big trees along the trail give us a sense of what the park looked like when Robert Palmer's grandfather first came to Cataloochee. Thank you, Boogerman.

Rounding a bend, the trail passes a huge, 50-foot sourwood, about as big as these understory trees get. Rattlesnake-plantain and squawroot grow near the tree's feet. Squawroot, whose pale protuberances grow in clumps directly from the earth, is a parasite, drawing nourishment from the roots of other plants, especially oaks, which tower above.

1.6 Boogerman Robert Palmer's homesite. A low, log bridge crosses Palmer Branch just before the trail reaches a broad flat area that was once the Boogerman's place. Nearby stands a double-trunked tuliptree shaped like a giant wishbone. What were once sunny fields are now full of young trees. Small pines grow in the sun and small hemlocks grow near the former field's shady edges. Striped maples with thin trunks and wintergreen grow here, too.

Records show that Palmer owned a three-room log house, a two-room log house, a four-stall barn, an apple house, and a springhouse. But, according to survey maps, his home and outbuildings were set back from this point.

The Boogerman's grandfather, George Palmer, was the first of the family to enter Cataloochee. In 1848, Palmer moved his family to isolated Cataloochee Valley in an effort to live down an embarrassing gambling incident. While drunk, he had gambled away his farm. George's efforts at a fresh start paid off. He and his sons George Lafayette (Fayte) and Jesse farmed, prospered, and became civic leaders in Cataloochee Township.

Although stories highlight characters in the Palmer family tree, such as Turkey George (see Little Cataloochee Trail) and the Boogerman, most of the Palmers were simply hard-working farmers, stalwarts of Cataloochee Valley. One, William Palmer, served as high sheriff of Haywood County for four terms. The Elizabeth Powers and Mark Hannah book *Little Cataloochee: Lost Settlement of the Smokies* describes a typical day in the life of Flora Palmer, Robert and George's sister.

She milked the cows, hoed corn, helped her siblings find the lead cow in the evening, cooked, carried spring water, chopped stove wood, pulled and tied fodder, cut tops, made hay stacks, helped make molasses, helped make breakfast, washed dishes, churned butter, and washed clothes before going to school. Some evenings she carded and spun wool while her mother wove or quilted.

Her uncle Fayte Palmer's house now serves as a museum near the beginning of the paved park road. And each summer Palmer Chapel, whose land was donated by Mary Ann Palmer in 1898, becomes the focal point for the Cataloochee Reunion. Descendants of the valley's original inhabitants come from near and far for chapel services and festive covered-dish picnics on the lawn beside the chapel.

Although Boogerman Palmer was somewhat eccentric, he too had to work. The flat area that spreads back from the trail was likely a farm field, full of corn and garden vegetables. Probably some of Palmer's corn crop was turned into moonshine because the Boogerman was known to like his liquor. Local experts have estimated that up to 95 percent of households in Cataloochee made their own liquor, which they used as medicine, for imbibing, and as a critical source of cash. It was sometimes called "saddlebag" because that is how they transported it out of the valley to distribution centers in Waynesville and other towns.

Behind Boogerman Palmer's place, between it and Caldwell Fork Trail, Harrison and Jane Sutton had a small farm where they raised four or five children. When the park was established, the Suttons moved just outside its boundaries, to Cove Creek.

Members of the Sutton family originally lived on the other side of Mount Sterling Gap, in the Cosby, Tennessee, area. But they migrated over to Cataloochee via the Cataloochee Turnpike, one of the first roads connecting Tennessee and

North Carolina in what is now the national park.

Just beyond the first clearing, another clearing on the right has been colonized by tuliptrees, those fast-growing poker-straight trees that provided most of the lumber in the Smokies. Near a black cherry, also on the right side of the trail, lies a broad, rusted metal wheel. In the late 1920s, the Boogerman himself cut a trail into this cove with hand tools. It was not as level as the present park trail, yet somehow he managed to bring a wagon or some other type of wheeled vehicle back to his property.

2.0-3.2 From the level terrain around the Boogerman's homestead, the trail rises, passing scattered wood rails, short fence sections, and a support post. These were all part of a worm fence, whose rustic, zigzag form was once a familiar sight in the Smokies. As the trail levels out, it passes rhododendrons and a couple of giant downed tuliptrees. Someone has marked the top of a cut trunk: 38 inches diameter, 220 rings, indicating the tree was at least 220 years old.

The trail crosses a number of small seeps whose banks are crowded with wildflowers: toothwort, Dutchman's britches, wild geranium, and foamflower, as well as sedge and clubmoss. A steep but brief climb crests at Sag Gap then descends gently past numerous fallen chestnuts, the bottoms of their trunks big, buttressed, and mounded with moss. Continuing downhill, the trail passes through rhododendron and hemlock, over a few more seeps until a waist-high stone wall comes into view.

3.2–3.6 Messer fields. More than 75 feet long, running perpendicular to the trail, the dry-laid stone wall marks the start of the Messers' property. Across from the end of the wall, on the other side of the trail, is some barbed wire. Where wire and wall face each other, the trail begins a brief descent to Snake Branch, a pretty piece of stream and an easy rock-hop across.

On the other side of the stream, a "cat-hole" tuliptree has a hollow at its base big enough for a person to stand in.

Elijah Messer and his son Carson.

The trail parallels Snake Branch, which flows downstream on the left. On the right, the eroded end of a rock wall seems to grow from the ground, rising to about three feet and running alongside the trail. A third wall, perpendicular, extends to meet the trail. The young trees and level land indicate this was once a field. More snatches of wall appear, including an "L"-shaped piece, just before crossing Snake Branch again.

Elijah ("Fiddlin' Lige") Messer built his second house along Caldwell Fork, probably near here along Snake Branch. This area held a cluster of Messer farms and homes. Lige Messer came into Cataloochee after the Civil War. Described to be as tall as Lincoln, he was a Union supporter in this mostly

Confederate valley. But residents of Cataloochee generally had a live-and-let-live attitude (see Little Cataloochee Trail).

Lige Messer was reputedly one of the best fiddle players in the region, and an avid reader, subscribing to the *Atlanta Constitution* and other periodicals. Apparently he passed his love of learning along to his son Will Messer, who did everything from carpentry and milling to commercial apple growing, and became Little Cataloochee's leading citizen.

3.7 Carson Messer homesite. Just beyond the branch crossing and flanked by yellow birches stand the rotting uprights of a doorframe. Rockwork lines a sunken structure about 15 by 20 feet, the rock now decorated with ferns, asters, and hepatica. Metal sheeting—the remains of a roof?—lies on the sunken floor. This structure may have been a root cellar. Clearly, this area is where Carson Messer's house, barn, and other buildings stood.

In her book, *Reflections of Cataloochee Valley,* Hattie Caldwell Davis quotes Thad Sutton: "Carson Messer built his house up against a bank where a two-inch stream of water came out of the bank into his house, then ran out under the house. He was the only one with running water," Sutton laughed.

Walnut trees are often an indication of human habitation in the Smokies, and the Messers' walnut trees stand close by. People of the Smokies ate the walnuts; used the husks to make a rich brown dye; gathered walnuts as barter or for cash at general stores; benefited from its shade, which cooled their homes in summer; and made fine furniture from its wood. Coffins and, later, sewing machine cabinets were often made of walnut.

From the Messer place back to the junction with Caldwell Fork Trail is less than 0.2 mile. Messer's place is so close to Caldwell Fork that he really belonged to the Caldwell community rather than the Boogerman loop outpost. In fact, Messer ran a gristmill just up Caldwell Fork, near where McKee Branch comes in. He was part of the larger Messer family, who were scattered throughout Cataloochee.

Caldwell Fork Trail
4.1/0.0 Junction with Caldwell Fork Trail. Turn right to return to the trailhead: it is two miles between the upper and lower ends of Boogerman Trail, then another 0.8 to the trailhead. On its way back to the trailhead, Caldwell Fork Trail crosses about a dozen footlogs over the fork. As before, the broad trail is obviously shared with horses.

CALDWELL FORK/ROUGH FORK TRAILS

DIRECTIONS: Best hiked using a two-car shuttle. The hike begins at the Caldwell Fork trailhead, near the beginning of Cataloochee Road, and ends at the Rough Fork trailhead at the end of Cataloochee Road. From Interstate 40, take Exit 20 (U.S. 276) and, almost immediately, turn right onto Cove Creek Road, which leads 10 miles over Cove Creek Gap and down into the national park. About three of these miles are on gravel road.

Where the paved park road begins, follow it into Cataloochee Valley, and pass the large campground on the left. Just beyond the campground, on the same side of the road, and just before the ranger station, lies the Caldwell Fork trailhead. Pass the trailhead, go to the end of the paved road, then continue across the bridge for 0.5 mile to the end of the unpaved road. Park one car in the small lot on the right, just before the gate across Rough Fork Trail. Take the second car back to the pulloff parking at the Caldwell Fork trailhead.

TOTAL HIKING LENGTH: 9.2 miles. Caldwell Fork Trail to Rough Fork Trail, 6.3 miles; Rough Fork Trail to Cataloochee Road, 2.9 miles. Optional side trip up McKee Branch Trail, 0.8 mile (0.4 mile one-way) for a total of 10 miles.

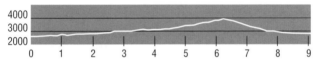

PHYSICAL PROFILE: The first part of the hike hugs Caldwell Fork, with numerous footlog crossings. Then the trail begins a relatively even ascent with a slightly steep section up to Rough Fork Trail. Rough Fork descends at a steeper gradient down to Cataloochee Road.

CULTURAL PROFILE: The Caldwell Fork community reveals the remains of about half a dozen homesites and two cemeteries, including one where two murdered AWOL Civil War soldiers were buried. Although the upper reaches of Rough Fork offer little of historical significance, the sturdy Steve Woody place, a preserved two-story home, caps the end of the hike.

*O*f all the once-populated parts of the Smokies, none retains the flavor of the early settlements more than Cataloochee

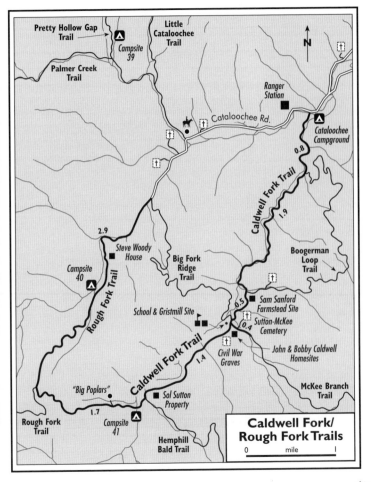

Pretty Hollow Gap Trail

Little Cataloochee Trail

Campsite 39

Palmer Creek Trail

N

Ranger Station

Cataloochee Rd.

Cataloochee Campground

0.8

1.9

2.9

Steve Woody House

Big Fork Ridge Trail

Boogerman Loop Trail

Campsite 40

Rough Fork Trail

0.5

Sam Sanford Farmstead Site

School & Gristmill Site

0.4

Sutton-McKee Cemetery

Caldwell Fork Trail

1.4

Civil War Graves

John & Bobby Caldwell Homesites

"Big Poplars"

McKee Branch Trail

1.7

Sol Sutton Property

Rough Fork Trail

Campsite 41

Hemphill Bald Trail

Caldwell Fork/ Rough Fork Trails

0   mile   1

Valley. Cataloochee lies at the southeastern edge of the national park, and to enter the valley is to take a trip back in time. Mown valley floors are open to the sun, as they were in the 1800s. Although Will Messer's barn was moved here from Little Cataloochee Valley, it looks like it still might hold hay for cattle brought down from high, grassy balds at summer's end. Down the road, Palmer Chapel stands facing Cataloochee Creek, its white steeple a peaceful statement of seeming permanence. Across the road stands Beech Grove School, where dozens of Cataloochee children learned to read and write.

In the early morning mist that rises off the fields, a string of Wild Turkeys may peck along the verge or an elk—reintroduced after an absence of decades—may trot toward the woods. One morning the resident ranger saw a bear run across the road, its mouth stuffed with apples from a tree planted by valley farmers many years before. Looking across the fields at the end of the road, near Caldwell house and barn, it is easy to see why the Cherokee called this Gad-a-lu-tsi—"standing in ranks." The trees march up the slopes that surround the narrow valley in tall, straight ranks.

Before white settlers began moving into Cataloochee, Cherokees lightly used the valley, mostly for hunting camps and small, semi-permanent settlements. As elsewhere in the Smokies, Indians forged the first paths, following the trails of deer, elk, woods bison, and other game.

In the early 1800s, drovers began entering the valley, driving their cattle and other livestock up to grassy balds for the summer. By the 1830s, level land from the piedmont to the foot of the Smokies had been bought up and was dotted with farms. People looking for land had to either move west or move up—into the mountains. In 1814, Henry Colwell bought 100 acres from Colonel Robert Love, a Revolutionary War veteran, a founding father of Waynesville, and a land investor who held title to all the land in the Cataloochee area.

In the mid-1830s, Jimmy Colwell, his son Levi, and their neighbor Young Bennett moved into Cataloochee, building log cabins near each other, not far from where the Caldwell house and barn now stand at the upper end of the valley. Soon other families began moving in: Hannah, Noland, Palmer, and Woody. Burgess, Cook, Hall, and Messer also were among Cataloochee's first families. The trees that covered the valley and lower slopes were cut, the land plowed and planted. Big Cataloochee Valley filled up with settlers willing to make a go of this rough, isolated place.

In the 1850s, the next generation looked for room to spread out. The sons and daughters of Cataloochee's settlers found what they needed along Caldwell Fork and in Little Cataloochee Valley. By 1870, Cataloochee Township had nearly 200 inhabitants. By 1900, the population in the three settlements had grown to 764 in 136 homes. And by 1910, the population had topped 1,200, making Cataloochee the largest single community in what would become the national park.

By the time the park was established, log cabins had mostly given way to large, weatherboard houses framed by flowers and set off by picket fences. Schools, churches, and stores were built; apple orchards planted. Although the logging companies that cut much of the Smokies in the late 1800s and early 1900s did not make many inroads into remote Cataloochee, valley residents sold their apples and beef to logging camps and beyond.

By the early 1900s, apples had become the major cash crop, but Cataloochee farmers sold honey, molasses, and tobacco as well. The community had grown relatively prosperous. Boarding with Cataloochee residents, tourists came to fish, ride horses, and enjoy the outdoors. Even a New York City opera singer came, allowing the clean mountain air to re-invigorate his voice. When the Depression years plunged the country into poverty, the hard-won self-sufficiency of those who lived in Cataloochee helped them endure.

In 1928, Reverend Pat Davis announced at Palmer Chapel that the government was buying all the land in the Smokies to

The Sam Sanford barn as it looked in 1937.

establish a national park. His congregation was stunned. Yet, by 1937, three years after the park was established, and a hundred years after their forebears had entered the valley, almost all the residents of Cataloochee had left.

Caldwell Fork Trail

0.0 A few steps from the parking pulloff, a 25-foot-long railed footlog crosses Cataloochee Creek at its confluence with Caldwell Fork. Paralleling Caldwell Fork, the four-foot-wide trail passes through a grove of tall hemlocks, then is edged by dense rhododendron and dog-hobble, with a sprinkling of tall Fraser magnolia. Crinkly sedge, pokeweed, ferns, and mosses take turns in the understory. The trail is shared with horses and, during wet weather, may be choppy from horse hooves. At 0.7 mile, another footlog crossing precedes the junction with the Boogerman Trail. Beeches, maples, and birches appear, along with a few sprawling witch-hazel trees.

0.8 Boogerman Trail junction. The semicircular Boogerman Trail intersects Caldwell Fork Trail twice: the first time here and the second two miles farther up the trail. Between the two intersections, Caldwell Fork Trail crosses the fork and a few side streams about a dozen times by footlogs.

2.7 Sam Sanford farmstead. The last side stream crossing before the second Boogerman Trail intersection (at 2.7 miles) is Snake Branch. Alongside Snake Branch Isam ("Sam") Sanford had a cabin, barn, springhouse, smokehouse, sorghum shed, and other farm buildings. Now the only hint of their existence is the once-cleared area that is filling up with skinny mountain laurels.

2.8 Second Boogerman Trail junction. Between the second Boogerman Trail junction and the junction with Big Fork Ridge

Trail, Carson Messer's gristmill once stood at Caldwell Fork, although rushing waters have washed away all signs. Gristmills were among the few gathering places in these mountain communities, because everyone had to grind their corn. Cornbread, or cornmeal in some other form, was "daily bread" in the Smokies.

The ruins of Carson Messer's extensive homesite and farm are still visible near the end of the Boogerman loop. He would have had to walk less than 0.3 mile from home to mill—not much of a walk in those days. The trail crosses another footlog before reaching the junction with Big Fork Ridge Trail.

3.2 Big Fork Ridge Trail junction. The first three miles of this hike make a pleasant, fairly level walk in the woods alongside Caldwell Fork, but that first section of trail was not much populated in the old days. The land along lower Caldwell Fork may have been too damp and enclosed for homes and farming. The historic part of the hike begins here, where the trail starts to rise slightly. About a dozen families once lived in this part of Caldwell Fork.

Big Fork Ridge Trail used to connect Caldwell Fork residents with the community in Cataloochee Valley. In fact, people coming from the Waynesville area would have traveled over Purchase Gap, down McKee Branch 2.3 miles, passing a few homesteads near where McKee Branch meets Caldwell Fork. Then they would have made a dogleg jog onto Big Fork Ridge Trail and continued to Cataloochee Valley. This route and the present-day car route over Cove Creek Gap were the two main ways into Cataloochee.

Although this hike continues on Caldwell Fork Trail, from the junction of Caldwell Fork and Big Fork Ridge Trails, it is 3.2 miles over Big Fork Ridge to Cataloochee Road and upper Cataloochee Valley. Near the end of Big Fork, Jim Caldwell built his home, not far from where his grandparents had built theirs. His grandparents, Levi and Mary Ann Colwell, were Cataloochee's first settlers, coming in the 1830s

Over time, the family changed the spelling of their name from Colwell to Caldwell, and Caldwells spread all over the Cataloochee area. Some moved to the narrow river valley now called Caldwell Fork. It was probably John Caldwell that gave the fork its name. John, who was Levi Colwell's sixth son and Jim's Caldwell's uncle, was one of the first to build along the fork.

Where it meets Big Fork Ridge Trail, Caldwell Fork Trail bends left, meeting McKee Branch Trail in 200 feet.

3.2 McKee Branch Trail junction. This broad trail junction, now flanked by hitching posts, was once the intersection for Caldwell Fork residents. The woods had been cut back and all around spread fields and homesteads. A short walk up McKee Branch Trail reveals a number of homesites and a cemetery.

Across from where the trails meet, between Caldwell Fork Trail and the stream, stood a school. Built in 1923, it was the last of the three schools in Cataloochee Township. (The other two were in Big Cataloochee Valley and Little Cataloochee Valley.) On Friday evenings parents gathered at the school to hear their children recite poems and speeches, proud that their children could become accomplished this far from a town. Now pine saplings mark the area where the school once stood.

The Jesse McGee - John Caldwell house in 1937.

A gristmill stood on the far side of Caldwell Fork where McKee Branch spills into the fork. The gristmill was probably the McGee gristmill. McKee Branch was named (if misspelled) for Jesse McGee, who also had a water-driven lathe that he used to make furniture for his family and the community. Pearl Rogers Sutton, who lived up McKee Branch with her husband Big Jim, once traded McGee a "gallon of corn" for a bedstead. That gallon of moonshine is long gone, but the bedstead remains in the Sutton family.

OPTIONAL SIDE TRIP: MCKEE BRANCH TRAIL.

Back in the late 1800s and early 1900s, McKee Branch was known as Long Branch, and a half-mile side trip on the trail alongside the branch shows off a number of homesites and a cemetery.

400 FEET John Caldwell homesite. Initially Jesse McGee's place, the original cabin was enlarged and enhanced over time, becoming a two-story weatherboard house. The house, graced by broad porches and a tall brick chimney, stood on the left of the trail, surrounded by fences and outbuildings. Although Caldwell Fork never produced apples commercially, as Little Cataloochee did, all the homes had apple trees in the yard.

Now only clumps of yucca and weedy fields colonized by pine saplings hint at that pleasant home. John Caldwell, who married Jesse McGee's daughter, Nicey, cleared a lot of land in the Caldwell Fork area, stopping at the Big Poplars near Campsite 41. The sight of big trees moved even industrious farmers such as the Caldwells. The trees that were left in historical backcountry areas were left on purpose.

John Mull Caldwell, John's nephew, lived in the house sometime later. He married Sol Sutton's daughter Annie, who was a midwife, just as her mother had been. Although Caldwell Fork was full of Suttons, Sol Sutton, who lived farther up Caldwell Fork toward Double Gap, was the first.

Bobby Caldwell, John's son, lived just across the trail, his homesite now marked only by a clump of yucca. Bear hunting was big recreation for the men of Cataloochee, and Bobby was an avid bear hunter who chose his dogs for their bear-hunting ability. Married and in his 30s, he and his wife invited her nephew to spend the summer with them. One Sunday, the teen decided he wanted to ride one of the horses, but Bobby said no, the horse needed rest because the next day it would be pulling heavy hay wagons. The nephew couldn't take no for an answer. He shot Bobby dead, then ran beyond the range of the local law, leaving a young widow.

400 FEET Cemetery turnoff. At the far end of the John Caldwell homesite, a path to the left crosses former fields for about 50 feet. There, a quick step over a small branch brings you to a path at the bottom of the hill, the upslope lined with 50 feet of eroding rock wall. Another 150 feet or so takes you to the flat, open top of the hill where a small, fenced cemetery holds ten graves. All but one are marked by small stones that bear no inscriptions. The one that rises above the rest reads "here lies Jesse McGee, 1823-1902, Confederate State Army." Jesse McGee was buried with honor. The soldiers who graves lie farther up Caldwell Fork had a more shocking end.

0.2 MILE J.H. Sutton homesite. Tuliptrees are now shooting up where J.H. Sutton's house and barn once stood. James Huston Sutton and his wife Addie boarded one of Caldwell Fork's teachers, who remembered Addie's good cooking and how their boys helped carry wood to the schoolhouse.

0.4 MILE Jim Sutton homesite. Up the hill from J.H. Sutton's place and a few steps over McKee Branch, the remains of fields, now filling up with trees, reveal what is left of Big Jim Sutton's homestead. He and his wife Pearl Rogers had 10 of their 11 children in the house on McKee Branch, before they reluctantly moved out to make way for the national park.

Like his father Sol, Big Jim was a blacksmith as well as a farmer. So, in addition to house and barn, a blacksmith shop stood here. Later Big Jim served as a deputy sheriff, but he had sowed a few wild oats earlier in his life. Once, when Big Jim and his brother George were making moonshine in Hells Half Acre, they imbibed too much of the product and were not as careful as they might have been. The still blew up, and a friend who was on duty as a fire guard at the Mount Sterling lookout tower told them he saw the result: a plume of smoke rising 80 feet through the trees.

Return to Caldwell Fork Trail.

3.4 Civil War graves. From the junction of Caldwell Fork and McKee Branch Trails, continue up Caldwell Fork about 400 feet. On the left, a well-worn path leads up

Graves of two men killed during the Civil War, above Jesse McGee place.

the steep slope about 100 feet. On the right, a small, open shelf of land fenced with wire and posts holds two graves marked only by low, rough stones. Pretty Dutchman's britches flutter close to the ground, but the story of the men who lie here is not pretty.

Although some mountain people had strong affinities for one side or the other during the Civil War, most just wanted to get on with the hard task of making a living. Many men, however, were mustered into Union or Confederate Armies. Generally, but not exclusively, men from the Tennessee side of the Smokies joined the Union Army and men from the North Carolina side joined the Confederate Army.

With fighting-age men gone, life in this difficult back-of-beyond became more difficult. Because it was remote, Cataloochee also became a haven for AWOL soldiers. Bands of raiders from both sides scoured the Smokies, supposedly looking for men avoiding duty. In fact, they used this as an excuse to loot and murder.

George Kirk was a renegade Confederate who had joined the Union, was made a colonel, and led a band that included deserters and criminals into Cataloochee during the last days of the war. Near Little Cataloochee, Kirk and his 600 men had already torched the house of Young Bennett, an outspoken Confederate supporter away in the war. Looking for other Confederates, they came into Caldwell Fork after Ellsworth ("Elzie") Caldwell and Levi Shelton, his brother-in-law.

Farmers often turned forests into cornfields by girdling, rather than falling, large trees.

When hiding men, livestock, or food from rapacious bands of raiders, women would sneak out at night and take a circuitous course to their hiding spots. This time, they were unlucky, because Kirk's Raiders followed the wives of Caldwell and Shelton. They murdered the two men and hastily buried them near where

Caldwell Fork and Rough Fork meet. Later, the two were disinterred and buried here, together in the same grave. The person buried in the second grave is unknown.

Follow the path past the graves as it arcs back down to Caldwell Fork.

3.5 Deadening Fields. From the Civil War graves, fairly broad Caldwell Fork Trail continues upward at a slight incline. Look for a large rock pile on the right, approximately 15 feet in diameter. Sometimes rock piles found in the Smokies are the result of crumbling chimneys. Many more are simply rock piles, gathered and heaped up when settlers were clearing land. A few minutes farther up the trail, the Deadening Fields are another clue that farm fields once lay here, open to the sun. Today a mix of young pines and hemlocks are filling up those fields.

One method of clearing trees was to chop them down. Before the logging era, early settlers used what they could of the downed lumber, then made huge piles of the excess and burned them. Another method was the one John Caldwell used here. He girdled the trunks by stripping off a broad band of bark so that no nutrients could nourish the trees. When the trees died, Caldwell burned the dry, dead wood.

Between the Deadening Fields and the junction with Hemphill Bald Trail a mile farther up the road, Caldwell Fork Trail is lined by a number of former fields and homesites. Clues include rock piles and groves of young trees.

3.7 Clontz Branch. Just before Clontz Branch, which is a narrow, step-over creek, Jim Evans had a home and a blacksmith shop. The branch is framed by rhododendron backed by big hemlocks. The shaded clearing among the big hemlocks is probably where Evans' log house stood. Now carpeted by partridgeberry, the ground once must have been scattered with nails, wheel rims, and chunks of metal ready for firing. Beyond Clontz Branch, the trail rises, offering fine views of the narrow Caldwell Fork valley below. As the trail levels off, winding below a ridge, squawroot hugs the feet of northern red oak and chestnut oak.

4.7 Hemphill Bald Trail junction. Hemphill Bald Trail generally parallels Double Gap Branch three miles up to Double Gap and the Cataloochee Divide Trail.

A few hundred feet before the trail junction, Sol Sutton owned property—the farthest farmstead up Caldwell Fork. Look for a rock wall on the left, about 3 feet high and 50 feet long; rock piles and clearings on the right; and a rusted pail hanging from a snag. It was a pretty place for a home.

Although Sol Sutton had a reputation for being…well…mean, he was tough and competent at a time when those qualities were key to survival. One of the first to move into Caldwell Fork, Sutton was a blacksmith as well as a farmer. His wife Easter was one of Cataloochee's midwives, and she traveled all over "Catalooch" delivering babies. The Suttons had relatives living near Cosby, Tennessee, and along Big Creek, North Carolina, in what is now the northeastern corner of the park. The Suttons on both sides of the Smokies were known as accomplished musicians and dancers. It is said that, in his 70s, Big Creek's Mitch Sutton could still fit in more steps than the musicians played.

Although Sol's son, Big Jim, moved to McKee Branch, his grandson Thad Sutton remained on Caldwell Fork in a two-story log house built by Big Jim up the trail from the Deadening Fields. Before the chestnuts died out in the 1930s, Thad once shoveled 60 bushels from the ground below two trees and sold the chestnuts in Waynesville for $3 a bushel—good money in those days.

During the Smokies logging era of the early 1900s, Thad Sutton worked for Suncrest Lumber Company and, during the Depression, he worked in one of the Civilian Conservation Corps (CCC) camps scattered throughout the Smokies. Back then, native brook trout were still plentiful, and Thad's wife claimed she could bring a pan out to the creek after a rain, dip it in, and scoop out as many fish as she wanted.

4.8 Backcountry Campsite Number 41. A footlog crosses Caldwell Fork, which rumbles gently down from ridges along the park's southern border. Just beyond the footlog, Campsite 41 flanks both sides of the trail. With its hitching post, it is used by backpackers and horsepackers alike.

The campsite reveals a few signs of former habitation: a rock pile at the base of a triple-trunk birch and another at the base of a double-trunk beech. The Suttons kept their milk cows here. Beyond Campsite 41, the trail rises. On the slopes the Suttons cleared three fields so steep that they said you could "dig out 'taters and just let 'em roll down the hill."

5.1 "Big Poplars." A sign points toward a narrow trail on the right that passes a hitching post and ends about 100 feet off Caldwell Fork in front of three enormous tuliptrees. These were the giants John Caldwell could not bear to cut down. The first one is about 25 feet in diameter at breast height. (Related to magnolias, tuliptrees are also known as tulip poplars and yellow poplars, although they are not poplars at all.)

Beyond the big trees, the trail continues to rise. Where it curves to the left, a line of three fence posts—part of the Sutton's fields—runs perpendicular to the trail. From this point to Rough Fork Trail, nature reigns: deep woods of maples, Fraser magnolias, and other deciduous trees mix with groves of hemlocks underlain with rhododendron.

Rough Fork Trail

6.3/0.0 Rough Fork Trail junction. From this high point of 4,000 feet, Rough Fork Trail descends three miles to meet the end of Cataloochee Road. (To the left, Rough Fork switchbacks, ascending 3.5 miles to Polls Gap.) Rough Fork Trail is steeper and rougher than Caldwell Fork Trail, parting forests of oak, red maple, striped maple, yellow birch, tuliptrees, and others—a typical casting call of a southern Appalachian forest.

1.4 Backcountry Campsite Number 40. As Rough Fork Trail descends, the sound of Hurricane Creek becomes louder until, finally, the trail begins to parallel the creek. Just before the confluence of Hurricane Creek with Rough Fork, where a footlog crosses the water, a narrow path heads left through a tunnel of rhododendron. Twenty-five feet off the main trail, Campsite 40 is a small rhododendron-walled retreat along Rough Fork.

Back on the main trail and across the footlog, Rough Fork Trail becomes broad and level, revealing gravel in places. Rough Fork, a gentle-enough stream, runs to the left of the trail. Soon an avenue of hemlocks announces the Steve Woody house.

The Steve Woody Place in 1940.

1.9 Steve Woody House. At the right of the trail, a small, white springhouse introduces the main event: a two-story, white weatherboard house with a broad covered front porch. Steve Woody's first dwelling was a log house that he built around 1880. Later he enlarged the original place, using sawn lumber. His was one of numerous frame houses that eventually dotted Cataloochee. One reason the Woody house remains intact is that the family remained in the house well after the park was established. Steve Woody stayed until 1942, just two years before his death.

About six feet tall, Woody was handsome, had an air of authority, and always rode a black horse, enhancing his imposing presence. He also had a good sense of humor and was known as a shrewd businessman. Once, when an apple buyer

came looking for his neighbor Hiram Caldwell, Woody told him Caldwell had sold all his apples. Woody suggested the buyer load up with Woody's apples so he wouldn't have to leave with an empty wagon.

Steve Woody at work with a shaving horse and draw knife.

Hiram Caldwell, whose house lies about a mile farther, was a co-conspirator with Steve Woody in burning down the original, too-small Beech Grove schoolhouse in order to force the county to help fund an adequately sized school, which still stands.

For those who do not want a long hike, but want only a short walk to see the Woody house, park at the end of Cataloochee Road and merely walk in a mile from the Rough Fork trailhead.

2.9 Cataloochee Road. In the mile between the Woody house and Cataloochee Road, the trail itself becomes as wide as a road and crosses Rough Fork three times via footlogs. The gate and the small parking lot at the end of Cataloochee Road mark the end of Rough Fork Trail. About 0.2 miles down Cataloochee Road from the Rough Fork trailhead, the Hiram Caldwell house looks out on picturesque upper Cataloochee Valley.

Hiram Caldwell was one of the sons of Levi and Mary Ann ("Granny Pop") Colwell, who were Cataloochee's original settlers. Hiram left Cataloochee for a time, working as a teamster in Greenville, South Carolina, for 10 cents a day until he saved enough money to return, buy land, and build this house. The nine-room, two-story house was finished in 1903.

Hiram met Mary Elizabeth Howell at a bean-stringing, a typical Smokies get-together that combined work and socializing. They married and she bore their four children in this house. Like his father and his son Eldridge, Hiram Caldwell was fluent in the Cherokee language and was able to communicate with the Cherokees who continued to travel through what were once their hunting grounds. Cataloochee was not only rich with game. Charlie Palmer, a son of another original settler, described how most felt about Cataloochee: "They was raspberries. And strawberries and June apples and all sorts of fruit, and it was more like livin' in the Garden of Eden than anything I can think of."

FORNEY CREEK TRAIL

DIRECTIONS: Best hiked using a two-car shuttle. The hike
begins at the Forney Ridge Trailhead at the Clingmans Dome
parking area and ends at the parking area at the end of
Lakeview Drive. In Bryson City, west of Asheville (via either
U.S. 74 or U.S. 19), turn north onto Everett Street at the old
Swain County Courthouse. The road crosses the Tuckasegee
River and becomes Lakeview Drive. It ends about 9 miles
from Bryson City at a tunnel. Park one car in the lot on the
right just before the tunnel.

Take either U.S. 19 or U.S. 74 to U.S. 441 and go north,
through Cherokee, to Clingmans Dome Road, which intersects U.S. 441 (Newfound Gap Road) just before Newfound
Gap. Turn left, drive about seven miles, and park the second
car at Clingmans Dome parking area, near the Forney Ridge
trailhead. The trailhead lies between a drinking fountain and
the beginning of the paved path to Clingmans Dome Tower.
(Clingmans Dome Road is closed in winter.)

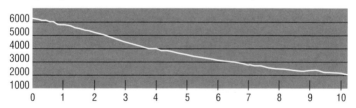

LENGTH: 14.7 miles, from the Forney Ridge Trailhead to the
end of Lakeview Drive.

PHYSICAL PROFILE: Sparkling cascades and one of the
Smokies' most exuberant creeks. Although the hike is almost

all downhill, the Forney Ridge section is steep and rocky.
Forney Creek Trail offers four challenging creek crossings. To
keep the challenge to a minimum, hike Forney Creek in dry
weather and at low water, which usually means the end of
summer or autumn. In addition, watch for hidden nails and
slippery moss on some of the railroad-tie footbridges. A flashlight for the 0.2-mile tunnel segment at the end of the hike is
handy, but not necessary.

CULTURAL PROFILE: From top to bottom, Forney Creek is a pre-
mier trail for telling the story of the Smokies' logging era,
with its railroad bed, retaining walls, cables, rails, and logging campsites. An imposing chimney marks the site of a former Civilian Conservation Corps (CCC) camp.

Forney Ridge Trail

0.0 If you start early in the morning, a good idea for this somewhat lengthy hike, Clingmans Dome may be wreathed in
clouds and mists. The vapors make an apt beginning to a

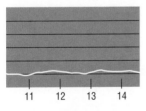

descent through the Fraser fir and
red spruce that clothe the top of
the ridge. This realm is part of the
thin finger of boreal forest that
crowns the Appalachians from
Canada southward. Few odors can
match the heady scent of fir. Berry
bushes, mountain ash, hobblebush, angelica, and yellow birch
also lie along Forney Ridge Trail. But it is good to watch your
feet because the trail is steep, rocky, and eroded.

As high and difficult as this region is, loggers and a logging

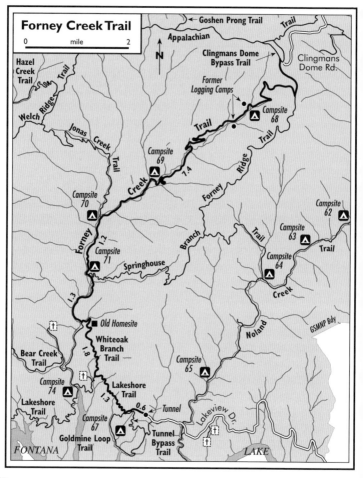

Forney Creek Trail

0   mile   2

Goshen Prong Trail →

← Appalachian

Trail

Clingmans Dome Bypass Trail →

Clingmans Dome Rd.

Hazel Creek Trail

Welch Ridge Trail

Former Logging Camps

Campsite 68

Jonas Creek Trail

Trail

Campsite 69

7.4

Forney Ridge Trail

Creek

Campsite 70

Forney

Campsite 62

Branch

Campsite 63

Trail

1.2

Campsite 71

Springhouse

Campsite 64

Trail

1.3

Old Homesite

Creek

Noland

GSMNP Bdy.

Whiteoak Branch Trail

1.8

Bear Creek Trail

Campsite 65

Campsite 74

Lakeshore Trail

1.3

Lakeshore Trail

0.6   Tunnel

Campsite 67

Lakeview Dr.

Goldmine Loop Trail

Tunnel Bypass Trail

FONTANA

LAKE

railroad were here. Norwood Lumber Company logged Forney Creek from 1910 to 1927. The company built a mill town more than 12 miles downstream, where Forney Creek poured into the Tuckasegee River. Because of Fontana Lake, which was created when Fontana Dam was completed in 1944, the mouth of Forney Creek and the site of the mill town are now under water. But in the early 1900s, the town ran a band mill, planing mill, and flooring mill as well as a dry kiln for drying lumber. Homes, school, church, store all clustered near the mouth of the creek as did a clubhouse where company executives stayed.

At one time, Norwood Lumber owned an estimated 30 million board feet of lumber "on the stump." In order to log out what they could, Norwood built a narrow-gauge railroad up Forney Creek and into many of its tributaries. Although the small Shay engines that powered the log flatcars were tough and relatively maneuverable, to haul the log cars up this last steep mile, Norwood used an incline with thick metal cables. Part of a wrecked Shay engine lies nearby, but vegetation now obscures it.

Although Forney's tributaries provided broad areas for farmland, Forney itself is narrow and steep. So, except for its mouth, the main creek was sparsely populated until Norwood came in to log hardwoods and evergreens. Then, logging camps and little "peckerwood" sawmills dotted the creek. During the early 1920s, a logging-related fire raged from the head of Forney Creek all the way to the present parking area on Clingmans Dome.

Forney Ridge Trail

1.1/0.0 Forney Creek Trail junction. At the sign, turn right, leaving the Forney Ridge Trail for the Forney Creek Trail. The trail becomes less steep and rocky. Airy groves of yellow birch now mix with hemlock as the trail leaves the spruce-fir zone.

During the first half-mile, look for "ball-hoot" gullies scoring the slopes. On the steepest slopes, loggers would fell trees, peel off the bark, and round the "nose" of the log. Then they would start the logs downhill. These huge missiles would pick up speed, "ball-hooting" their way to the bottom of the slope. They also rolled logs sideways. The ponderous wood crushed everything in its path, scarring the slopes for decades.

Ball-hooting was the hardest job on the mountain. In his book *Last Train to Elkmont*, Vic Weals says there was a superstition among loggers that most men killed were those who stayed on the same job too long: "Ninety days, ninety dollars, and a hundred days a dead man."

1.4 Meeting Forney Creek. In a relatively open area canopied with maples and tumbled with boulders, the trail first encounters Forney Creek. Look for some light-colored quartz, but do not cross the creek here. Keep the creek on your left and pick your way over rocks for about 75 feet and the trail will soon become obvious. The trail is edged with wildflowers: white snakeroot, blue aster, and goldenrod.

1.8 Steeltrap Creek crossing. Steeltrap Creek pours into Forney Creek less than a mile downstream. Spiked rails lie across the boulder-strewn stream, a prelude to the old logging camp com-

ing up on the left of the trail. Just before the camp, Forney
Creek sheets down a long, smooth slab of rock. This elegant
cascade is one of the finest water features in the park. Scoring
the dark rock are veins of white quartz so symmetrical they
look like painted highway lines.

2.0 Former logging camp. Campsite 68. Where the slab of rock
flattens out, a logging camp once occupied the adjacent apron
of land. A railhead may have been located here as well. The
ground is covered with gravel. A heavy piece of rusted metal
grate has fused with a yellow birch. Metal cable twists here
and there. And, on the far side of the cascade, iron spikes are
imbedded in the rock. At the bottom of the cascade, boulders
block the water's progress and a long piece of rail arcs over the
pooling water like a rusted, miniature St. Louis Arch.

More recently, this area was used as an illegal camping
area. Heading back to the trail, look for pipe wrapped around a
birch and, lying
across the trail, a
piece of rail serving
as a water bar.

2.5 Logging Camp.
A short, left-hand
fork off the main
trail leads to a broad
area next to the creek.

**A Norwood Lumber Company building on Forney
Creek. 1937 photo.**

This, too, was probably a former logging camp, as evidenced by
the gravel scattered across the ground. When Norwood was

71

logging Forney Creek in the early 1900s, this and other sites along the creek were clear-cut. The ground was choppy with stumps and cluttered with piles of brush. Near the tracks, stacks of logs waited to be loaded on flatcars.

The Shay locomotive engines billowed steam, the rail cars clanked, and men shouted instructions to each other, working hard to cut and load timber without getting maimed or killed. Tents and boxcar-type houses provided rough accommodations.

As they moved men and equipment from site to site, the lumber companies often off-loaded the precursor to prefab housing: boxcar-shaped "car shacks" that could be hoisted off a flatcar and set down as instant housing alongside the tracks. Sometimes several car shacks set in a row were run as a boarding house, with one car shack serving as the dining room. Breakfasts were especially hearty: huge "cathead" biscuits, gravy, side meat, fried potatoes, and coffee. Loggers loaded up calories they would soon burn off.

Vic Weals, who reported extensively on the logging era in the Smokies, wrote that Sally Messer and her husband Walter Sluder, a logging train brakeman, lived along Forney with their two young sons. In 1919, Sluder was killed in a train accident and Sally moved her family to the Tennessee side of the Smokies, where she helped her sister run a logging camp boarding house. Some of the large logging camps even had rudimentary dance halls, which drew people from all over the mountains.

From this point downward, the trail follows an old railroad bed: broad and even, except where retaining walls have crumbled at the backs of coves. Segments of rock retaining walls line the trail in a number of places, and the trail passes through three or four road cuts. Building this railbed was no easy matter.

Further along are several easy crossings of small tributaries: Little Steeltrap, Steeltrap again, then Buckhorn. Low trestles once bridged even smaller, unnamed tributaries. Now all that remains are timbers serving as footbridges across these small waterways. But use caution—nails dot the timbers. The nails are sometimes hidden by moss, which make the timbers slippery.

A Climax Locomotive Type A on Forney Creek. Equipment at the front of the engine sprinkled sand on the rails for better traction on steep grades.

The railbed snakes down the mountain, at one point winding through a tight "S" curve where it is easy to imagine the squeal of wheels as the logging train rounded the bend. In the upper reaches of the Smokies, trains averaged four to five cars, each loaded with about 12 logs, each 16-foot log weighing between one and two tons. With loads this heavy, brakes needed supplementary help, so sand was sprinkled on the tracks to slow the wheels as the train descended.

At a sharp switchback, the trail seems to end at the creek, where a "No Camping" sign is posted. This was probably a siding or the start of a spur line. The trail does not cross water here, but continues down the switchback, passing a two-foot-high retaining wall. More curves, side creeks, and low trestles, one with enough cross ties to give a sense of what these trestles looked like.

Ferns, pipsissewa, partridgeberry, and other groundcover carpet the forest floor. Yellow buckeyes, tall tuliptrees, hemlocks, and rhododendron are part of this second-growth forest. Before Forney Creek was logged, it was full of giant old-growth trees, a quiet cathedral forest with such a high, dense canopy that little vegetation grew on the shadowed floor.

The bottom of another switchback is secured by an enormous retaining wall: 10 to 12 feet high and about 75 feet long. After the next switchback, look for a low rock channel that carries a side stream along the left edge of the trail. Just beyond is the first of four hard creek crossings. As tributaries have poured in along the way, Forney Creek has become a boisterous, bubbling stream, one of the fastest-flowing in the Smokies. Almost immediately after the first major crossing, Campsite 69 lies on the left side of the trail.

6.0 Backcountry Campsite Number 69. Not a big campsite, Campsite 69 is a pleasant place that reveals some scattered metal parts and other detritus of human use. It is called Huggins Camp for Huggins Creek that flows into Forney just downstream. It is also known as Monteith Camp. The Monteiths were among the first white settlers in what became Swain County. In the early 1800s, some of them moved up Forney Creek. The Coles, Woodys, and Welches, for whom Welch Ridge is named, were also among Forney's first families.

Catherine Proctor Welch, related to the Proctors of Hazel Creek, married into the Welch family of Forney Creek. She remembered that, before the Civil War, the Welches owned slaves. Sometime before the war, looking for a sign of hope, the slaves along Forney Creek took a meteor shower to be a signal of Judgment Day, when they would be freed.

Although not many mountain people owned slaves, the few who did usually lived on the North Carolina side. Unlike plantation owners on the coastal plain, who owned dozens of slaves, farmers in the Smokies had much smaller fields, thus owned fewer slaves. The vast majority of mountain farmers, however, cleared, plowed, planted, and harvested their tough, steep fields by themselves.

The next three challenging creek crossings occur within less than a mile, one after the other, each about a quarter-mile apart.

7.4 Jonas Creek Trail junction and Backcountry Campsite Number 70. Forney Creek Trail continues straight, but a sign points right to Jonas Creek Trail, which begins at a footlog over Jonas Creek. Campsite 70 lies in the "V" of land between the two creeks. On the left side of Forney Creek Trail, Norwood Lumber Company owned a building.

Just before it pours into Forney, Jonas Creek is swelled by the waters of Scarlet Ridge Creek. At about that point, in 1912, a spark from a train engine on the spur line ignited a fire. The fire quickly jumped to the canopy and, racing through the crowns of 80-foot hemlocks, burned three miles up the mountain in four hours.

From this point down, horse traffic is allowed on Forney Creek Trail. When it is wet, the trail can be choppy with horse hoofprints. A few dozen feet beyond the junction, look for a rusted rail along the right side of the trail. Less than 0.5 mile from this point, follow the sign that points left onto a bypass trail, which skirts more Forney Creek crossings by traversing a small ridge.

Near the beginning of the bypass, Slab Camp Branch joins Forney from the right. Although the Woody family homeplace was at the junction of Forney Creek and the Lakeshore Trail, at this confluence Tom Woody ran a tub mill from 1890 to 1920. Tub mills were small, about the size of an outhouse. Unlike large gristmills, whose grindstones were turned by huge water-wheels, the tub mills were turned by water hitting a circle of wooden blades only a few feet in diameter. The grind-stones, too, were small.

Tom Woody's tub mill in 1937. Built in 1890, the water-powered mill was frequently used for grinding corn to make moonshine.

Woody's mill could have ground enough meal for his family and a few neighbors, but it was mostly used to grind corn for moonshine. Woody would grind sprouted green corn to make the mash that would ferment into liquor. In those days, stills dotted the hills.

In *Strangers in High Places,* his book on the making of Great Smoky Mountains National Park, Michael Frome tells the story of a logging superintendent on Forney Creek who worked with six bootleggers selling moonshine to loggers during

Prohibition. The man's wife was sick of the clutter and smell of liquor jars in their house, so she turned him in.

The government "revenuer" came and poured out all the whiskey, but that did not stop the logging boss. A few months later, the revenuer picked him up at a hotel in Bryson City, where he had come to sell liquor. Afraid of the notoriously tough prohibitionist Judge E.Y. Webb, the logging superintendent agreed to help the revenuer trap his confederates on Forney. For that, the superintendent was given only a year's sentence. Frome says he probably would have served even less time had he not assaulted the revenuer in the hotel and been half-drunk at trial.

8.6 Backcountry Campsite Number 71. Not far beyond where the bypass trail rejoins the railbed, Campsite 71 lies on the left side of the trail. Campsite 71 was once a Civilian Conservation Corp (CCC) camp. Just beyond the camp, Springhouse Branch Trail forks left. (This trail, which crosses Forney Ridge, leads 8.3 miles to Noland Creek Trail, passing an old springhouse and eventually paralleling Noland's Springhouse Branch tributary.)

The branch that feeds Forney at this point is called Bee Gum Branch. Mountain farmers who wanted to collect honey would make bee gums to house hives of bees. The bee gums were cut from sections of black gum trees, which develop heart rot. Although the heart of the tree rots, creating a hollow interior, the outer bark remains whole, making a convenient container when lid and bottom are nailed on.

Bee Gum Branch is undoubtedly named for the bee gums that once lined a section of the branch. David Monteith, whose

Civilian Conservation Corps (CCC) camp barracks on Forney Creek. 1945 photo.

family was from Forney, said that several homesites preceded the CCC camp here. But most families, including his, lived along Forney's tributaries.

Campsite 71 centers on the most prominent remains of the CCC camp: an enormous stone chimney more than 20 feet high and about half as wide with a large, brick-lined fireplace near its base. Scattered around the broad, flat area are other remnants of the Forney Creek CCC camp, which was built in 1933, during the Depression.

The Forney CCC camp included the usual complement of buildings: barracks, mess hall, bathhouse, officers' quarters. When they were not building trails and bridges or planting trees, the CCC men here added a library, a post office, and a commissary.

Jack Woody, who grew up on Forney Creek, wrote in the *North Shore Historical Association Newsletter* that his father worked as a cook in this CCC camp. When his father's dog was "discharged" from the camp for bad behavior, Woody's father left, too.

His parents, Lawrence Woody and Bertie Mae Collins, were married on Forney Creek in 1920. "The Lord said, go forth and be fruitful," said Bertie Mae, "and by golly we did." They raised 10 of their 11 children to adulthood. They also raised all their own produce and meat. Bertie Mae had a big garden and bee gums. Jack Woody remembers there was always plenty of honey and it tasted good on homemade biscuits.

They raised chickens and hogs and kept a cow for milk and butter. Woody had to milk the cow before and after school, in addition to other chores. Each of the boys had two pair of overalls and two shirts. Each of the girls had two outfits. Monday was washday and, once a week, the children changed to clean clothes.

Undoubtedly, the Woody children wore some hand-me-downs, but buying new clothes required cash. So, Lawrence Woody worked other jobs besides those on the Woody farm. Before he was a CCC cook, he worked for the lumber company and lost a few toes in a lumber accident. In that, he was luckier than some.

After Campsite 71, another bypass skirts the creekside railbed, then returns to it.

Whiteoak Branch Trail
10.0/0.0 Whiteoak Branch Trail junction. At the junction, take the left fork onto Whiteoak Branch Trail. This two-mile trail is

79

an alternate, shorter route to the Lakeshore Drive parking area. Although Forney's story is primarily one of the logging era, the people who called Forney Creek home generally lived between here and where Forney once poured into the Tuckasegee River.

In the late 1800s, John Monteith was born along Bear Creek, the next tributary downstream. In addition to farming, he worked for Norwood Lumber Company as a brakeman on the incline that spanned the last mile or so to Clingmans Dome. Later, he and his wife, Mary, moved their family closer to the mouth of Forney, where he ran a general store. They had five children, including David Monteith and Beatrice Monteith Douthit.

Born in 1927, Beatrice was one of three Monteith children born on Forney Creek. Eight months a year, she went to the upper of the two grammar schools on Forney, a one-room schoolhouse with a pot-bellied stove, one teacher, and about 25 students ranging over seven grades. Back then about 20 families lived along Forney Creek and its tributaries.

Although a circuit-riding preacher came once a month, Beatrice, her siblings, and friends went to Sunday school weekly. Afterwards, the children would meet at one of their homes, eat Sunday dinner, then play baseball or some other game. In summer, they swam and fished in Forney's deep pools.

Beatrice also helped in her father's store. She and her siblings helped with other work as well: farming fields of corn and sweet potatoes, canning produce from the garden, picking wild blackberries and blueberries and, in early autumn, wild grapes. They had chickens and a milk cow. In summer, they brought their hogs up to Silers Bald to fatten them up. The

Monteith cabin near Silers Bald served many herders who brought hogs and cattle to the grassy balds.

But this was the end of an era. With the coming of the park in 1934, residents moved to the lower reaches of Forney. With the coming of the dam and Fontana Lake in 1944, they moved out altogether.

0.9 Old homesite. From its junction with Forney Creek Trail, Whiteoak Branch Trail rises, then descends into a pocket creek valley at 0.9 mile where an old homesite spreads. The trail rises again, crests a hill, then descends briefly before meeting the Lakeshore Trail. Just below where the two trails meet is another homesite.

Lakeshore Trail
1.8/0.0 Lakeshore Trail junction. Turn left onto Lakeshore Trail, which ends at the parking area in 1.9 miles. Along the way, Lakeshore Trail passes Goldmine Loop and Tunnel Bypass Trails. The families along Forney Creek and Goldmine Branch formed one community and attended summer revivals and other community events together.

1.9 Tunnel. Lakeshore Trail ends at a 360-yard-long tunnel. This imposing, two-lane tunnel was built as the start of a north shore road that was supposed to stretch from Bryson City to Fontana Dam, but environmental concerns ended the road right here. (See the Fontana Dam story at Lakeshore Trail: Eagle Creek.) Upon exiting the tunnel, the parking area lies within sight on the left.

GOLDMINE LOOP TRAIL

DIRECTIONS: In Bryson City, west of Asheville (via either U.S. 74 or U.S. 19), turn north onto Everett Street at the old Swain County Courthouse. The road crosses the Tuckasegee River and becomes Lakeview Drive. It ends about nine miles from Bryson City at a tunnel. Park in the lot on the right just before the tunnel.

LENGTH: 3.1 miles. This is a loop hike: Lakeshore Trail through

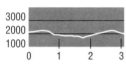

tunnel to Goldmine Loop Trail, 0.6 mile; Goldmine Loop Trail to Tunnel Bypass Trail, 2.0 miles; Tunnel Bypass Trail to Lakeview Drive, 0.4 mile.

PHYSICAL PROFILE: This unassuming little trail provides a lot of variety in a short distance. It descends quickly from the Lakeshore Trail, meets Fontana Lake, then ascends just as quickly over a few low ridges. A flashlight for the 0.2-mile tunnel segment is handy, but not necessary.

CULTURAL PROFILE: Two extensive homesites lie along this hike as well as homesite remnants at Campsite 67. Since this is not a heavily traveled trail, the discoveries are singular treats.

Lakeshore Trail

0.0 The imposing tunnel at the hike's beginning was built as the start of a north shore road intended to connect Bryson City and Fontana Dam, but environmental concerns halted the road right here. (See the Fontana Dam story at Lakeshore Trail: Eagle Creek.) Because Lakeview Drive dead-ends at the tunnel, nearby residents also call it The Road to Nowhere.

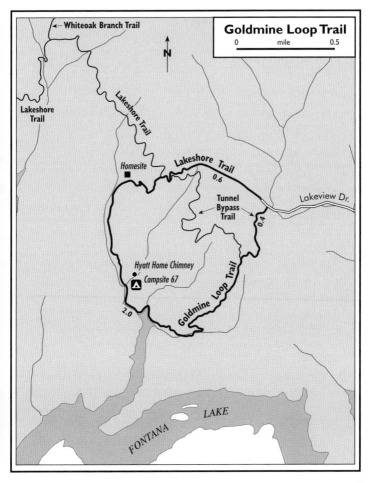

Whiteoak Branch Trail

Lakeshore Trail

Goldmine Loop Trail

0   mile   0.5

Lakeshore
Trail

Lakeshore Trail

Homesite

Lakeshore Trail   0.6

Tunnel
Bypass
Trail

Lakeview Dr.

0.4

Hyatt Home Chimney

Campsite 67

2.0

Goldmine Loop Trail

FONTANA   LAKE

Although the tunnel is fairly dark at the center, light from the arched entries on either side is always visible. And the side beyond the paved road is hardly "nowhere." A second-growth pine and oak forest with an understory of mountain laurel covers the sloping terrain. Pass the first trail junction sign on the left, which is the far end of the Tunnel Bypass Trail.

Goldmine Loop Trail

0.6/0.0 Goldmine Loop Trail junction. A sign at this junction points left to Campsite 67. Turn left onto Goldmine Loop Trail, named more out of hopefulness than any serious gold deposits. The trail descends down a narrow, forested ridge full of oaks with American hollies dotting the understory. Watch out for the strands of barbed wire wrapped around a tree near the bottom of a short, steep section.

Where the trail bottoms out at a saddle at about 0.25 mile, go right, following a more moderate descent. In less than 0.2 mile, the trail reaches a "T" where a creek edges a clearing that was once part of a farm. Go left at the "T." The trail curves around the back of a small spring in a thick understory of mountain laurel, then emerges at an old homesite.

0.3 Old homesite. Goldmine Branch runs along the right side of the trail. Step across this gentle, sandy-bottomed stream to see the sprawling homesite on the other side. This is one of about 10 homesites that used to lie in the Goldmine Branch drainage.

Beautyberry shrubs mark the 25-foot-long path to what was someone's home. The most obvious remnant of that home is its chimney. About 12 feet high, 5 feet wide, and 4 feet deep, the chimney stands in the middle of a clearing full of New York ironweed, rosinweed, and other lanky wildflowers and shrubs. Planted long ago, honeysuckle still grows near the chimney. The house foundations are still visible, but barely. All around are scattered other remnants of some family's life: part of a blue enamel pail, shards of glass, a piece of brown pottery. Park artifacts are protected by law, and these poignant pieces of the past remain for us to see because no one has removed them.

Head of Slab Camp, Forney Creek Sawmill. 1925 photo.

Although Hyatt, Cole, and Hall were the main family names of those who lived along Goldmine Branch, this property likely belonged to Will Jenkins. It is hard to say who lived here, though, since people did move around a lot.

The Goldmine Branch community was closely tied to the Forney Creek community just to the west. So, when Norwood Lumber Company came into Forney Creek with logging opportunities, people in this area became loggers. North shore residents often moved to follow the logging jobs up and down creeks and their tributaries.

From this homesite, the trail follows an old roadbed. Dog-hobble, mixed with American holly and common alder, lines Goldmine Branch on the right. Beyond the stream, the clearings—once cornfields and gardens—are filling in with young trees. The slope on the left is thick with rhododendron canopied by hemlock. Look for a segment of wire fence on the left.

The trail forks left off the roadbed at about 0.75 mile. Just beyond the fork, on the right side of Goldmine Branch, is another old homesite in a weedy clearing.

0.7 Old homesite. Step over Goldmine Branch again to explore this homesite, which is now, occasionally, home to grouse. Two tall boxwoods announce the entry to the house. This once looked quite proper and trim, but now the boxwoods have outgrown the site, and all that remains of the house are a cellar and some moss-covered steps. Beyond that, an old roadbed ends at the base of a slope.

This homesite probably belonged to a member of the Hyatt family, perhaps Cole Hyatt who lived along Goldmine Branch just about at this spot. Nearby stands a black walnut tree—a clue to a nearby homesite because farmers usually planted walnut trees near their homes. The ground all around has been rooted and rumpled by wild hogs. Returning to the trail, follow the fork to the left and up a low rise full of white oak with some hemlock and mountain laurel. The trail and roadbed meet again, paralleling Goldmine Branch.

0.9 Path to Backcountry Campsite Number 67. A short path to the left parallels Hyatt Branch upstream less than 0.2 mile to Campsite 67. On the right side of the turn toward Campsite 67, look for old washtubs next to Hyatt Branch. Not surprisingly, the branch is named for other members of the Hyatt family who lived up this way.

A 20-foot-tall chimney that once heated the Hyatt home distinguishes this long and narrow campsite, which is dotted with flowering dogwoods. Just below the path leading into the campsite, an old road is visible. The roadbeds once were traveled by wagons, even cars. The first cars on this part of the north shore were ferried over to a marina that lay along the Tuckasegee River between here and the mouth of Forney Creek.

Back on the main trail, which bears right, pass over a rocked culvert and look to the right for a small cascade under a fringe of rhododendron. Soon Fontana Lake comes into view, signaling that you have reached the lowest elevation of this walk.

1.1 Junction with Fontana Lake and Tunnel Branch. At this point, Goldmine Branch slips into Fontana Lake. Rounding the back of a small cove, now an embayment of the lake, step across a small branch. Just beyond, where Tunnel Branch tumbles down toward the lake, Goldmine Loop Trail leaves the roadbed and bears left up the hill for the return to Lakeview Drive.

The view of the lake is soothing, but has been a feature of the scenery only since 1944. That was the year Fontana Dam flooded the Tuckasegee River to form Fontana Lake. Before then, the river flowed two-thirds mile downstream from this point.

From where Goldmine Trail passed Campsite 67 around to Tunnel Branch and partway up the hill—all this land once belonged to Evan O. Hall. Hall was one of those rare people who could do everything. He was a teacher and a preacher, and former students and neighbors lauded him for his many skills and his personal qualities. Born in Bryson City in 1888, Hall moved to Goldmine Branch to take up teaching on Forney Creek. In 1913 he married a former student and they had 10 children.

In addition to teaching, Hall served as a Baptist minister, preaching at Forney Creek and other north shore communities. He taught shaped-note singing, ground cornmeal for neighbors at his gristmill, sawed lumber at his small sawmill, cut tombstones at his blacksmith shop, where he also shoed horses and mules. In short, he was a community treasure.

Using the power of a waterwheel and his own ingenuity, Hall wired his home for electricity. His electrically lit home was one of the first that north shore residents had ever seen. In remembering his former teacher, Jack Woody, who grew up on Forney Creek, said that when someone in the community died, either Hall or Chasteen Cole would make the coffin. Hall himself died in 1969.

Ascending steeply for about 0.2 mile, the trail parallels Tunnel Branch through hemlocks and mixed hardwoods. Where the land flattens for a few hundred feet, the trail bears left, then switchbacks up a moderately steep slope. Following the back of a low, narrow ridge, the trail provides splendid views of distant ridges and close-up looks at a forest floor carpeted with wintergreen and trailing arbutus.

Tunnel Bypass Trail

2.0/0.0 Tunnel Bypass Trail junction. A sign at this junction points your direction: Lakeview Drive 0.5 mile to the right. The Tunnel Bypass Trail was built so that horseback riders, whose horses might be skittish in the tunnel, would have a way to reach Lakeshore Trail. Over the next half-mile the Tunnel Bypass Trail winds among hardwoods, then through groves of hemlock and rhododendron dotted with low pipsissewa before ending across the road from the tunnel parking lot.

HAZEL CREEK TRAIL

DIRECTIONS: The easiest access to Hazel Creek is by boat. From the park's Oconaluftee Visitor Center near the town of Cherokee, travel west on U.S. 74. Then take Route 28, winding along the south side of Fontana Lake toward Fontana Village. Or, from the western edge of the park, take the western Foothills Parkway to Highway 129. Turn left and travel south to the intersection of Route 28. Turn left here and follow the signs to Fontana.

Two miles east of Fontana Village, take the spur road north. Almost immediately the road will fork. Take the right fork to the Fontana Village Marina (the left fork goes to Fontana Dam). To arrange boat transportation, call the Fontana Village Marina at 800-849-2258 ext. 277. The boat ride across Fontana Lake takes about a half-hour. Another way of reaching this trail is by foot or horseback along the Lakeshore Trail from Fontana Dam.

LENGTH: 18.1 miles. This hike goes from the boat docking point on Fontana Lake near Campsite 86 to Campsite 82 and back (9 miles, one way). Lakeshore Trail: boat dock to Hazel Creek Trail, 0.7 mile; to Campsite 82, 8.3 miles. This hike can be shorter or longer. To see the town of Proctor, the mill ruins, and Proctor Cemetery is about a 4-mile roundtrip. A hike that includes the farthest historical points of interest, just above Proctor Creek, is a 21.6-mile roundtrip. A walk to Proctor Cemetery from Proctor adds an optional 0.8 mile (0.4 mile, one way). A walk to Higdon Cemetery from the Sugar Fork junction adds an optional 0.7 mile (0.35 mile, one way).

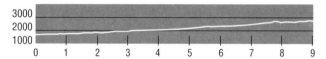

PHYSICAL PROFILE: The trail was once a railroad bed, so it is broad and fairly even much of the way. Bridges cross the creek until Campsite 82. After that, creek crossings are rock hops.

CULTURAL PROFILE: Hazel Creek was once the most populous place along the north shore of Fontana Lake (an impoundment of the Little Tennessee River). Remnants of the town of Proctor, the Ritter mills, and homes that lined the upper sections of the creek echo that busy period. Frame houses, foundations, cemeteries, a huge, ruined mill with associated structures and millponds, old fields, and many other constructions lie along Hazel Creek.

The story of Hazel Creek is the story of many Smokies communities, but Hazel Creek history was writ large. The Cherokee had been here for perhaps a thousand years—— hunting, fishing, setting up summer camps, even small settlements, along the tributaries of Hazel Creek. The first non-Cherokee residents arrived in the early 1830s. Following an established Indian trail from Cades Cove via Eagle Creek,

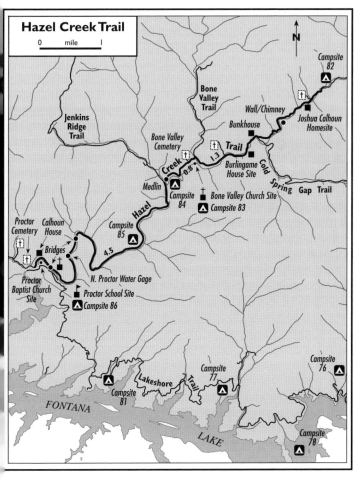

Hazel Creek Trail

0 — mile — 1

N

Campsite 82

Jenkins Ridge Trail

Bone Valley Trail

Wall/Chimney

Bunkhouse

Joshua Calhoun Homesite

Bone Valley Cemetery

Trail 1.3

Creek

0.8

Burlingame House Site

Medlin

Campsite 84

Bone Valley Church Site

Campsite 83

Cold Spring Gap Trail

Proctor Cemetery

Calhoun House

Campsite 85

Hazel

4.5

Bridges

N. Proctor Water Gage

Proctor Baptist Church Site

Proctor School Site

Campsite 86

Campsite 81

Lakeshore Trail

Campsite 77

Campsite 76

FONTANA

LAKE

Campsite 78

Moses and Patience Proctor and their young son William moved from where her relatives lived in Cades Cove to a magnificently isolated hill above Hazel Creek.

Over the next 80 years, the homesite would become a cemetery, its first grave that of Moses Proctor. And the hill would overlook the town of Proctor, a bustling community that eventually grew to more than a thousand people. School, church, barbershop, theater, train depot, ball field, ice cream shop, even a photo shop— Proctor had all this and more.

Calhoun's Store. Proctor, Hazel Creek.

In 1835, Samuel and Elizabeth Cable with their seven children made the trip from Cades Cove, settling closer to the Little Tennessee River on what became known as Cable Branch. (The Cable family name is still found in Cades Cove in the John Cable Mill and the Gregg-Cable House.)

Slowly, other families filtered in. In 1852, Josiah and Sarah Bradshaw came. He built the first gristmill on the creek and became Hazel Creek's first justice of the peace. But it was not until after the Civil War that settlement swelled.

In the late 1870s, Jesse Craten ("Crate") Hall and his young family camped out in Bone Valley, six miles from their nearest neighbor, while he built their first cabin in this Hazel Creek side valley. Their second cabin still stands at the end of the Bone Valley Trail. Baptist preacher Joshua Calhoun, who came with his family about 1886, helped establish the first church and school along Hazel Creek. One of his sons, Granville, became the recognized "squire" of Hazel Creek. Marion Medlin established the first post office in 1887 in his store at the mouth of Sugar Fork.

Mrs. Cunningham. Proctor, 1920.

Grace Pullum and family of North Proctor, 1920.

By the end of the nineteenth century enough people lived on Hazel Creek to support two post offices, three stores, and four combination church-schools. Almost all residents were farmers, but farming would soon be supplemented by a touch of mining and a lot of logging.

The Adams Copper Mine opened in 1889. Modest logging operations began in the 1890s. By far, the biggest impact began in 1902, when the W.M. Ritter Lumber Company, based in Columbus, Ohio, decided on an extensive plan for logging Hazel Creek and its tributaries. Ritter was one of the biggest lumber operations in the Smokies and certainly one of the most deliberate. Timber "cruisers" had scouted

the north shore for Ritter and reported that the biggest and best trees were in the Hazel Creek drainage.

Ritter did not begin logging until 1910. During the intervening years, the logging company built the town of Ritter at the mouth of Hazel Creek where the creek met the Little Tennessee River. Ritter had convinced the Southern Railroad to extend its rail line along the north shore of the river. Then Ritter built a spur line up into Hazel Creek.

From mountain forests, narrow-gauge trains hauled logs down to the mill Ritter built at Proctor. From there the trains carried finished lumber down to the Southern Railroad depot to ship to market. Ritter also ran a daily passenger train that connected with the Southern Railroad. Instantly, travel to places such as Bryson City became easy.

At Proctor, Ritter built the mills, dry kilns, millponds, bridges, and other structures needed to run a successful logging operation. It also built the entire mill town of Proctor:

Logs arrived by narrow-gauge railroad at Ritter's Mill.

workers' homes, train depot, schools, and more. The company even ran phone and electric lines up to Ritter operations.

By the time Ritter pulled out, in 1928, the company had logged all the way from the town of Ritter, at the mouth of Hazel Creek, 20 miles into the creek's upper reaches and into its tributaries. It had taken 201 million board feet of lumber from the Hazel Creek watershed, enough to build 20,000 homes. Before the lumber company came, Proctor was a settlement with a sprinkling of log homes. Ritter turned Proctor into a full-fledged town with frame houses, stores, cafes, and amusements.

Those who remained after Ritter left struggled through the Depression, some working for the Civilian Conservation Corps (CCC) camp at Proctor. Great Smoky Mountains National Park was established in 1934, and the park boundary reached halfway down the North Carolina side of the mountains. More people left Hazel Creek.

In the 1940s, the Tennessee Valley Authority built Fontana Dam and Lake as part of the World War II effort to generate electricity and increase manufacturing capacity. As a result, the remaining north shore lands became part of the national park and the remaining residents had to move out. (See the Fontana Dam story at Lakeshore Trail: Eagle Creek.)

The story of Hazel Creek remains an integral part of the park story. Duane Oliver, himself descended from the Proctor, Welch, and Farley families of Hazel Creek, tells this richly textured story in his book *Hazel Creek From Then Till Now.*

0.5 Backcountry Campsite Number 86. Because the docking

point on the Fontana Lake embayment changes with the lake level, the walk from boat to Campsite 86 can vary from 0.3 to 0.7 mile. Hazel Creek was named for the American hazel trees growing alongside it.

Shaded by trees, broad and flat Campsite 86 lies between Hazel Creek and the trail. When Proctor was flourishing, the

portion of the creek just below the camp was used as a swimming hole and for baptisms. Before the CCC replanted this spot with trees, it was sunny, spread with sand, and used as a playground and

Proctor School, Hazel Creek, 1923.

ball field by the children of Proctor. At some point, the playground even held a basketball court. As trains clacked by on the railbed—now the trail—children must have stopped to wave.

On the right of the trail, overlooking the ball field, stood Proctor School. Built by Ritter to replace a smaller school across the creek, it opened about 1915. A big step up from the more common one-room schools found in mountain communities, Proctor School was a white frame building with gables, four classrooms, a school bell, and other amenities. In 1923, 138 students attended Proctor School. In 1934, when extra classrooms were built and high-school grades added, it was renamed the Calhoun-Coburn School. In 1944, when Fontana

Dam flooded the Little Tennessee River Valley, the school closed.

0.7 Bridge. This was once the heart of the town of Proctor. Straight ahead was Main Street, the nicest of the workers' streets. Despite the fact that the train ran right along the street, the women who lived here were quite proud of their homes, so it became known as Struttin' Street.

Struttin' Street was where the foremen and their families lived, in good-sized houses: three bedrooms, a hallway, living room, dining room, and kitchen. Most every building in Proctor had running water, piped in from concrete reservoirs. Some homes had outhouses, some had indoor bathrooms.

Cars came into Hazel Creek once North Carolina Route 288 (a gravel road) was built. The October 1924 issue of *Hardwood Bark*, the Ritter Lumber Company newsletter, mentions a total of six cars belonging to residents of Hazel Creek and says, "Mrs. W.C. Bearden has the distinction of being the first woman to drive an automobile on Hazel Creek."

At the far end of Struttin' Street, just before the next bridge where the train crossed the creek, stood the train depot, Ritter's offices, and the commissary, which sold groceries and other supplies.

Cross the bridge and pick up Hazel Creek Trail.

Calhoun House. After crossing the bridge, turn left down the daffodil-lined path that edges the creek to reach the Calhoun house. After the park was established, it was used as a ranger station for a number of years. Beside the house is a pleasant, tree-shaded picnic area.

The restored, white frame house looks like a place anyone might want to live: a broad, covered porch runs the length of the front. Inside are a foyer, five rooms, and a kitchen, plus an attic. A separate room, which does not afford access to the house, might have been for a lodger, such as a teacher or a circuit-riding preacher. Such lodger rooms were fairly common in the southern Appalachians.

Called the Calhoun house, it was bought by Granville Calhoun in 1928, but the house was built earlier than that by George Higdon. Higdon's family had moved to Hazel Creek in the late 1800s. At one point, Higdon carried mail from Ritter to Proctor and farther up Hazel Creek via horse and buggy.

Granville Calhoun, who bought the house about the time that Ritter left, was one of those energetic and accomplished people who seemed to rise up in each flourishing Smokies community. Born in 1875, Granville Calhoun died in 1978 at the age of 103. He had seen the whole arc of Hazel Creek development in his lifetime: from backwoods wilderness to a string of mountain communities connected by trains and roads, to acres of stumps left by lumber companies, to a return to something approaching wilderness.

Over time he told his story to John Parris, a columnist for the *Asheville Citizen*. When he was nine, his parents moved up Hazel Creek from Wayside, a town along the river now flooded by Fontana Lake. His father, Joshua Calhoun, lamed by a childhood accident, nevertheless built the family's log cabin on Hazel Creek above Bone Valley. Joshua Calhoun farmed and, in summer, grazed cattle on the balds. He also established the first church on Hazel Creek and served as a preacher.

As a child, Granville spent spare hours fishing for foot-long trout in the creek, still known as one of the park's best trout streams. He started hunting bear when barely older than a boy, and became renowned as one of the great bear hunters of the Smokies.

Granville Calhoun worked as a timber cruiser, dam builder, and dam tender for Taylor and Crate, the New York lumber company that selectively logged ash and tuliptrees from Hazel Creek in the 1890s. The north shore rail line had not been built, so Taylor and Crate let the creeks and river do the work.

The logging company built three splash dams on Hazel Creek: one near Crate Hall's cabin in Bone Valley, one near Josh Calhoun's place, 15 miles from the mouth of the river, and one here, just below the Calhoun house at Proctor. In the early days of logging, splash dams were used throughout the Smokies to run logs from the tops of mountains to rivers where they would be corralled in huge booms and floated downriver to market.

The splash dam that once crossed Hazel Creek just below the Calhoun house was typical. It spanned the creek and then some. It was about 18 feet high and, in the middle, had a 16-foot gate. To move logs down the creek, Calhoun and other dam tenders let water build up behind the dam gates, then opened the gates, loosing the water. The powerful surge carried everything with it: logs, debris, and men who did not jump out of the way quickly enough. A number of men were killed on Hazel Creek, tending splash dams and breaking up logjams.

Tenders had the two upper splash dams timed so that the rushing heads of water met on the main creek at the same time, creating a deluge. As Calhoun told Parris, "When that happened, the logs went rolling and tumbling and the water roaring, you could hear it for a mile. It was like a storm, the logs bumping one another and hitting the rocks."

The roiling water washed native brook trout onto the banks, where people scooped them up by the bucketful. Splash dams nearly annihilated native trout.

When Ritter Lumber came in 1903, Calhoun was hired to build the first six miles of the company's railroad. In 1904, when Horace Kephart arrived at Hazel Creek, Calhoun owned a general store and post office at Medlin on Sugar Fork. He and his wife and three children lived nearby in a six-room house, a considerably better dwelling than most of his neighbors' log cabins.

Because he was a larger-than-life figure in the community, Calhoun had been asked to show Kephart around, but what he found when he met Kephart was a man suffering from alcohol withdrawal. So Calhoun took Kephart home and nursed him back to health.

Kephart was trained as a scholar and librarian. When a young man, he worked under a mentor in Italy and in the libraries of Rutgers College and Yale University. Eventually, he headed the Mercantile Library of St. Louis and was building its collection, with special focus on frontier communities. But he found his life stifling and allowed alcohol to bring him down. In 1904, Kephart fled his job as well as his wife and six children for a frontier community: Hazel Creek. There, he lived in a small cabin up Sugar Fork.

Once he regained his health, Kephart reveled in the life and customs of mountain folk, especially in the masculine realms of moonshining and bear-hunting. *Our Southern Highlanders*, which tells the story of his time on Hazel Creek, is Kephart's look at southern Appalachian mountain life. He lived on Sugar Fork for three years, then moved to Bryson City, but stayed in close touch with his Hazel Creek friends.

Kephart came to Hazel Creek just as the era of intensive logging began. While he watched what saws, skidders, railroads, and mills did to his beloved forests, he became increasingly convinced that the only way to protect the Smokies was as a national park. Kephart became a leading park advocate and instrumental in establishing Great Smoky Mountains National Park.

Horace Kephart moved to the mountains of western North Carolina and wrote prolifically about his outdoor adventures for national magazines.

He wrote in the July 19, 1925, *Asheville Citizen*:

"When I first came to the Smokies, the whole region was one of superb forest primeval….Not long ago I went to that same place again. It was wrecked, ruined, desecrated, turned into a thousand rubbish heaps, utterly vile and mean."

In 1931, just three years before the park was established, Kephart died in an automobile accident near Bryson City. His grave is marked by a boulder in the Bryson City cemetery.

When Ritter Lumber left in 1928, Granville Calhoun moved down to what is now called the Calhoun house. He took in lodgers who came to Hazel Creek for rustic vacations. He also bought Proctor's community building and a number of other buildings. In 1944, when he had to move to make room for the park, Granville Calhoun owned 17 houses on Hazel Creek. He was the last to leave.

Proctor's community building was adjacent to the Calhoun house and directly across from the bridge, not far from where the National Park Service maintenance barn and corral stand. The two-story building was a center of activity. Outside steps led up to the second-story barbershop where girls got their hair bobbed in the 1920s. The upper floor also housed a pool hall.

Downstairs, a large room served as an auditorium for school plays and dances. Sometimes box suppers were a highlight of the dances, young men bidding on suppers brought by young women, who were the real focus of the bidding.

Most of the time, it was the community movie theater. As Oliver explains in *Hazel Creek From Then Till Now*, Calhoun managed the theater from 1913 to 1918 and showed silent films—mostly westerns and Charlie Chaplin—on Wednesday and Saturday nights. A seat cost 10 cents and rows of benches held 200 to 300 viewers. To keep customers happy when films broke, Calhoun hired a family band of black musicians who lived in North Proctor. Next to the community building was a café that sold soft drinks, tobacco, and ice cream.

OPTIONAL SIDE TRIP, PROCTOR CEMETERY.

For an optional 1.2-mile side trip (0.6 mile, one way) to see Proctor Cemetery, continue along the trail that passes the Calhoun house. This old roadbed parallels Shehan Branch in Possum Hollow, which was once lined with the homes and fields of Bradshaws, Welchs, and others.

Between the Calhoun house and the path to the cemetery, W.A. Franklin built a home and a store on the slope to the right of the trail. Here, too, was Proctor's first school. After about 0.25 mile, a log-railed path rises on the right. Take this up to Proctor Cemetery.

Once the site of the Proctors' home, this cemetery is the largest of the nine that lie in the Hazel Creek drainage. In fact, with 192 graves, it is one of, if not the largest, on the north shore. Most of the gravestones are small slate slabs whose inscriptions have been worn away by time and the elements. One plot bears the graves of twins, one who lived less than two weeks, the other only a few days longer. The surnames on the gravestones—Cable, Cook, Walker, and others—belonged to families who helped establish the Hazel Creek community. The most prominent gravestone, however, belongs to the first family: Moses and Patience Proctor.

Their daughter, Catherine Proctor Welch, was the first white girl born on Hazel Creek. Back then, a few Cherokee families still lived in the area and the Proctors were acquainted with one family, in particular, who lived in Possum Hollow.

Catherine Proctor Welch.

Back then, the mountains were still full of wolves and panthers. One day, Catherine Proctor Welch was riding her horse home from the nearest gristmill, on the river, her baby in one arm. Panthers began following her over what is now called Welch Ridge. They continued following her through the forest, screaming occasionally. The big cats turned back only when Catherine approached Hazel Creek.

Wildlife was not the only threat. During the Civil War, when all the men were off fighting, deserters came through and stole Welch's horse. After figuring out the thieves had taken her mare to Cades Cove, she walked the 25 miles to demand her horse back. She got it, and for the remainder of the war kept it in her cabin at night.

0.7/0.0 Return to the Calhoun house. Heading upstream, Hazel Creek Trail overlays what was once Calico Street. Calico paralleled Struttin' Street, across Hazel Creek, but the houses were smaller. At about 0.3 mile, look for the foundations of the Proctor Baptist Church alongside the trail.

Most churches on Hazel Creek and in other mountain communities were one-room log structures that served as both church and schoolhouse. Circuit-riding preachers usually came once a month. Because it served a relatively large community, Proctor Baptist Church did not do double-duty as a school and preachers led services and delivered sermons on a more regular basis. The church even had a second floor for meetings and Sunday school classrooms.

Until the Ritter era, families celebrated Christmas with stockings hung above the hearth, at most. Few had seen a Christmas tree. W.M. Ritter instituted a Christmas celebration at the church, complete with tree and bags of apples, oranges, nuts, and candy. The 1921 Christmas celebration revealed that

435 children between the ages of 1 and 14 lived on Hazel Creek.

Proctor Church.

Near where the church stood, the railroad bridge crossed over Hazel Creek from the depot at the end of Struttin' Street. On the other side of Calico Street, opposite the bridge, a road rose up what was known as Clubhouse Hill. Atop the hill stood the Clubhouse, a three-story building with verandas on the first two levels and two dining rooms on the main floor. The Clubhouse hosted visiting Ritter executives as well as the company's doctor and dentist. Having a resident doctor was a real luxury for many mountain communities.

In 1923, Grace Lumpkin, a socialist writer from New York, lived at the Clubhouse for a few months while interviewing people for a story. Whereas Kephart favored the ripsnortin' view of life in the southern Appalachians, Lumpkin and others caught up in the social activism of the early 1900s saw mountain folk as both downtrodden and exotic. Although both revealed aspects of the Hazel Creek community, the truth was more complex.

After Ritter Lumber left Hazel Creek in 1928, the Clubhouse was not completely abandoned. Several families would get together to rent the place for the summer.

A boarding house also stood atop Clubhouse Hill. It provid-

The sprawling Ritter sawmill complex at the old town of Proctor, NC.

ed housing for mill workers and had a hallway that ran from one end of the building to the other. Alice Posey remembers that when Ritter left and the boarding house stood empty, she and her friends would roller-skate from one end of the long hall to the other.

0.4 Ritter Mill. Less than a half-mile from the bridge at the Lakeshore Trail junction, a deep rut on the left side of the trail signals the edge of the Ritter millpond. The rut widens to a broad, pond-sized depression, now filled with grasses and weedy wildflowers. In the early 1900s, the pond was filled with water. In winter, when temperatures dipped below freezing, boys slid and skated over the frozen ice.

Nearby spread the lumberyard, which held thousands of

boards neatly set atop rows of low scaffolding to keep them off the moist ground. Between 50 and 75 men were employed in the lumberyard alone. In the late 1930s, nearly a decade after Ritter moved out, the CCC built a camp on the site of the lumberyard. The CCC camp was abandoned in 1942, about four months after World War II began.

Just beyond the pond rises a mournful-looking giant of a ruined dry kiln. The sawmill once stood adjacent. The sawmill consisted of a band mill, which could cut thousands of board feet of lumber a day and a planing mill. The planing mill turned out strip flooring and parquetry. A coal-powered generator provided electricity for the mill—and the town. All that is left of the mill complex is the brick-and-concrete kiln, which dried lumber for market. The mills and kiln employed about 50 men. Past the millpond and the dry kiln, look for a couple of small concrete pump sheds.

Between the farming community, the railroad, and the mills, which attracted workers from all over the region and beyond, Hazel Creek was a busy place in the early 1900s. In 1910, Ritter provided the Hazel Creek community with a resident doctor, Dr. J.G. Storie, who lived in the Clubhouse. In his decade on Hazel Creek, Dr. Storie officiated at the births of 685 children.

A more precise population count came in 1918. Because of his stature in the community, Granville Calhoun was asked to take the official census that year. Calhoun found that 2,000 people lived along Hazel Creek and its tributaries.

1.0 Site of North Proctor. Look for a cylindrical, 15-foot-tall concrete water gauge standing on the right side of the trail on the bank above Hazel Creek. Ritter used this to gauge water levels in the creek. Not far beyond the water gauge, the homes of North Proctor clustered in a fairly flat area shaded by walnut trees.

Here lived the small community of African-Americans who worked for Ritter Lumber. Their community lasted only a decade or so at the height of the Ritter era, and they held religious services in each other's homes. Although the two communities did not mingle much, occasionally whites would walk up to sing with members of the North Proctor community on Sunday mornings. A man from this community is buried in the Sugar Fork Cemetery, one of the few African-American graves in the Smokies.

1.2 Second bridge. Like other bridges on Hazel Creek, this one is broad and sturdy, capable of bearing the park vehicles that maintain the Hall cabin in Bone Valley and the park bunkhouse farther up the road. Parallel to the trail and about 10 feet above, cut into the slope, is an old roadbed, once used by the Hazel Creek school bus. Hemlocks and hardwoods shade the road, with mountain laurel edging the trail. The third bridge lies at about 1.5 miles.

3.0 Backcountry Campsite Number 85. Campsite 85 lies at the end of a huge horseshoe curve along Hazel Creek. This broad, former clearing is now filling in thinly with trees. Campsite 85 is also called Sawdust Pile because a small sawmill operated here. Beyond Campsite 85, bridges four and five come in quick succession just before Hazel Creek Trail's junction with Jenkins Ridge Trail.

4.5 Jenkins Ridge Trail junction. Hazel Creek Trail continues right. Jenkins Ridge Trail bears left, following Sugar Fork Branch. In the V formed where Sugar Fork meets Hazel Creek was the community of Medlin: a handful of homes, a store, and a post office.

It was named for Marion Medlin, who moved here with his family in 1887, marking the arrival of Hazel Creek's third preacher. Medlin applied to open a post office in the tiny store he built; both post office and town bore his name. The store carried only a few basic supplies, which Medlin sold in barter, including ginseng roots that eventually reached Asian markets.

The Adams-Westfeldt Copper Mine was located about 2.5

miles farther up Sugar Fork and Little Fork. Although a thick, rich ore body runs from Eagle Creek to the Adams-Westfeldt Copper Mine, neither Adams nor Westfeldt was able to take advantage of it. In fact, they would be appalled to find their names so linked.

In the mid-1880s, Jacob Fonslow ("Fonzie") Hall, brother of Bone Valley's Crate Hall, discovered copper at the mine site. In 1889, New York mineral developer W.S. Adams heard of the discovery and came down to purchase and develop the site. In

order to move supplies up and ore down to the closest railhead, 25 miles away, Adams built the first wagon road on Hazel Creek. The Adams mine was the first outside economic force in this far-flung community.

New Orleans land speculator George Westfeldt, who had

Cable winch used to haul ore from an Eagle Creek copper mine. 1988 photo.

bought property on Sugar Fork back in 1869, heard about the Adams mine. Westfeldt believed the Adams mine was actually located on his property and he rushed up to contest the mineral deposits as his. Court battles ensued. In 1901, after only two years of operation, the mine was closed until the courts cleared ownership. Property lines were confused and overlapping, based on ax marks on trees. The litigants battled through the courts over which ax marks meant what.

In *Hazel Creek From Then Till Now,* Oliver says, "In 1927, after 26 years of litigation, the suit was finally decided in favor of Adams. By then, however, both litigants were dead. They had each hired 11 lawyers and had, together, spent about a half-million dollars in court costs." The case was like a story line straight from Charles Dickens.

By 1904, Granville Calhoun owned the community store and post office, which served 42 households scattered up Sugar Fork and Haw Creek. At least seven tiny tub mills dotted the edges of these streams. Farm fields and apple orchards spread back from the streams. That was the year that Calhoun escorted Horace Kephart to his home in Medlin, where Kephart stayed until he recovered his health. Then Kephart moved into the empty caretaker's cabin at the Adams-Westfeldt Copper Mine.

William Calhoun, one of Granville's brothers, ran the store at Medlin, and his wife, Nora Lee Davis Calhoun, served as postmistress. In the North Shore Historical Association Newsletter, Verayle Calhoun Franks remembered the goods in her parents' store: candy, tobacco, cornmeal, flour, lard, various meats, bolts of cloth, shoes, lamps, kerosene, and wagon and buggy supplies. Two to three logging trains came through every day, plus a passenger/freight train that delivered their supplies.

At that time, Sugar Fork had a school with 35 to 45 students, with some students walking down from Bone Valley. The schoolteacher boarded with the Calhouns.

Franks told of her grandparents' hundred-plus bee gums and the bee-robbing parties. Everyone who volunteered to help went home with a winter's supply of honey. Most of the honey was poured into 10- to 50-pound tin cans and sold to logging crews. Ritter Lumber even ran a special train up to Sugar Fork for Proctor residents who wanted to buy Calhoun's apples and honey.

OPTIONAL SIDE TRIP, HIGDON CEMETERY.

For an optional 1.1-mile side trip (0.5 mile, one way) to see Higdon Cemetery, continue left on the Jenkins Ridge Trail approximately 0.25 mile to a path on the left that leads upward about 0.1 mile. The path splits: one side is steep, one ascends moderately via switchbacks. They meet at the top where a wire fence surrounds 20 graves.

To the left of the cemetery, set by itself behind a forked tree, lies the grave of an African-American, whose gravestone is simply inscribed: "A Black Man." It is said that this man helped nurse many members of the Hazel Creek community hit by the influenza epidemic that spread through the country in 1918-1919, right after World War I. In carrying out his ministrations, the man contracted the disease and died.

Return to Hazel Creek Trail.

4.5 Backcountry Campsite Number 84. On the right, immediately past the sixth bridge, Campsite 84 lies near the confluence of Hazel Creek and Sugar Fork. An extremely pleasant spot, Campsite 84 was once William and Nora Calhoun's vegetable garden.

5.2 Backcountry Campsite Number 83. Just before the junction of Hazel Creek and Bone Valley, Campsite 83 lies alongside Hazel Creek. Above the campsite, just to the right of the trail, is a flat-topped knoll. The slope from campsite up to the knoll is covered with large patches of vinca, also known as periwinkle. This nonnative plant is sometimes known as "graveyard grass" because it was planted as a decorative evergreen groundcover in cemeteries.

The knoll was once the site of both the first and the second Bone Valley Baptist Church. About 15 feet from the road, foundation stones from the second church lie nearly flush with the ground. This second, newer Bone Valley church had store-bought pews and a pump organ. At the upper edge of the knoll lies a section of rusted rail, evidence of the railroad that once cleaved this valley.

Directly across the trail from the campground and knoll, a path rises about 0.3 mile to the Bone Valley Cemetery. About halfway up, just past a small, step-over branch, the trail splits. Take the right-hand fork, which switchbacks to the cemetery. (The left-hand fork is part of the old Hazel Creek road.)

The four ranks of graves all face east, anticipating resurrection. With 82 graves, Bone Valley Cemetery is the second largest in the Hazel Creek drainage. Oaks and a couple of tall pines canopy this high prow of land, with mountain laurel adding beauty to the understory. Most of the markers are small slabs whose inscriptions are no longer visible.

Jacob Fonslow ("Fonzie") Hall, a Civil War veteran who discovered copper nearby, lies here. So does Marion Cook, another Civil War veteran. Orson Paul Burlingame, who came to Hazel Creek as Ritter's civil engineer, owned a magnificent home about a mile farther up Hazel Creek. He is buried here, too.

Peter and Nan Laney, part of Hazel Creek's large and prominent Laney family, lie here. Willa Mae Hall Smathers, a great-granddaughter, tells the story of how they met. During the Civil War, Pete and his companions came upon enemy soldiers trying to molest Nan, then only 13 years old. Pete rescued her and asked her to wait until the war was over, when he would return to marry her. She waited and he returned two years later. When they went to get their marriage license, she bluffed the office staff into believing she was 18.

5.3 Bone Valley Trail junction. Just beyond Campsite 83 and immediately after the seventh bridge, Bone Valley Trail angles off to the left. Our hike bears right, continuing up Hazel Creek Trail. Bone Valley, however, was an integral part of the Hazel Creek community and is historical enough to warrant its own inclusion. (For more on Bone Valley, see the Bone Valley Trail hike.)

For the next mile or so, signs of old homesites flank Hazel Creek Trail. About 0.1 mile past Bone Valley, an old rusted pipe lies parallel to the trail. Another 0.1 beyond that, a pit, perhaps once a cellar, lies on the left of the trail. Directly across, in a broad flat area between the trail and Hazel Creek, an old homesite centers on a pile of red chimney bricks. Adjacent to it lie the remains of a root cellar. Root cellars were often located near a corner on the chimney side of a room. The flat area alongside the creek at this "terraced" homesite was most likely a vegetable garden or cornfield.

Nearby are other piles of rocks that look like they might have been footers for a house. Log cabins usually stood above the ground on sturdy rock pilings. As houses became more sophisticated, wooden latticework was used to face the spaces between footers. The best houses had complete stone foundations.

Close to the trail, a washtub forms a necklace around a tree—fairly common at homesites. It happens this way: a washtub lies on the ground, its bottom rusting out. A tree seed sprouts in the middle, becoming a sapling that flourishes with the extra water funneled to it by the sides of the washtub. As the sapling grows to a tree, its expanding trunk grows to meet the encircling washtub. Near the necklace tree, patches of shiny-leaved vinca remain from someone's gardening efforts. Shards of glass and other historical litter lie scattered alongside the trail.

A small eroding road continues to parallel the trail as it once did the railroad. About a mile beyond Bone Valley, a 10-foot-wide wooden bridge crossed Hazel Creek to the Burlingame house on the other side. The Burlingame house was reputedly the most splendid on Hazel Creek. It was built for Ritter's chief civil engineer, Orson Paul Burlingame, who relocated to Hazel Creek in 1902 from Racine, Wisconsin.

Although he had been married previously, Burlingame came as a single man and fell in love with Lillie Lucille Brooks. Brooks was raised here, but when she was 14, she moved to Boston for some years to work as a seamstress and a hat decorator. He was 60 and she 30 when they married in 1911. Ruth Burlingame Brown, the second of their four children, told of her family's history in the North Shore Historical Association newsletter.

The Burlingame house had 14 rooms, paneled with different species of woods and finished with hardwood floors throughout. The first floor included a living room and dining room with beamed ceilings and fireplaces, a laundry, a canning room, and a furnace room. The second floor held three bedrooms, a sewing room, and a large playroom. Burlingame piped water into the house from a nearby spring.

Lillie Brooks Burlingame's parents owned about 2,000 acres of land on Hazel Creek, some of it in orchards up near Ritter's Campsite 7. Burlingame was so devoted to his mother-in-law, Matilda Brooks, that he asked to be buried next to her.

6.5 Cold Spring Gap Trail junction. Hazel Creek becomes narrower at this point. Cold Spring Gap Trail veers off on the right side of the trail, heading toward Welch Ridge. Perched on a slope, a park bunkhouse with a screened porch looks down on the trail across from the junction. In the 1930s, members of the Cable family, among the earliest to settle on Hazel Creek, lived here. Now park personnel stay overnight when doing maintenance on this and other trails in the vicinity.

Beyond the bunkhouse, Hazel Creek Trail becomes steeper and rockier, with a number of step-over branches crossing the trail. At about 7.3 miles, a 2.5-foot-high rock wall flanks the left side of the road and, above it, stand the remains of a stone chimney. Pretty pipsissewa grows in the rubble of rock at the foot of the chimney.

Judd Hall, Granville Calhoun's brother-in-law, lived on the left of the trail very near here. Perhaps this was his place. Although lower Hazel Creek gets more use by anglers, trout are found on the upper stream as well. In 1898, Hall and Calhoun caught 476 brook trout in 4.5 hours not far upstream from here.

At about 8 miles, look for a homesite on the right in a flat, expansive area open to the sun. This place belonged to Joshua Calhoun. His fields spread all around, and it is still possible to make out the extent of these clearings, which continue to Campsite 82.

Joshua and Susan Crisp Calhoun, who arrived about 1886, had six children, including Granville Calhoun ("squire of Hazel Creek") and John Calhoun, who built his home farther upstream, just below the mouth of Walker Creek.

Although he made his living farming, keeping bees, and raising cattle, Josh Calhoun was a preacher by inclination. He spoke against the evils of alcohol and ran revivals on Hazel Creek and in other communities, including Cades Cove. Because he was lame, he rode a mule wherever he went, and he taught his mule to kneel so he could get on and off more easily. Community-minded Calhoun also helped build schools and churches on Hazel Creek.

8.3 Backcountry Campsite Number 82. At Campsite 82, horse-packers camp on the left side of the trail, and backpackers on the right, under trees along Hazel Creek.

Remnants of rock walls line both sides of the trail. In the mountains, rock walls were built around vegetable gardens and fields to protect them from livestock, which were allowed to roam free.

For those who continue beyond Campsite 82, Hazel Creek Trail becomes progressively more backcountry. No bridges cross the creeks above this point. The next homesite up the trail was Pink Martin's, Josh's son-in-law and John Calhoun's brother-in-law. Here, too, was the site of one of Hazel Creek's three splash dams, used by Taylor and Crate when they logged during the 1890s. John Calhoun's place lay just up the trail from Martin's, and before Walker Creek.

9.2 Walker Creek crossing. Rock-hop across to where the Walkers and other families had homes and fields. To reach Walker cemetery and its half-dozen graves, walk through the field on the left, following a faint path. Cross Walker Creek just before the cascade and circle upward to the top of the knoll and the cemetery; return to the main trail.

The trail then crosses Hazel Creek twice, in quick succession. Or take the path above the left bank of the creek, which meets the trail beyond the creek crossings.

10.1 Proctor Creek. Ritter Lumber's highest camp, Camp Seven, spread across this level area. Across the creek lie old homesites. George and Matilda Brooks, Orson Burlingame's in-laws, had a large peach orchard here. Of the 2,000 acres they owned on Hazel Creek, much of it was planted in apple orchards and vineyards. Until the Ritter era, which brought a resident doctor and dentist, George Brooks, with his wife's help, delivered more than 300 babies on Hazel Creek. "He died in 1938," Duane Oliver said, "the last surviving Civil War veteran in Swain County."

KEPHART PRONG TRAIL

DIRECTIONS: Take Newfound Gap Road (U.S. 441) approximately 8.8 miles south from the top of Newfound Gap to pulloff parking on the left. Or, from Smokemont in North Carolina, take Newfound Gap Road approximately 5 miles north to pullout parking on the right. Kephart Prong Trail starts at the broad footbridge across the Oconaluftee River adjacent to the pulloff parking.

LENGTH: 4 miles. This hike goes from the Kephart Prong trailhead to Kephart Prong shelter and back (2 miles, one way).

PHYSICAL PROFILE: Kephart Prong remains nearly level the first half-mile, than rises steadily but gently to the shelter. This easy to moderate walk crosses Kephart Prong by four railed footlogs.

CULTURAL PROFILE: Remnants of a Civilian Conservation Corps (CCC) camp and a WPA fish hatchery near the start of the trail are rife with evocative bits of history. Farther up, remnants of the logging era are scattered alongside the trail. At the end of the trail lies Kephart Prong shelter.

0.0 Begin by crossing a stout wooden bridge that spans the Oconaluftee River. Rollicking over rocks, the river makes a pleasant beginning. Its name is derived from the Cherokee word Egwanulti meaning "town by the river." Somehow, the name became attached to the river itself and white people shortened it further to Luftee.

Dorie Woodruff Cope, whose story is told in *Dorie, Woman of*

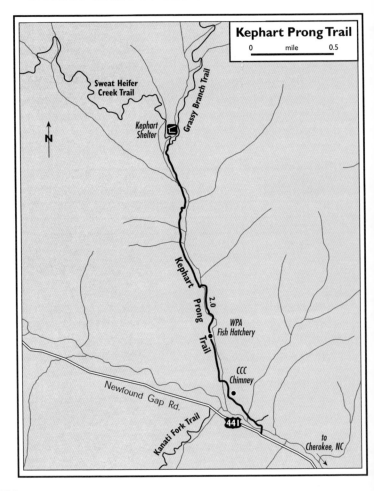

Kephart Prong Trail

0   mile   0.5

Sweat Heifer
Creek Trail

Grassy Branch Trail

Kephart
Shelter

N

Kephart Prong Trail

2.0

WPA
Fish Hatchery

CCC
Chimney

Newfound Gap Rd.

Kanati Fork Trail

441

to
Cherokee, NC

the Mountains, was born in 1899 in a one-room log cabin farther down along the river. Their Cherokee neighbors, who
taught Dorie's mother how to make bean bread and chestnut
dumplings, called one part of the river Ya'nu-dine hunyi,
"where the bears live." This part of the river might be called
"where waters sing."

The broad trail on the other side of the bridge was once a
paved road, and chunks of asphalt lie scattered here and there.
It winds past yellow birch, beech, tuliptrees, and rhododendron. The first sign of human endeavor is also a plant, one that
would not naturally grow in the Smokies.

0.2–0.3 CCC camp. On the left, a scraggly evergreen boxwood
stands behind a low section of stone wall. When Company 411

**Men from the Kephart Prong Civilian Conservation Corps (CCC) camp
pose behind the officer's quarters. Circa 1934.**

of the Civilian Conservation Corps (CCC) was stationed here, the boxwood was trim, just like the camp. From 1933 to 1942, the young CCC men stationed here improved 6 miles of Route 107, constructed 22 fish-rearing ponds, 65 miles of trails, 14 miles of mountain highway, parking areas for 600 cars, and a water system for Newfound Gap. They also planted 100,000 trees. Some of those trees were planted in this area because, a decade or so earlier, the slopes had been denuded by logging.

Beyond the first boxwood stands another boxwood, near two-foot-high stone pillars flanked by low stone walls. The remains of a stone-edged trail leads toward the river. This was once a formal entryway, perhaps to the officers' quarters. In addition, the camp, which housed about 200 corpsmen, included barracks, mess hall, recreation hall, education building, latrine, and woodworking shop.

Pieces of pipe lie scattered beyond the "entryway," engulfed by ferns, sedge, Dutchman's britches, and other wildflowers. The CCC occupied both sides of this broad, flat, weedy area, which is slowly reverting to its natural forested state. On the right side of the trail, opposite the pillars, stands a three-foot-high rusted wellhead. A masonry "notice board" once held news and information. A bit farther up the trail a hearth, approximately six feet high and wide, stands before a huge old oak.

A pair of big boxwoods stand sentinel on the right side of the trail and, behind them, an evergreen arborvitae twists 15 feet high and wide. Boxwood, arborvitae, and the clumps of yucca growing in this old CCC camp are always signs of human habitation in the Smokies, for none are native. Behind the arborvitae is a classy stone drinking fountain that looks as though you might be able to turn a knob and drink.

A few steps up the trail, again on the right, rises a 20-foot-high chimney with a hearth large enough for cooking. Back toward the high bank overlooking the camp, lie a rusting metal frame, metal stove or chimney tops, and a bit of rusting barrel. This was a well-used place. And it was used beyond the CCC era.

During World War II, the camp became a facility for conscientious objectors. The "conchies," as they were called, carried out a variety of chores in the park, even tutoring children of park rangers in reading, writing, spelling, and arithmetic.

Beyond the CCC camp, the trail narrows. A short side trail leads to a pebbled place along Kephart Prong. The main trail passes mountain laurel, rhododendron, and hemlock. The trail then bears left at a fork and, shortly, reaches the first of four railed footlogs over the stream. On the far side of the bridge, remnant stonework is embedded with pipe that once carried water to the camp. Oaks, tuliptrees, and Fraser magnolia add to the forest mix. After a broad bench of land, the trail rises slightly.

0.7 WPA fish hatchery. On the left of the trail and a few yards up the bank lie all that remains of a Work Projects Administration (WPA) fish hatchery: a 9- by 11-foot concrete platform with a 3- by 3.5-foot cistern in one corner. Nearby stand two concrete tanks, each 3 feet square and 3 feet deep.

Like the CCC, the WPA was initiated by the federal government to help relieve unemployment during the Depression. In 1936, the WPA built a fish hatchery on Kephart Prong com-

A 1937 photo of the fish hatchery on Kephart Prong.

prised of several buildings, a house, and nearly two dozen fish pools. Each rock-rimmed pool was approximately ten feet in diameter. In contrast to the forest-shaded Kephart Prong of today, the broad fishery area of the 1930s was cleared of trees and so open to the sun that two small, cloth-covered decks were built at the sides of each pool to provide shade for the fish.

Smokies tourism had begun in the first decades of the 1900s, and streams once flush with fish were being fast depleted by recreational fishing. The WPA project supplied trout and bass to park waters. In December 1936, the Kephart Prong fishery hatched a half-million trout eggs. As the trail continues upward, Kephart Prong tumbles prettily over mossy boulders below on the right.

1.0 Second footlog. This and the two upcoming footlogs cross Kephart Prong just above where the trail fords the water. The CCC made the footlog's stone supports. Between this and the third footlog—about 0.2 mile upstream—look along the left side of the trail for several lengths of railroad track.

In the early 1920s, Champion Fibre Company built a narrow-gauge railroad line up Kephart Prong. The logging company was after red spruce, which grows near the ridgeline between Newfound Gap and Dry Sluice Gap. The company constructed numerous switchbacks, building a railroad as far as they could into the mountains. To transport logs from the ridges to the railroad's loading platform, they used overhead skidders. These steam-powered skidders used overhead cables to carry logs downslope from as far as half a mile away.

Champion Fibre eventually clear-cut spruce from about 2,200 acres of the upper Oconaluftee and its tributaries. Like the other logging companies that cut much of the Smokies, it left piles of

Logging railroad on Kephart Prong of Oconaluftee River, 1925.

brush that became tinder-dry. In 1925, an extremely dry year, fire consumed the Oconaluftee watershed, burning to the tops of the peaks and over into Tennessee. A few years later, torrential rains pummeled the scorched earth, shearing off soil, in some places down to bare rock.

1.6 Fourth footlog. The trail follows the path of the old railbed, winding past tuliptrees, yellow birch, beech, and oak. Downy rattlesnake-plantain and partridgeberry spread at the feet of understory rhododendrons.

2.0 Kephart Prong shelter. This stone-and-wood shelter and its fireplace mark the end of the hike. Once this cove served as a logging camp and was busy with Shay locomotives toiling up and down, loggers' tents, torn-up terrain, noise, steam, the clanking of cables, and the like. Now it is a quiet and pleasant place for lunch. For those who want to go farther, Sweat Heifer and Grassy Branch Trails start just beyond the shelter.

Shelter, trail, and Mount Kephart, which rises just to the northwest, are named for Horace Kephart. A complex man, Kephart was one of the early and ardent supporters for establishing a national park in the Smokies. But he came to the area by a circuitous route. Raised in a family where he learned a love of the outdoors, Kephart first followed an academic life.

After a number of years as librarian in Missouri, Kephart, plagued by alcoholism and depression, left his wife, children, and the life he knew and set out for the Smokies. Here, he spent his first three years living in the mountains along Hazel Creek. After moving to the nearby town of Bryson City, North Carolina, he still spent much of his time outside, talking with mountain folk and recording their customs and lives in his book, *Our Southern Highlanders*.

LAKESHORE TRAIL: FONTANA DAM TO EAGLE CREEK

DIRECTIONS: From the park's Oconaluftee Visitor Center near the town of Cherokee, travel west on U.S. 74. Then take Route 28 west, winding along the south side of Fontana Lake toward Fontana Village. Or, from the western edge of the park, take the western end of the Foothills Parkway to Route 129. Turn left and travel east to Fontana Village.

Two miles east of Fontana Village, follow signs on the side road that goes north to Fontana Dam. Cross the dam, bear right, and park near the Lakeshore trailhead, about 0.5 mile from the dam. If the dam is closed to cars because of repairs, park in the Fontana Dam Visitor Center parking lot. Walk over the dam and bear to the right to the Lakeshore trailhead.

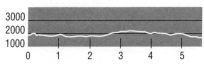

LENGTH: 11.3 miles. This hike goes from the western terminus of the Lakeshore Trail to Eagle Creek/Campsite 90 and back (5.6 miles, one way). If the dam is closed to cars because of repairs, add another 1.4 miles (0.7 mile, one way) from the visitor center parking lot to trailhead, totaling 12.2 miles.

To cut the mileage by half, make arrangements with the Fontana Village Marina (800-849-2258) for a dropoff by boat at Eagle Creek. The marina is conveniently located near the road to the dam.

PHYSICAL PROFILE: This segment of the Lakeshore Trail follows old North Carolina Route 288, then traverses a number of ridges—lots of moderate up and down—before reaching

Eagle Creek's Campsite 90. A few easy creek crossings. Fine views of Fontana Lake punctuate the hike.

CULTURAL PROFILE: Signs of human habitation all lie within the first 2.5 miles: first an old homesite. Then, along what was Route 288, are the highlights: the near-complete hulls of a number of old cars. Fontana Dam and the lake it formed are a critical part of this hike's history.

View of Fontana Lake from near Fontana Dam. 1955 photo.

The story of Fontana Dam begins with the original park boundaries, established along with the park in 1934. In places, these boundaries reached into North Carolina little more than a mile from the crest of the Smokies at the

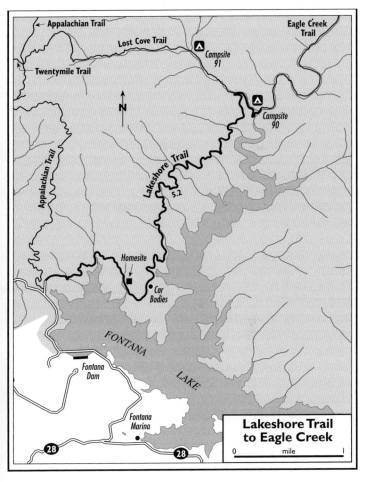

Lakeshore Trail
to Eagle Creek

0   mile   1

129

Tennessee-North Carolina border.

The park citizens group and the National Park Service wanted the North Carolina borders to extend from mountain crest to mountain base at the Little Tennessee River. Such boundaries would be logical for managing visitors, ecology, and hydrology. But a subsidiary of Tennessee Copper Company wanted $500 per acre for its lands, an inflated figure that was twice the amount anyone else had received. By 1940, the park was resigned to obscure, illogical boundaries. Then a solution appeared.

A decade earlier, the Aluminum Company of America (ALCOA) purchased land along the Little Tennessee River with the idea of building a large hydroelectric dam at Fontana to supply the aluminum company's electrical needs. The idea remained on the back burner until 1941, when World War II started. Suddenly the government needed to produce more aluminum for aircraft and other defense-related products.

A deal was made. The Tennessee Valley Authority (TVA), a federal agency, bought ALCOA's lands so the company had the money to speed aluminum production. To supply the necessary electricity for aluminum production, TVA began building Fontana Dam on the Little Tennessee River at the west end of the Smokies. Construction started in January 1942 and finished in November 1944—less than three years, a record for a dam this size.

At 480 feet high, Fontana Dam is the tallest dam east of the Rockies. It covers more than 10,000 acres and, at peak production, delivers 225,000 kilowatts of energy. Fontana Lake, which took a few months to fill, backs up 30 miles from the dam.

TVA also bought the land between ALCOA's property and

the park. The agency gave lands not flooded by the dam to the park, so that parkland reached from the crest of the Smokies to the water. In exchange, the park was to construct a paved road along the north shore of the newly created lake.

For area residents who did not serve in World War II, due to age and other circumstances, the dam provided employment in a historically underemployed area. Approximately 5,000 people, working in shifts around the clock, seven days a week, helped construct the dam. But the area paid a price. Although citizens received money for their property, all 600-plus families had to move. Fontana and five other towns, plus numerous smaller settlements, had to be dismantled before the rising lake water covered them. More than a thousand graves in 28 cemeteries had to be reinterred elsewhere.

By the 1970s, conservation issues arose, issues not even considered in the 1940s when TVA negotiations took place. TVA lands given to the park were returning to their natural state. Those with environmental concerns said a north shore road would permanently destroy any possible natural state. In addition, mineral leaching from road construction and quarrying would cause toxic minerals to spill into streams and Fontana Lake. Construction of the road was halted, though proponents of finishing the road continue to be active.

The period of settlement in the Smokies lasted little more than a hundred years. Yet, this era was recent enough that the road issue remains a sensitive point with descendents of those settlers. To compensate for the lack of a road, the National Park Service transports descendants across the lake and up to cemeteries to hold annual grave decoration days.

0.0 The Lakeshore Trail heading east begins on an old roadbed with a view of a Fontana Lake embayment far below to the right. You may see large cages within the first few hundred yards. These are traps for the non-native wild hogs that still inhabit the park, tearing up the terrain and competing with native animals for food.

0.3 At this point, the trail narrows, begins skirting hills, and switchbacks down along a side-stream drainage. The canopy is full of oaks: chestnut, northern red, southern red, and white. This is second-growth forest, the old-growth having been logged by the Whiting Manufacturing Company in the early 1900s. The trail continues to hug the hillside, curving around the back of a small cove, then passing mountain laurel, large rock outcrops along the left side of the trail, and another peek-a-boo view of the lake on the right.

0.8 Cross Payne Branch. The back of this cove is greened with hemlock, rhododendron, and dog-hobble. The narrow trail continues to curve around the sides of hills, then climbs briefly over a ridge of Shuckstack. The trail descends into a new drainage with a moist streambed on the right. Nearing the bottom of this tiny valley, at mile 1.5, look for remains of autos and an old homesite.

The small stream was originally called Mill Branch, along with a couple dozen other streams in the Smokies. To avoid confusion, it was renamed for the Payne family, who settled along its banks in the 1880s.

The Eagle Creek area has always been a connecting route

between North Carolina and Tennessee. The first to forge routes around the west end of the Smokies were Native Americans. In the mid-1800s, Cades Cove residents came this way, headed for new starts on Hazel Creek. During the early 1900s, Daniel and Verna Payne and their six children made the 15-mile trip to Cades Cove to visit relatives for a couple of weeks every year. And people came to the Payne house. Verna Payne had a trunk full of songbooks that drew neighbors to their house on Payne Branch to sing and tell stories and ghost tales.

In the mid-1920s, Daniel and his oldest son Marcus worked as loggers. Marcus saved his money and bought a Model-T Ford and a Victrola. Neighbors appreciated the new technology, but thought the Paynes were getting "bigity."

1.3 Old homesite and old autos. On the right, near the stream, lie the remains of a car plus a few chunks of concrete and part of a washtub. Just beyond, sparse American hollies and weeds have begun the process of filling in what was once cleared farmland. Although the house is no longer there, the black walnut tree and the four shrubs that form a precise 90-degree corner signal its former position. Because of their many uses— for shade, for dye, for the nuts themselves—black walnut trees were often planted near mountain homes.

A few hundred feet from the clearing, the remains of another old car lie at the base of a double-trunk sycamore alongside the stream. Here the trail comes to a "T," with an unpaved roadbed coming in from the right and continuing up toward the left. Go left, on what was once North Carolina Route 288. At the "T" intersection, look downslope for the remains of a rock retaining wall.

Route 288, a winding, sometimes tortuous gravel road, ran from Bryson City, at the eastern end of the present lake, to Deals Gap, about 10 miles west of Fontana Village on Route 129. It roughly paralleled the north shore railroad, which was the first transportation line connecting the towns and settlements that once dotted this side of the national park. (After the lake was filled, a south shore road was completed which connects Bryson and Fontana Village.)

In the 1930s and early 1940s, Route 288 was *the* road along

Jack and Lula Anthony and their Model T Ford.

the Little Tennessee River, curving past towns, settlements, and farms on the north shore of the river. The lake created by Fontana Dam flooded most of Route 288, but this section gives a sense of what was here before.

Back in the late 1800s and early 1900s, logging companies had been at work throughout the Smokies. The land on both sides of Route 288 and on the slopes was cleared. After the logging companies were finished, land speculators J.E. and Bland Coburn bought huge swaths of the clear-cut land, which they later sold to TVA.

1.75 Old cars. Starting with an old, upside-down car, approximately four vehicles line the edges of Route 288 for the next quarter-mile. These 1930s-era autos were left to rust because tires were needed for the war effort, and civilian tires were generally not available. North shore residents drove their vehicles until the tires wore out, then left them by the side of the road. After the war, with Fontana Lake as an obstacle, owners found it far too difficult to claim their vehicles. So here they sit.

2.2 Rock outcrops. Beyond where the road curves at the back of a small cove, outcrops of Nantahala Formation rock bulge along the left side of the road. Slate, mica, and schist are some of the minerals that comprise this formation. But the most sought-after minerals along Eagle Creek were copper and gold. Ed Trout, a park historian, described the Smokies' mineral deposits this way: "Over geological time, the mountains turned and turned like a marble cake. North Carolina got it all and Tennessee nothing."

By the late 1920s, logging companies had finished stripping trees from the Smokies and were pulling out. In 1927, the Fontana Mining Corporation opened a mine opposite this point on the other side of Eagle Creek. The Depression was close at hand, and the mine proved a lifesaver for workers who had lost logging jobs all along the north shore.

Between 1927 and 1944, when the mine closed, more than half a ton of high-grade copper ore was processed, plus more than 250 pounds of gold and 14,500 pounds of silver. Yielding the most significant amount of minerals in the Smokies, the Fontana ore body runs from the mouth of Eagle Creek to the old Adams-Westfeldt Mine on Hazel Creek.

2.5 Trail forks. Although Route 288 swings toward the right, stay with the Lakeshore Trail, which becomes a footpath at the left side of the road. As the trail ascends, it parallels a stream on the right. After an easy stream crossing, the trail tops a small ridge, then winds up and down, in and out over the undulating terrain of Shuckstack Ridge.

3.2 Cross Birchfield Branch. Just down the trail, a view of the lake appears. The trail continues to wind from cove to cove, some with tiny, step-over streams. At about 3.8 miles, the trail crosses a stream at the back of a cove just before rising over the lower flanks of Snake Den Ridge. The trail bears left, passing through pines, then begins to switchback down through rhododendron. This part of the hike is simply pleasant walking through varied terrain and a variety of forest types, with glimpses of Fontana Lake.

5.2 Lost Cove Trail junction. Narrow here, Lakeshore Trail descends to meet Lost Cove Trail, a broad old railroad bed coming in from the left. Turn right onto this broad path as the trails converge, paralleling Lost Cove Creek, which descends toward Campsite 91 where Eagle Creek meets Fontana Lake. The railbed was a spur line for the Montvale Lumber Company, which logged the Eagle Creek area.

The Myers family was one of the largest extended families across the mountain in Cades Cove. Part of the family moved over to the Eagle Creek area and one Will Myers lived up Lost Cove.

A trail sign 0.2 mile farther points ahead to Campsite 90.

5.6 Backcountry Campsite Number 90. The broad flats of Campsite 90 lie beneath a high, light canopy of trees and overlook the confluence of Lost Cove and Eagle creeks. It is a pretty place, accommodating both backpackers and horsepackers. A bay of Fontana Lake backs up this far,

A building on the Will Myers place. 1935 photo.

covering the site of Fontana with its waters. Fontana was the lumber and mining town that lay at the mouth of Eagle Creek, where the creek added its waters to the Little Tennessee River.

Although people passed through Eagle Creek, moving west from North Carolina, or east from Cades Cove, far fewer settled here than in other north shore creek valleys. Eagle Creek is simply too narrow for farming. By 1900, only seven families lived on the creek. One was Orville Welch, who lived on Ecoah Branch. One day in the 1890s, an eagle flew over his yard, dropping a piglet. In his book *Hazel Creek From Then Till Now* Duane Oliver says, "This strange gift from the heavens…grew into a fine hog."

Another was Aquilla "Quill" Rose and his wife Vicie, who was half Cherokee. They lived farther up Eagle Creek near where Ekaneetlee Creek comes in. Quill was one of the most famous moonshiners in the Smokies: famous for his whiskey and famous for not getting caught.

He had a gristmill where he ground green corn for his own and others' moonshine mash. He also had a blacksmith shop. Quill rarely went anywhere without his fiddle and his Winchester; he was good with both. When the U.S. government was paying bounties on wolf pelts, he was paid $5 for one as late as 1869. Once, after killing and skinning a bear, Quill wanted to show the measure of the bears found in the Smokies. He hoisted the hide as high above his head as he could. Still, four inches of the hind end trailed on the ground. Quill was nearly six-foot-two.

Aquilla Rose with a scythe.

And when it came to guns, Quill had his standards. Horace Kephart, who adopted the Smoky Mountains way of life and became one of its most famous chroniclers, was a friend of Quill's. One day, Kephart asked Quill if he wanted to buy a .30-.30 carbine he happened to have. In his book, *Our Southern Highlanders,* Kephart says Quill answered him this way: "I don't like them power-guns; you could shoot clar though a bear and kill your dog on the other side."

Through it all, Quill kept moonshining. Finally, though, the law caught up with him and he was brought before an Asheville, North Carolina, judge—who let him off with a warning. That was in 1912 when Quill was in his 80s.

Settlement on Eagle Creek picked up when Montvale Lumber Company established the logging industry and the town of Fontana. During that era, Eagle Creek was a much different place. In 1904, Montvale Lumber Company began building up the Eagle Creek area. Just downstream, where Eagle Creek once poured into the Little Tennessee River, stood the lumber town of Fontana. Some say the town was given its name by the wife of a Montvale executive, who thought the romantic name matched the views.

From Fontana, Montvale's narrow-gauge rail line ran 14 miles up the creek. With spur lines up the side creeks, railroads in Eagle Creek totaled 28 miles. By the time Montvale finished logging in the mid-1920s, they had cut 108 million board feet of lumber in the mill at Fontana.

Today it is hard to imagine the naked swaths of land that edged Eagle Creek and its tributaries. The music of the creek is pleasant, and Campsite 90's trees provide just enough shade for a relaxing respite before retracing the trail back to Fontana Dam.

LITTLE CATALOOCHEE TRAIL

DIRECTIONS: Best hiked using a two-car shuttle. The hike begins at the Pretty Hollow Gap trailhead in Cataloochee Valley and ends at the Little Cataloochee trailhead at Route 284. From Interstate 40, take Exit 20 (U.S. 276) and, almost immediately, turn right onto Cove Creek Road, which leads ten miles over Cove Creek Gap and down into the national park. About three of these miles are on narrow, winding gravel road.

Where the gravel road over Cove Creek Gap meets the paved park road at the head of Cataloochee Valley, Route 284 forks to the right. Take this gravel road approximately 5.5 miles to the Little Cataloochee trailhead. Park at the side of the road, but do not block the park gate. Drive the second car into Cataloochee, to the end of paved Cataloochee Road, where a small parking lot on the right lies at the trailhead for Pretty Hollow Gap Trail.

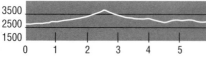

LENGTH: 5.9 miles from Cataloochee Road to Route 284. Pretty Hollow Gap Trail to Little Cataloochee Trail, 0.8 mile; Little Cataloochee Trail to Route 284, 5.2 miles. Optional 1 mile (0.5 mile, one way) on Long Bunk Trail for a total of 7 miles.

PHYSICAL PROFILE: Little Cataloochee Trail ascends steeply and quickly to a high point at Davidson Gap. The trail then generally descends with a few gentle ups and downs in between.

CULTURAL PROFILE: Little Cataloochee is one of the park's most culturally rich trails, with the Cook Cabin, applehouse ruins, Little Cataloochee Baptist Church and cemetery, Hannah Cabin, and more.

From the small parking area at the Pretty Hollow Gap trailhead, Beech Grove School is visible through the trees. Built in 1907, it replaced a smaller school building that, in 1880, was crammed with 85 schoolchildren. The story goes that Steve Woody and Hiram and George Caldwell made the long ride to Waynesville set on convincing the county commis-

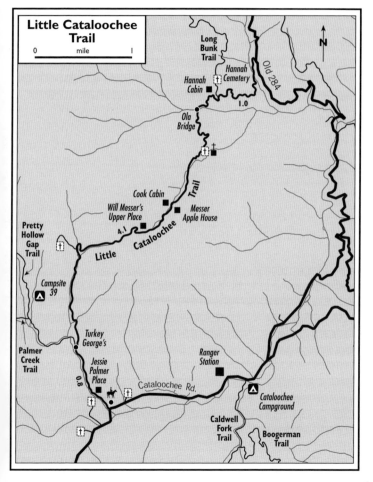

Little Cataloochee Trail

0   mile   1

N

Long Bunk Trail

Hannah Cabin

Hannah Cemetery

Old 284

1.0

Ola Bridge

Cook Cabin

Will Messer's Upper Place

Messer Apple House

Little Cataloochee Trail

4.1

Pretty Hollow Gap Trail

Campsite 39

Palmer Creek Trail

0.8

Turkey George's

Jessie Palmer Place

Cataloochee Rd.

Ranger Station

Caldwell Fork Trail

Cataloochee Campground

Boogerman Trail

HISTORY HIKES OF THE SMOKIES

sioners that they needed a larger school. Their request fell on deaf ears.

On the way home, they concocted a plan that they swore they would reveal to no one. Carefully, they removed all materials from the tiny school, then they burnt the building down, knowing that the law would require the county to fund its replacement. They got their new school, but few knew how until decades later.

Pretty Hollow Gap Trail

0.0 Pretty Hollow Gap Trail, which once served residents as a road, winds through second-growth woods 0.2 mile to a horse camp. In the 1850s, Jesse Palmer built a two-story house and a small gristmill where the horse camp now lies. Jesse's father George was the first Palmer to settle in Cataloochee.

In 1848, George Palmer was 54 years old when he, Polly, and their youngest children, Jesse and George Lafayette, moved to Cataloochee. While the Caldwells, Hannahs, and other first families of Cataloochee came looking for land, George Palmer came to put an unpleasant incident behind him and make a new start. A successful farmer elsewhere in North Carolina, Palmer had a bit too much to drink one day and suffered significant gambling losses. Some say he lost his farm, others all his money. In any case, he was so embarrassed that he fled with his family to Cataloochee, where the Palmer family thrived.

When Jesse Palmer built his gristmill here on Palmer Creek, the whole area was cleared of trees. Creek water provided the power to turn the heavy granite millstones. As corn was the main grain, eaten every day as cornbread and in dozens of other ways, gristmills were a necessity and a social focal point of every Smokies' settlement.

Eventually Jarvis Caldwell bought the mill from the Palmers and ran it until the park was established in the 1930s. Although the Caldwells and Palmers had many connections through marriage, through most of the hundred years of Cataloochee settlement, this was Palmer land.

In 1890, "Turkey" George Palmer, one of Jesse's sons, built his house about a half-mile farther up Palmer Creek, just below where Pretty Hollow Creek adds its waters to Palmer Creek. Back then the creek was called Indian Creek, and the area where Campsite 39 now lies was Indian Flats. While plowing the flats, which lay just beyond his house, Turkey George turned up Indian arrowheads, flints, and a rock corn-grinding bowl.

"Turkey" George Palmer in 1935.

Turkey George's garden area included a small patch of "sang." In the 1790s, botanist Andrew Michaux scoured the southern Appalachians for new plants to introduce to Europe and discovered wild ginseng in the mountains. He taught mountain people how to prepare this prized root for the China market and, like moonshine, "sang" became a way of earning cash. From his garden and from digging wild plants, Turkey George figured he earned about $50 to $60 a year. Unfortunately, digging wild ginseng became so popular that ginseng populations in the Smokies have since become threatened. All plants and artifacts in the national park are protected by law.

Although everyone planted corn and other crops, Turkey George basked in his reputation as a bear hunter. He claimed 105 kills and insisted he be buried in a steel coffin when he died so bears could not dig him up in revenge. But he got his name from a Wild Turkey-trapping adventure. He built a pen near his house, dug an opening at the bottom of one side, and planted a trail of corn kernels through the opening. The idea was that turkeys would scuttle into the pen after the corn, but would try to escape by flying upward—impossible.

The next day he discovered he had trapped about ten turkeys. When George entered the pen to grab one of them, the other turkeys thrashed him furiously with wings and feet. The name stuck.

0.8 Little Cataloochee Trail junction. Just below where Turkey George's house once stood (now marked by yuccas), Little Cataloochee Trail veers upward to the right.

Little Cataloochee Trail
0.0 Climbing steadily, following Little Davidson Branch briefly, then Davidson Branch, Little Cataloochee Trail crosses the latter several times within a half-mile. The water is generally ankle-deep, making for easy rock-hops, but this section of trail can be choppy from horse traffic. The branch was named for the Davidsons, who owned land on Long Bunk.

1.7 The first signs of Little Cataloochee history lie just below Davidson Gap: a four-foot-high section of stone wall runs across the slope and behind it are clumps of daffodils and the swordlike leaves of yucca, both planted for pleasure by settlers. A wire trap may also stand near the top of the wall to trap wild, non-native hogs that compete with native wildlife. Just beyond, another rock wall, this one about three feet high and nearly 75 feet long, parallels the trail. These were once fenced fields belonging to residents of Little Cataloochee.

1.8 Davidson Gap. On the shoulder of Noland Mountain, Davidson Gap connects Cataloochee and Little Cataloochee, but the last 0.3 mile is steep and deeply rutted from horse traffic. A few rose bushes, descendents of those planted by settlers, dot the edge of the trail. The windy top of the gap is flanked by hitching posts.

Levi and Mary Ann Colwell were the first family to settle in Big Cataloochee, but two of their daughters moved to Little Cataloochee. One married a Cook, the other a Bennett. Although the daughters' surnames changed, so did the spelling of their maiden name, from Colwell to Caldwell.

Mary Ann Colwell would walk five miles over Davidson Gap to see her daughters. Once, so the story goes, while she was on her way home, she spotted a mountain lion crouched in a tree, ready to pounce. With no defense at hand, Colwell tore off her apron and flung it on the path, hoping to slow down the big cat by tempting its curiosity. The mountain lion took the bait and stopped to sniff, but was soon back on her track. In her book *Reflections of Cataloochee Valley,* Hattie Caldwell Davis, a descendent, tells how Colwell kept dropping articles of clothing, finally making it home…nearly naked.

Today's hikers see neither mountain lions nor wolves. Neither can we see Little Cataloochee Valley spread below full of fields, orchards, and houses. The forest is growing back, full of tuliptrees, hemlocks, maples, rhododendron, and other natives. At the height of habitation, however, between 1890 and 1920, Little Cataloochee Valley was mostly cleared from edge to edge. It held 11 houses (four log houses and seven frame houses) plus springhouses, barns, applehouses, smokehouses, corncribs, and other outbuildings. Apple orchards and cornfields spread out around each cluster of farm buildings. And the church overlooked all from its hilltop position in the valley. It still does.

Most residents were descended from the dozen or so families that originally populated Big Cataloochee; they formed an interdependent network through marriages. There were, however, the Canadians, Bill and Nancy Ewart; but everyone substituted "Canadian" for their surname. That's how Canadian Top, the mountain that lies just southeast of Noland Mountain, got its name.

1.9 Signs of the Messer farm begin with a stone wall running across the slope. Another bit of moss-covered wall stands on the right. Nearby, on the left, a 9- by 12-foot cavity is set into the slope, lined on three sides by rock. This is the remains of Will Messer's applehouse. Back in the late 1800s and early 1900s, apple orchards marched up the slopes on both sides of Little Cataloochee Valley.

Apples that were not immediately sold were stored in applehouses many of which, like this one, were dug into a bank and thickly lined with stone. Usually two levels with a gabled roof, the half-buried applehouses afforded cool, moderate temperatures that helped preserve the apples. Messer's applehouse was moved and reconstructed—although not set into a hillside—at the Mountain Farm Museum near the Oconaluftee Visitor Center.

2.0 Messer homesite. A rock wall parallels the trail on the left and, nearby, large clumps of rosebushes rise behind a patch of bloodroot, the bloodroot native, the roses not. A flat weedy area thinly sprinkled with young trees signals the site of Will Messer's home.

His father Elijah ("Lige") Messer, who came to Cataloochee after the Civil War and settled on Caldwell Fork, was an accomplished man, and Will carried on the tradition. Born in 1870, Will moved into Little Cataloochee in 1894, when he married Rachel Cook, the daughter of Daniel and Harriet Cook, one of the first families to cross Noland Mountain.

The Messers lived with the Cooks until their first child was born, then Will built a log home here on upper Coggins Branch, followed by a barn, springhouse, and applehouse. Relocated by the National Park Service, the Messer barn now stands beside the ranger residence on Cataloochee Road. Messer's second house—the big house—lay farther down the valley across from Ola, the name of the post office and store that formed the center of the community.

Eventually, Messer became the most prominent citizen in

Little Cataloochee, and his wife a renowned homemaker. Although most mountain farmers had to learn skills from carpentry to animal husbandry just to survive, Messer became expert at most of them. He had a sawmill, a gristmill, and a blacksmith shop. He established Little Cataloochee's first store

The W.G.B. Messer store as it looked in December, 1937.

and post office, which he named Ola after his daughter Viola. He ran a prosperous farm, built coffins, and introduced Cataloochee's first cattle scale, charging between five and 10 cents per head for weighing.

Like Turkey George and other mountain dwellers, Messer had a "sang" patch where he grew ginseng for the Asian market. Whereas Turkey George Palmer had an 8- by 16-foot patch, Messer's was 40 by 100 feet. He was paid about 25 cents per pound of dry ginseng root, good money back then. In fact, it's said that everything Messer touched turned to money.

It was Messer, along with neighbors John Burgess and Mack Hannah, who introduced apple-growing to Little Cataloochee and transformed the community's economy. Messer's orchards brought him an average of $2,000 per year. Apples from Little Cataloochee were sold in Knoxville and Newport, and to logging camps that had begun dotting the Smokies near the end of the 1800s. Cash from orchards and other endeavors allowed Little Cataloochians to order clothes, dishes, treadle sewing machines, and items from "wish books" such as Sears and Roebuck.

2.0-2.5 A row of fence posts reaches down the hill from the Messer homesite. The trail, which has been running alongside Coggins Branch, is lined by a section of rock wall on the right. On the left, another rock wall runs perpendicular to the slope just uphill of where Coggins Branch crosses the road. For a hundred feet or so, the shallow stream and the trail intertwine before the trail claims its bed again. From this point on, the trail is actually the old roadbed that ran from Route 284 to this point.

A line of fence posts strung with barbed wire runs perpendicular to the trail. Nearby are a rock wall and a grove of young hemlocks. Wall, fence posts, and young trees hint that this area was once an enclosed field.

2.5 Cook Cabin and applehouse. Where the valley flattens out, the Cook Cabin stands on the left side of the trail. Across the road, a short footpath leads to the ruins of Cook's applehouse. Daniel Cook and Creighton Bennett were the sons of two of Cataloochee's original settlers. They both married daughters of Levi and Mary Ann ("Granny Pop") Colwell, another original Cataloochee family, and moved onto adjoining tracts here on Coggins Branch. Back when Little Cataloochee was the most remote settlement in the region, it must have been comforting for the Colwell sisters to live so near each other.

Cook built his cabin about 1856 on 100 acres of land. The

finest log cabin in the valley, it was Dan and Harriet Cook's home for more than 50 years. When vandals damaged the structure in 1975, the National Park Service dismantled what was left of the 17-by-20-foot cabin and stored it in a barn until the late 1990s, when it was reconstructed on its original site.

Park carpenters replaced rotted and broken timbers, hewing to historical accuracy, but they had to work hard to match Dan Cook's skills. Cook was known as an expert carpenter and cabinet-maker. When a Cataloochee house- or barn-raising began, the family often called on Cook to be the "corner-man." He would be the one to notch the ends of logs or timbers accurately so they would lock securely at the corners of the structure.

He built furniture for his own home: dressers, beds, chairs, and a cherrywood corner cabinet embellished with a star and moon motif. He also made the family's shoes. His wife Harriet grew flax, which she wove into cloth from which she made the family's clothes. She prepared and preserved all of their food and organized family trips to gather wild foods. Although Cook apparently preferred preaching to plowing, he cleared land and planted orchards on both sides of the path.

In the early 1890s, the Cooks divided their property among three of their eight children, giving daughter Rachel their home if she promised to care for them as they aged. Rachel's husband, Will Messer, took over much of the farming in the Cooks' later years. The applehouse, whose remains lie nestled against the hillside opposite, is called the Cook applehouse, but it was built by Messer a few years after Daniel Cook's death in 1908. The unusually large structure served as a community apple storehouse because most everyone had apple trees.

The high terrain of Cataloochee provides cool growing conditions, making it one of the best areas for apple-growing in the Smokies. Cataloochee farmers bought many of their trees from Stark Brothers Nurseries in Missouri: red and golden delicious, winesap, Stayman, and varieties once common but now hard to find. Late-ripening fruit, such as winter Johns, were stored in applehouses, while sweeter varieties would be used first. Near the applehouse lie the remains of an old road that once connected Big and Little Cataloochee via Bald Gap.

The community apple house built on the Dan and Harriet Cook farm.

2.6-2.8 This fairly level area was part of the Cook homestead. A fence strung with wire parallels the right side of the road. Adjacent, old metal buckets and other vestiges of farm life lie strewn across a broad area of sunny, once-cleared land. On the left is a section of eroding rock wall and more fencing. From this point, the road begins to rise above Coggins Branch and the valley bottom below on the right.

3.2 Little Cataloochee Baptist Church. The most ornate of the park's six churches, Little Cataloochee Baptist Church rests on a broad shelf of land overlooking the valley. From the scalloping on the eaves to the graceful steeple atop the gabled roof, this lovely white-painted church was a visible focal point of the community.

A 1937 view of the Little Cataloochee church and cemetery.

Built in 1889, the 20- by 24-foot church sits on land donated by J. Valentine Woody. William J. Hannah donated the 400-pound bell. Will Messer built the steeple and pulpit. Circuit-riding preachers from Waynesville came once a month, receiving between $5 and $10 dollars from the collection plate for each trip. During those years, the only wedding held in the church was that of Flora Messer (Will and Rachel's oldest child) to Charles Morrow. Most weddings were held at home before the hearth.

The church still serves as a focal point. Each year, on cemetery decoration days, descendents of those who settled Little Cataloochee reunite for services and a community picnic. But the tenor of services has changed somewhat. Back then women sat on one side of the aisle, men on the other, and the sermons were loud and fiery.

Still, men would edge outside to sit on the steps, pass the news, regale each other with stories, and barter: a hog for blacksmithing work, chickens for corn, and other trades. Boys ran around the grounds, taking advantage of the time off from the daily round of chores.

Church, the local store and post office, and the community gristmill were the places hard-working mountain folks could meet regularly, and they made the most of it. After church people might gather at each other's homes for Sunday dinner. With the large families that everyone had, it might take three "seatings" to get everyone fed at the Messers' long, 14-place table.

Revivals, held at the church in late summer, were all-day social events and feasts. Women would bring platters of fried chicken, biscuits, preserves, sweet potatoes, beans, pies and cakes. People would participate in shaped-note (Old Harp) singing, each tone designated by a circle, a triangle, and the like. Singing hymnal songs such as "Amazing Grace" and "Blessed Assurance," voices floated across the valley.

On one side of the church, the fenced cemetery holds approximately 60 gravestones. Messer, Palmer, Hannah, Hall, Burgess, Cook, Woody, and Bennett—the gravestone names confirm the settlers of Little Cataloochee. Dan (1831-1908) and Harriet (1837-1903) Cook are both buried here. Two of Will and Rachel Messer's children are buried here: Loretta and Ollie

Messer both died in 1920. Although the influenza epidemic that raged around the world near the close of World War I took time to reach Little Cataloochee, it took these two and others.

During fall and winter months, the church was used as a classroom. Eventually, Little Cataloochee had a separate schoolhouse, actually two successive schoolhouses. Both were substantial frame buildings. The first had a men's club on the second floor. The second, built in 1909, lasted until the park was established. Flora Messer Morrow served as one of the valley's schoolteachers. During one year she earned $50 a month for teaching 72 pupils.

A school year back then lasted only a few months. Mark Hannah, who was born in Cataloochee, a descendant of one of the valley's original settlers, said that youngsters such as 'Tine Bennett went to school only three months a year, and they looked forward to it. Otherwise, much of their time was filled with chores, such as pulling fodder and cutting tops in the cornfields and picking apples.

Most were sent to school with a woven basket packed full of food, which usually included a sampling of the following: biscuits, molasses and butter; green beans, cucumber, tomato, or corn; apple or blackberry pie; sometimes ham and sweet potatoes. Slates, rags, and chalk served as supplies. Although school was a treat, that did not prevent students from whooping it up during their 15-minute recess.

3.2-3.7 The road switchbacks downhill from the church and, where the land flattens out, patches of daffodils, planted long ago, announce the presence of a small, rocked-up spring at a

The W.G.B. Messer "big house" had gaslights and hot and cold running water. The Messer family poses out front.

curve in the road. Pieces of rusted metal lie strewn nearby. A low rock wall on the left, just before the confluence of Conrad Branch and Little Cataloochee Creek, signals the site of Ola.

3.7 Ola. Named after Viola, one of the Messers' daughters, Ola was the commercial center of Little Cataloochee. To the left stood Will Messer's general store and post office, as well as a blacksmith shop, gristmill, and other structures. To the right of the road stood the Messer's "big house," set approximately 75 feet back. Now all that marks its presence are two tall ornamental evergreens.

In its time, the Messers' second house was the largest and fanciest in Little Cataloochee Valley. Finished in 1910, the frame house had a tall gabled roof, a large wrap-around main-floor porch, and a second-story balcony porch. It had hot and cold running water, and its 11 rooms were lit by an acetylene gas lighting system. Messer was also the first in this valley to own a car. Like most, the Messers had a large family, and Will Messer was proud of his 11 children; 10 daughters and a son. He boasted that he had "ten daughters and everyone of them's got a brother."

Messer was also community minded. Although he was an ambitious businessman, the cherrywood coffins he built and sold for $7 were free to those he knew could not afford it. Like most mountain storekeepers, he accepted produce such as butter and honey, as well as foraged nuts and berries, in exchange for coffee, sugar, salt, thread, nails, tools, toys, and other items. He also extended credit to those who were caught short.

3.7-4.0 A short, wide bridge crosses Little Cataloochee Creek. On the near side of the creek stands a section of mossy rock wall, another remnant of Ola. Upstream, Woody Branch adds its waters to Little Cataloochee Creek. The branch is named for J. Valentine "'Tine'" Woody, who built a home and small gristmill there.

Most mountain people would have preferred to ignore the Civil War, but

"Uncle" J. Valentine "'Tine'" Woody.

Young Bennett, an original Cataloochee settler, and his sons were strong supporters of the Confederacy. Son Creighton Bennett, who married Louisa Matilda Colwell, Rachel Messer's sister, moved into Little Cataloochee in the 1850s, on property adjoining the Cooks. A decade or so later, Creighton died as a prisoner at Camp Douglas, Illinois. In 1880, when she was 42, his widow married 'Tine Woody and moved up Woody Branch. 'Tine Bennett, her son, was nicknamed for his stepfather.

The James Hannah house in 1937, two years after James and Melissa moved to make way for the establishment of the national park.

Like many property owners in Cataloochee, Woody rented to tenant farmers. One of his renters ran the mill, and it became known as a moonshine mill. Moonshine mash is made from sprouted corn, called "green corn." Most millers avoided grinding green corn because revenuers could easily spot its remains on the millstones. During Prohibition, moonshiners could make a decent amount of money in the Smokies' cash-poor economy, so hidden stills dotted the slopes. Green-corn millers, too, made more money from the moonshine business than from grinding an equal amount of cribbed corn.

4.0 Hannah cabin. A little way up the hill from Little Cataloochee Creek, the Hannah cabin stands on the left at the end of a short but steep path. An apple tree grows at the front, and banks of daylilies and daffodils grow on the slope next to the cabin. A covered porch that runs the length of the cabin looks out toward the flowerbank. Inside the 18- by 22-foot home, stairs set against one wall lead to a sleeping loft. Windows flank the brick fireplace, and the finely crafted puncheon floors are made from logs nearly 30 inches wide.

Missing are the railed fence, springhouse, corncrib, bee gums, and vegetable garden that stood on this property. Nearby was the Hannah apple orchard, reputed to have one of the world's largest apple trees.

This was the homeplace of Martha and John Jackson Hannah, he the son of Evan Hannah, one of Cataloochee's first settlers. The extended Hannah family was probably the largest in the valley, and a few of the Hannahs remained in Cataloochee long after the park was established, long after everyone else had gone. The reason? One of the Hannah's 11 children, Mack, had a son, Mark, who became the first park ranger in Cataloochee Valley. He served there for more than 30 years.

Although most of Cataloochee's dozens of homes, barns, and outbuildings were torn down and the forest allowed to reclaim its millennia-old realm, Mark Hannah did what he could to preserve the valley's human history. Perhaps his best preservation effort is found in *Little Cataloochee: Lost Settlement of the Smokies*, the book Hannah wrote with Elizabeth Powers.

Sited as it is, the Hannah cabin was in a perfect location for John Jackson Hannah to catch the latest news. John Jackson was interested in politics. A staunch Republican, he named his son Mack after a Republican senator from Ohio, and Mack was known as "Senator" when he was a boy. As an adult, Mack became one of the most successful commercial apple-growers in the valley.

Another of John Jackson's sons, James, carried mail between Big and Little Cataloochee, taught Sunday school, served as justice of the peace, and farmed. He also cut timber during the logging era. Known as Uncle Jim to all, he had a reputation for finding bee trees, and his wife Melissa tended bee gums. Uncle Jim and Melissa lived in the Hannah cabin until 1935 when they were displaced by the establishment of the national park.

A third son, William, left Cataloochee as a young man, attended college, then law school, and settled in Waynesville—the nearest large town—to practice law. It was William who donated the bell for Little Cataloochee Baptist Church.

4.1 Long Bunk Trail junction. Little Cataloochee Trail continues uphill from the Hannah cabin. Where the trail flattens out, it meets the junction with Long Bunk Trail, which splits off to the left toward Mount Sterling, six miles distant. A half-mile detour down Long Bunk reveals another cemetery and a homesite.

OPTIONAL SIDE TRIP: LONG BUNK TRAIL.

Like the eastern half of Little Cataloochee Trail, Long Bunk Trail is more old road than narrow footpath. A moderate uphill, its edges are lined with mountain laurel, trailing arbutus, and galax. In summer, Little Cataloochee residents drove their hogs and cattle onto Long Bunk Mountain: the cattle to graze and the hogs to fill up on chestnuts and other mast. Owners notched their livestock's ears in order to tell them apart. As early as the 1840s, cattle drovers such as the Davidsons took their herds onto Long Bunk to fatten them up for market.

This was also the route David Nelson took to reach school in Little Cataloochee. Mark Hannah said that Nelson, who lived near Mount Sterling Gap, had the longest hike of any Little Cataloochee pupil: a 10-mile round-trip. He got to school by 10 a.m. and had to leave by 3:30 p.m.

0.2 Hannah Cemetery. To the right of the trail spreads Hannah Cemetery. Here, Martha and John Jackson Hannah are buried, along with other members of the Hannah family. A few of the 50-some gravestones in the fenced cemetery mark the graves of war veterans, from the Spanish-American War and World War II. A huge stump stands before the cemetery gate, perhaps the remains one of the great chestnuts that dominated Smokies' forests before the species fell prey to an imported fungal disease. Yuccas, planted by settlers, stand in clumps.

Long Bunk Trail continues uphill another 0.2 mile, then descends 0.1 mile to a flat area that reveals the remains of an old homesite.

0.4 Homesite. Behind a large, gnarled oak on the right side of the trail lie the remains of a building. All that is left is a corner of the building, one to two layers of logs high. A flat, once-cleared area spreads out on the left. Violets and yellow ragwort dot the ground and young hemlocks promise to fill it in, but a couple of old metal buckets say someone once lived here. Although Long Bunk saw human activity all along its route, few signs are left, and this is a good place to turn around and rejoin Little Cataloochee Trail.

4.2–5.2 From its junction with Long Bunk, Little Cataloochee Trail remains level for a bit, then descends to a bridge across Correll Branch. Trillium, false Solomon's seal, and crested dwarf iris edge the trail, which parallels the tumbling branch upstream for part of the final 0.3 mile.

5.2 Trail's end at Route 284. Parallel to Route 284 and sometimes just out of sight, Asbury Trail (an unofficial trail near the park boundary) was the probable route of the "Cataloochee Turnpike." Completed in 1860, the turnpike was the first real road connecting the North Carolina and Tennessee sides of the Smokies. For the most part, it followed older tracks made by Cherokees and white pioneers after them.

In the mid-1850s, North Carolina passed legislation to build Cataloochee Turnpike as a toll road, charging 75 cents for a six-horse wagon, 10 cents for a man on horseback, and one cent for each hog or sheep. Each spring and fall, Cataloochee men were required to take a week or so to clear debris and fix washouts on the road. George Palmer, the first of the Palmer clan to settle in Cataloochee, died of a heart attack at the age of 65 on a cold day in 1859 while working on the turnpike.

Although the turnpike made getting to markets such as Newport, Tennessee, and Waynesville, North Carolina, easier, it also invited trouble during the Civil War. Renegades from both Union and Confederacy came into Cataloochee via the turnpike, usually to hide out or steal horses, food, and other supplies.

A Captain Albert Teague, who rounded up Confederate draft dodgers and tracked down Union sympathizers, captured three men on the Tennessee side of the turnpike. He and his rabble marched the men over Mount Sterling Gap toward Cataloochee. Not far from the gap, they stopped the prisoners and made one of them, Henry Grooms, a well-known fiddler, play for them. Grooms chose "Bonaparte's Retreat," a poignant and mournful tune known afterward as "Groom's tune." But the music did not soften Teague's heart: his men shot the three and left them dead in the road.

George Kirk, a renegade east Tennessee Confederate who joined the Union side and led a band of deserters and criminals, came into Cataloochee via the turnpike during the last days of the Civil War. The first house they passed was Young Bennett's second house, which likely stood near the intersection of Route 284 and the road into Big Cataloochee that follows Cataloochee Creek.

Young Bennett strongly supported the Confederacy. Six of his boys fought for the South and three of them died for that cause. He himself was away in the war. Hearing that Colonel Kirk and his 600-some men were approaching, Bennett's wife Allie hid their food and ran down the road to warn others. When she returned, she found the ruins of their house. Kirk and company had burned it down.

NOLAND CREEK TRAIL

DIRECTIONS: In Bryson City, west of Asheville (via either U.S. 74 or U.S. 19), turn north onto Everett Street at the old Swain County Courthouse. The road crosses the Tuckasegee River and becomes Lakeview Drive. About 8 miles from Bryson City, just before the viaduct over Noland Creek, park in the parking area on the left side of the road. The Noland Creek trailhead is in the corner of the parking area closest to the viaduct.

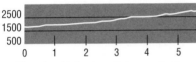

LENGTH: 11.2 miles. This hike goes from the Noland Creek trailhead at Lakeview Drive up to Campsite 63 and back (5.6 miles, one way).

PHYSICAL PROFILE: The broad, even trail follows a gentle grade all the way to Campsite 63, the turn-around point for this hike, a pleasant and easy meander along a lovely creek. Bridges and footlogs cross Noland Creek.

CULTURAL PROFILE: After Hazel Creek, this was the most heavily settled area along the north shore. Noland Creek Trail is a former roadbed that passes a number of homesites, cemeteries, old fields, and the remains of a large, waterwheel-powered mill and power plant.

0.0 Noland Creek Trail begins with a steep descent from the trailhead, but quickly makes a switchback and arrives at a broad roadbed running parallel to Noland Creek. A sign points left to Fontana Lake and right toward Springhouse Branch

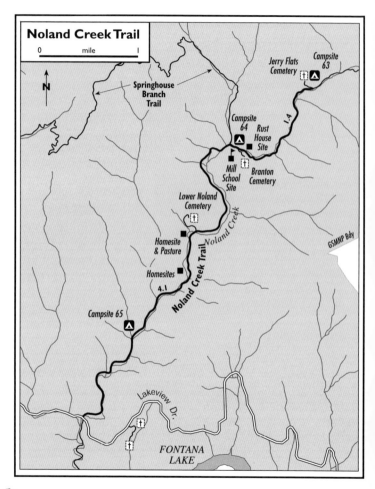

Noland Creek Trail

0   mile   1

N

Springhouse
Branch
Trail

Jerry Flats
Cemetery

Campsite
63

Campsite
64

Rust
House
Site

1.4

Mill
School
Site

Branton
Cemetery

Lower Noland
Cemetery

Noland Creek

Noland Creek Trail

GSMNP Bdy

Homesite
& Pasture

Homesites

4.1

Campsite 65

Lakeview Dr.

FONTANA
LAKE

Trail and Noland Divide. Go right.

In less than 0.2 mile, the trail will pass under the Lakeshore Drive viaduct and immediately cross a broad, vehicular bridge. Here sycamore and beech trees shade the trail, and the creek bank is dense with dog-hobble. Most of this trail is reminiscent of a walk up a country lane. Back in the early 1900s, it was exactly that.

Of all the main drainages on the north shore, Noland Creek was the only one never scarred by a logging company railroad. Noland Creek was a more pastoral valley, full of farmers. Noland's heyday was from the 1880s through the early 1900s. Although this period was also the logging era in the Smokies, only a modest amount of logging occurred here. Farmers selectively cut timber and, in the 1880s, Eversole Lumber Company came in to cut hardwoods in the upper reaches of the main creek. The company used cattle teams to bring logs down to its mill at the mouth of Noland Creek.

About 1905, the Harris-Woodbury Lumber Company purchased 17,000 acres that included Noland Creek, and they did some cutting, especially from 1905 through 1908. They went up as far as Bald Branch, near present-day Campsite 61, where they operated a portable mill. They also built a flume to bring logs down to the mill.

One of the Harris-Woodbury partners said, "We manufactured nine or ten million feet of hardwoods, with just a little bit of spruce." The total area cut was about 3,000 acres, but "we just cut out the large poplars, some selected oak and chestnut." In 1916 the company sold these lands to Champion Fibre Company, which held them in reserve. As a result, the top of

Noland Creek Trail still supports large, old trees.

Although the creek bears the name of the Noland family, Nolands are more closely associated with Cataloochee. In fact, William Noland was one of the first settlers on the North Carolina side of the Smokies. In 1839, he came into Cataloochee with his daughter and son-in-law, Elizabeth and Evan Hannah. Noland Mountain, which separates Big Cataloochee from Little Cataloochee, was also named for him.

During the first mile, rock outcrops appear on the left as the trail ascends past white oak and rhododendron. Just before Campsite 65, look for a bit of berm, the remains of a side road on the left, and a flat area that was probably once a field and is now filling in with trees.

A bearpen, used for killing bears.

1.4 Backcountry Campsite Number 65. Where the trail bears right, following the creek, a broad path leads straight ahead to Campsite 65. The path passes through a rhododendron tunnel to reach the small campsite, which is little more than 0.1 mile off the main trail. Not much is left to see at Campsite 65, although a few old homesites dot the edges of Bearpen Branch.

One of Noland Creek's two elementary schools was located here. The other was up at Mill Creek and, when the upper school closed, Swain County paid Noland Creek resident David

Payne to drive children from upper Noland down to the Bearpen school and back each day.

At about 1.8 miles, the main trail passes a white pine grove where young hemlocks and shade-tolerant hardwoods such as beech grow in the understory. Just before the second bridge, what might have been a rocked spring edges the left side of the trail.

2.1 Second bridge. About 300 feet beyond this broad bridge is the first of several old homesites along Noland Creek. Even before this homesite, an old road once angled off to property owned by Arby Gass. Each spring, Gass came up to Noland Creek from Bryson City, where he owned a bakery. He lived in a small house alongside his Noland Creek orchard, which was planted with apple, peach, and pear trees. He tended the orchard and, in autumn, brought back what he had harvested to his bakery and winter home in Bryson City. His bakery was known for its fruit pies.

By the early 1900s, it was possible to drive from Noland Creek to Bryson City. Back in the 1880s, the Southern Railroad built a railroad along the north shore of the Tuckasegee and Little Tennessee Rivers to serve logging operations. By the 1930s, the state had built Route 288, a gravel road that roughly paralleled the railroad and connected north shore communities: Noland, Forney, Hazel, Eagle Creek, and others.

The first man to own a truck on Noland used the truck to haul out "acid wood," which Champion Fibre Company bought for the chemicals they could extract. But it took a tank of gas just to get from Noland Creek to Bryson City, so this entrepreneur paid a fellow in Bryson City to send him a five-gallon can of gas every day via the train.

2.05 Old homesite. This homesite marks the trail's approach to the Solola Valley area of Noland Creek, where most of the Noland Creek community lived. Two big boxwoods planted long ago style the entryway to what was once Bob Patterson's home. Roses and privet grow next to the boxwood. Although these non-native plants look healthy, all that remains of the house are the remnants of a chimney. Bob Patterson, who served as sheriff of Swain County for two terms, also had a general store and post office up the trail.

About 0.3 mile farther up the trail on the right lies another old homesite. Here, three pair of evergreen boxwoods flank the entryway to the house. Once these shrubs were clipped and neat. Now they are so overgrown it is difficult to pass between them.

A set of low steps still leads up to where the front door once stood. The house remains are extensive: sections of stone foundation, one 35-feet long; tin sheeting; parts of plumbing pipes; a concrete pad centered on a round piece of grating that looks remarkably like an old shower grating.

Behind the house grows another huge ornamental shrub, an arborvitae. Near it, a pit was once some sort of cellar and, to the left of this cellar, stands a five-foot-square concrete cistern. Although he did not own the property, the last to live here was probably schoolteacher Ernest Lindsey.

2.8 Third bridge. Immediately after crossing this broad bridge, take the side road on the left less than 0.2 mile up a hill to another homesite on the left of that road. Farther up, a small cemetery perches atop a sharp ridge. At the homesite stands a tall, fieldstone chimney with a brick-lined fireplace on either side, the remains of three metal bed frames, plumbing pipes, an old sink and the white-sided cabinet that once held the sink, part of the foundations, and chunks of metal. Where the side road ends at a flat area above the homesite, parts of a water-delivery system edge the left side of the road.

After the property became part of the park, rangers used the house as a base for patrolling the Noland Creek area, especially during hunting season. The house burned down in 1979, some say the work of hunters who wanted to keep rangers from taking too close a look at what they were doing.

Where the flat area ends at the base of a slope, a sketchy path leads up the steep slope to a ridge and a small cemetery. About 0.4 mile from the main trail, it is somewhat difficult to find. The dozen graves lie in a single line because of the shape of the sharp, narrow ridge. Roy Payne, whose grandfather drove the Bearpen school wagon, said the ridge was so narrow that they had to be careful while burying people so their feet did not stick out the side of the hill.

Back at Noland Creek Trail, the land between bridges three and four is Solola Valley proper and was heavily settled. The valley post office bore the name "Solola," a corruption of the Cherokee word salali, for "squirrel." Salali was also the name of a renowned Cherokee who was an equally adept inventor, storyteller, and metalworker.

Just past the third bridge, the land on the right side of the trail belonged to Phillip Rust, who was an important property owner on Noland Creek. Allow your eyes to remove all the young trees in order to see the 600-acre sheep pasture that was here. A seven-strand barbed-wire fence ringed the pasture to keep the sheep in and the bears out. The top and bottom wires were electrified. Electrified? How was that possible? The answer lies about a mile up the trail.

For the next mile, broad aprons of land slope down to Noland Creek on the right and a few old homesites are visible. The rubble from a chimney stands in a former clearing down by the creek. Farther on, plantings of walnut trees and a stone foundation stand alongside the trail. Just before the fourth bridge, a large clearing steps down toward the right.

4.0 Fourth bridge. Mill Creek braids into Noland Creek immediately upstream from the bridge. Also immediately upstream are the remains of a large power plant: a concrete base and 10-foot-tall stone supports for the waterwheel that Rust used to generate electricity for his electric fence and for his house. Only a few people living in the north shore creek valleys had electricity. The structure probably served as a community gristmill as well. The foundations of Rust's house stand less than 0.5 mile up the trail from here.

4.1 Fifth bridge. The fifth bridge crosses the creek a very short distance beyond the fourth bridge. Mill Creek school once stood just before the fifth bridge, on a rise to the right. It was also called the Rust school because most of the pupils were children of people who worked for Rust, so Rust paid for the teacher.

4.2 Backcountry Campsite Number 64 and Springhouse Branch Trail junction. Immediately past the fifth bridge, a sign points forward for the Noland Creek Trail and to the left for the Springhouse Branch Trail, which leads over to Forney Ridge and Forney Creek trails. Campsite 64 is atop a small rise on the left of this junction, with hitching posts and open-air stalls for campers on horseback. The picnic tables in the sunny clearing make a fine place to eat lunch.

By the late 1890s, people had settled near the confluence of Mill Creek and Noland Creek, or a bit farther up, where Springhouse Branch adds its waters to Mill Creek. The lower section of Springhouse Branch Trail is studded with homesites, and it was so-named for the remains of a rocked springhouse.

Josh and Bertha Payne Lowe had settled along Mill Creek, and their son Eugene was born here in 1918. Josh Lowe farmed and worked for a time building Norwood Lumber Company's narrow-gauge railroad up Forney Creek. The Lowes moved to the mouth of Noland Creek when Gene was three years old, and his father got a job with the Southern Railroad, whose line ran along the north shore. Ironically, Gene was in charge of the crew that took up the last vestiges of railroad when the Tennessee Valley Authority bought up that property in the 1940s. (See the Fontana Dam story at Lakeshore Trail: Eagle Creek.)

Even earlier, during the Depression of the 1930s, Gene Lowe got his first job working with the Civilian Conservation Corps (CCC) on Clingmans Dome. By then, his family had moved west of Bryson City, anticipating the coming of the park. Only 17, he lied about his age, adding a year to make the CCC cut.

Every morning, before dawn, he walked five miles to Bryson City where he caught a bus for Clingmans Dome, put in a full day's work, took the bus back, and walked five miles back to his house, arriving after dark.

He was paid $2.40 a day, 40 cents of which went for the bus ride. In those hard times, people were thankful for that much. Later, Gene Lowe married Willa, a young woman whose family came from Hazel Creek.

On Noland Creek Trail, a few hundred feet beyond Campsite 64, look for a rocked spring at the left edge of the trail.

4.3 First footlog. After crossing the footlog, the Noland Creek Trail bears left. But continue straight about 30 feet to see the remains of the Rust house. Look for remnants of a chimney and a cellar. Just past that remnant structure, three sides of a well-built stone foundation are set against the base of a slope with dog-hobble gracefully arching over one wall.

Phillip Rust was the equivalent of landed gentry on Noland Creek. He had sheep pastures, power plants, electric lighting, a cook, and a fish hatchery, among other amenities and improvements. The clearing to the right of the housesite held Rust's fish hatchery. Water from the rocked springhead, at the back of the clearing, fed the pools.

To the left of the Rust house, a steep path ascends about 0.1 mile to Branton Cemetery where 30 people are buried in 29 graves: one grave holds a mother and baby. Many of the Branton family lie here, as well as some from the Woody family, and baby Ruth P. Laws. Cornelius Laws, the Rust's gamekeeper, managed the fish hatchery.

Like almost all graves on the North Carolina side of the Smokies, these have headstones and footstones, and all face east, anticipating resurrection. On decoration days, the descendants of those buried here mound the graves with fresh soil and decorate their relatives' graves with bouquets of flowers.

Return to the trail. On the right, Rust had cabins that he rented to summer visitors looking for a rustic vacation. One of his workers would drive down to Bryson City in a precursor station wagon to pick up vacationers arriving by train.

On the left, look for a five-foot-high quartzite boulder on the way to the next footlog. After the first footlog, the trail remains wide, but is rockier and less level. Low, damp spots are choppy from horse traffic.

5.0 Second footlog.

5.6 Backcountry Campsite Number 63. Campsite 63 spreads across both sides of the trail at Jerry Flats. Lightly canopied by trees, broad, level Jerry Flats was once planted with extensive cornfields. The farmer who owned and tended the fields lived along Mill Creek in the winter and had a small summer place overlooking Jerry Flats. His home was on the way to the tiny graveyard on the ridge.

On the left side of Campsite 63, a small footbridge crosses an equally small stream and the path beyond winds up about 0.1 mile to the ridge overlooking Jerry Flats. Here lie three graves, all believed to be the graves of children, one marked with Indian writing and one with a stick figure.

The remaining 3.6 miles of Noland Creek Trail, though very scenic, offer no signs of human habitation.

History Hikes

OF THE SMOKIES

TENNESSEE

COOPER ROAD TRAIL

DIRECTIONS: Best hiked using a two-car shuttle. Because the drive between trailheads spans about 30 miles, and traffic on the 11-mile Cades Cove Loop Road is often slow going, especially on weekends, it is good to get an early start. The hike begins at Cooper Road trailhead near Abrams Creek Campground and ends at the Elijah Oliver cabin about one-third of the way around Cades Cove Loop Road.

From Sugarlands Visitor Center, go west to Cades Cove on Little River Road and Laurel Creek Road. Or, from Townsend, take Route 73 to Laurel Creek Road west to Cades Cove. Take the Cades Cove Loop Road 4.3 miles. Look for the trailhead sign on the right and park on the left, between the stops for the Missionary Baptist Church (#7) and the Elijah Oliver place (#10). Leave one car here.

Continue around the loop road, take the park road east and turn toward Townsend. Take U.S. 321 to the western arm of the Foothills Parkway, then take the parkway to its end, where it meets Route 129. Turn left onto Route 129, then almost immediately turn left again onto Happy Valley Road and take it seven miles to Abrams Creek Campground. Park in the hikers' lot and walk about 0.4 mile through the campground to Cooper Road trailhead.

LENGTH: 10.5 miles.

PHYSICAL PROFILE: Cooper Road Trail rises in fits and starts,

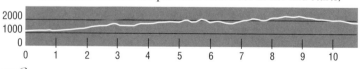

but never rises very far. This was, after all, an old road and its generally gentle grade and broad width reminds hikers of its original use.

CULTURAL PROFILE: Although no obvious remnants of human use lie along this trail, Cooper Road was the major commercial route in and out of Cades Cove. Without too much effort it is easy to imagine the many and various journeys people took as one walks along this classic Smokies country lane.

*R*oads can be metaphors as much as they are ribbons of asphalt or old tracks full of dusty ruts. Roads symbolize the transmission of culture and ideas as well as serving as real-life networks for products and goods. Roads tell the stories of war and politics, advance and decline, and the vicissitudes of a community.

Cooper Road embodies all of these and more. Unlike many other historical trails in the Smokies,

Land sleds generally traveled better on very rough roads than wagons with wheels.

where rock walls, old barns, and log cabins provide visible hooks for history, Cooper Road provides little in the way of human artifacts. Yet, the road itself evokes the Cades Cove era of the Smokies.

Cooper Road may have been an Indian track in the early

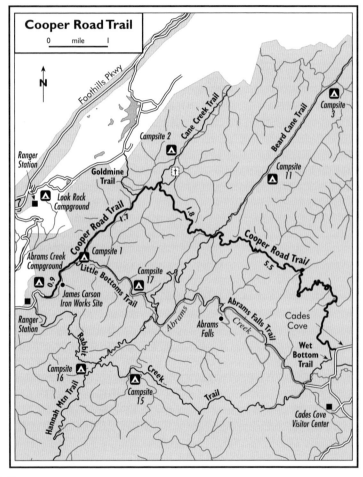

Cooper Road Trail

0   mile   1

N

Foothills Pkwy

Ranger
Station

Look Rock
Campground

Goldmine
Trail

Cane Creek Trail

Campsite 2

Campsite
3

Beard Cane Trail

Campsite
11

Cooper Road Trail

1.7

1.8

Cooper Road Trail

5.5

Abrams Creek
Campground

0.9

Campsite 1

Little Bottoms Trail

Campsite
17

Ranger
Station

James Carson
Iron Works Site

Abrams

Abrams
Falls

Creek

Abrams Falls Trail

Cades
Cove

Wet
Bottom
Trail

Rabbit

Campsite
16

Creek

Campsite
15

Trail

Hannah Mtn Trail

Cades Cove
Visitor Center

1800s, but the first white settlers in Cades Cove came by another Indian trail over Rich Mountain. The first route popularized by settlement, the Rich Mountain trail connected Cades Cove with a similar broad, level valley: Tuckaleechee Cove.

In 1818, John and Lucretia Oliver came over Rich Mountain from Carter County, Tennessee, as a sort of test case, to see whether white settlement could take hold in Cades Cove. They came at the suggestion of land speculator William Tipton, who promised to pay them for this experiment. Oliver had little to lose in Carter County because he was too poor to purchase land there. That first winter in the cove, the Olivers inhabited an old Cherokee hut and feared that Cherokee families living in the cove might attack them. In 1818 the land still belonged to the Cherokee. Yet it was the Cherokees of Cades Cove who shared their food stores and kept the Olivers from starvation.

In 1819, the U.S. government convinced the Cherokee to sign the Calhoun Treaty, thus giving up Cades Cove and the rest of the Smokies. After that, a small but steady stream of settlers entered Cades Cove.

Named for Chief Kade, a Cherokee leader, Cades Cove is unusual for the Smokies in that it is so level and fertile. Four miles long, a mile wide, and ringed by mountains, Cades Cove still seems something of a hidden never-never land. In the mid-1800s, most who settled here eked out livings as farmers, growing vegetables, corn, and lesser amounts of other grains. In summer, they took cattle and hogs up on the grassy balds to fatten them for market. Peter Cable, who became a great friend of John Oliver, used his skills to drain swamps, build irrigation networks, and generally improve the land. Daniel David Foute had other ideas entirely.

A man with many entrepreneurial interests, Foute built a bloomery forge near Forge Creek in Cades Cove in 1827. The chunks of iron he produced were made into farm tools that he

sold within the cove and beyond. In addition, Foute owned a hotel and sold merchandise in Montvale Springs. He was also clerk of the circuit court of Blount County and, from that position, saw that cove land speculation might prove profitable. He began buying land in Cades Cove in the 1830s, eventually owning 15,000 acres. In 1849, Foute built a home of his own in the cove and called it "Paradise Lost." For a number of years Foute served the cove community as justice of the peace.

Daniel David Foute was a major land owner in Cades Cove.

Although Cooper Road was used as a way to get to Maryville in the 1830s, it was little more than a trail. Foute mapped out a road that would allow him to transport the products of his forge and his Montvale businesses more easily. Joe Cooper supervised the final improvements to the road, which the Tennessee General Assembly authorized in 1852. It connected the folks of Cades Cove with markets in Maryville and Knoxville and, thus, the wider world.

0.0 The hike begins in Abrams Creek Campground, which is named for Old Abram, a Cherokee chief who was part Cherokee, part white. His village, Chilhowee, stood along its namesake creek southwest of what is now the park boundary.

At the beginning, Abrams Creek flows along the right side of Cooper Road Trail with maidenhair ferns decorating rock outcrops on the left.

Past the gate at the end of the campground, the trail is broad and flat, welcome entry for those on foot, horseback, wagon and—later—in automobiles. Mail service into Cades Cove began in 1833, even before Cooper Road was fully improved. Although post offices shifted over the years, Cades Cove enjoyed continual mail service until 1947. At first, however, the 96-mile roundtrip through a number of small communities at the western end of the Smokies brought mail into the cove only once a week.

From edges bordered by berry bushes, Cooper Road passes into shadowed hemlock groves. The road rises with Abrams Creek, whose wide, silky surface shines below. Within the first half-mile, however, Abrams Creek leaves the road and veers off to the right.

Kingfisher Creek pours into Abrams Creek just where the latter turns toward the east. Copper Road will now parallel Kingfisher Creek on and off for a mile or so. Here at the confluence, near the mouth of Kingfisher Creek, stood the James Carson Iron Works. Although later purchased by Foute, the James Carson Iron Works served the Happy Valley community in the 1830s. Remains from the forge were still visible as late as 1950.

Along with Foute's forge in Cades Cove, this was one of a number of forges that dotted the western end of the Smokies. The reason for the forges was that the western end of the Smokies held all minerals found in these mountains: iron, silver, lead, and others.

Small tributaries of Kingfisher Creek cross the road and, as the road rises, the forest community changes to hickories, maples, white oaks, and northern red oak. Then the road plunges through a shadowed hemlock grove dense with an understory of rhododendron and dog-hobble.

0.9 Little Bottoms Trail junction. Little Bottoms Trail veers east to parallel Abrams Creek toward Abrams Falls, 4.2 miles away, intersecting Hatcher Mountain Trail halfway along. Cooper Road continues straight ahead, paralleling the western park boundary.

0.9 Backcountry Campsite Number 1. Campsite 1, which serves both backpackers and horsepackers, lies on the right, bordered at the back by Kingfisher Creek. Perhaps this pleasant, level site also saw the wagons and blanket rolls of Cades Cove farmers, on their way to markets in Maryville and Knoxville, approximately 24 and 40 miles, respectively. In his book *Cades Cove,* Durwood Dunn says:

"Every fall a train of wagons left the cove loaded with a wide variety of crops. Usually the family took four days going and coming, camping along the road at night.... These annual trips accounted for the main part of the typical family's hard cash."

Their wagons might be loaded with corn and smaller amounts of wheat, oats, and rye. Garden crops such as peas, beans, and potatoes, white and sweet, might take up one corner, while a variety of orchard fruits, apples especially, would fill the rest. Butter, eggs, molasses, chestnuts, honey, beeswax, and tobacco were other produce Cades Cove farmers sold. Wood products, too, went to market, including some finished products, such as coffins fashioned of walnut and other fine wood.

With the cash they received, Cades Cove residents purchased shoes, kerosene, sugar, tools, slates for schoolchildren and, later, tablets and pencils as those school supplies replaced slates. Pre-Civil War, most women still grew, carded, spun, and wove flax to produce the cloth with which they made clothes for their families. After the war, when store-bought cloth became relatively cheap, bolts of cloth were added to the harvest-time shopping list.

One of the more popular and high-priced items that Cades Cove farmers sold in Maryville and elsewhere were the brandies and whiskeys made from orchard fruit and corn mash produced in the Chestnut Flats section of the cove. Chestnut Flats was a community socially cut off from the rest of the cove because of its lax morals and bad characters. But its liquor sold well.

Beyond Campsite 1, ruts made long ago furrow the road. Hemlock and pine shade the road's sandy soil. Soon hickory and oak add to the forest mix. Below, the road is edged by galax, wild ginger, and—in sunny patches—blueberry. Near where seeps cross the road, baneberry and partridgeberry grow. Look for a rock retaining wall running parallel to the trail.

At about 2 miles, another Kingfisher Creek tributary shallowly crosses the road. As Cooper Road rises slightly from the stream, Fraser magnolia and mountain laurel become obvious. Pines take over the higher, drier ground with a substory of blueberry, wintergreen, and the occasional American holly as the trail rises to Gold Mine Gap.

2.5 Gold Mine Trail junction. At Gold Mine Gap, Cooper Road continues straight and Gold Mine Trail angles left, reaching the park's western boundary in 0.8 mile. This road, too, was a D.D. Foute effort, connecting to his Montvale Springs resort hotel, which lay between here and Maryville. Foute was no slouch at creating networks to make his market reach farther.

Until this high point, Copper Road has seemed a pleasant country lane, displaying little sense of the mountains that rise nearby, but that is about to change. From this relative high point, the road drops back down to Cane Gap, a half-mile farther.

3.1 Cane Creek Trail junction. At Cane Gap, Cane Creek Trail bears left and Cooper Road continues 7.4 miles to Cades Cove, bearing right on an easterly course. Cane Creek Trail was once a main route connecting Miller Cove and Happy Valley, two broad, level valleys that lie just west of the park boundary.

Perhaps it was at such a junction where cattle drovers spent the night, bringing herds into the cove. In 1956, University of Tennessee professor Henry Duncan recalled experiencing the sounds of a cattle drive. The year was about 1904 and he was with his aunt and uncle, Sarah and Noah Burchfield, who were residents of Cades Cove. Back then, Knox County farmers hired Cades Cove drovers to bring cattle into the cove and up onto the balds to graze. The drovers took Cooper Road in and out of the cove, camping along the way.

"Bells could be heard for miles as they passed and this 'cow-bell serenade' put on in the spring and fall when the cove was full of hundreds of cattle wearing many-toned bells was a memorable thrill," Duncan wrote. The experience made such an impression on him that when Professor Duncan led a hike into the cove in 1955, he had members of the Smoky Mountain Hiking Club wear cowbells to re-create this auditory event.

Immediately after this meeting of trails, Cooper Road begins ascending a switchback; the trail becomes steeper and chocked with boulders. It is hard to imagine a wagon having an easy time of this section.

When Cooper Road was built, in the first half of the 1800s, it improved the lives of those who lived in Cades Cove, giving them critical connections with outside markets. As the years passed, the need to reach outside markets became more important. Improvements to Cooper Road, however, did not keep up with the times.

Until the state took over road building, each district levied its citizens in either time or money. In the district that included Cades Cove, able-bodied men between the ages of 21 and 45 were required to work on the public roads five to eight days a year, or pay the district road commissioner a dollar a day for each of those days.

As the nineteenth century wore on, Cooper Road and others wore out. The number of days' labor and the road tax were not enough to keep up repairs, and cove residents complained. By 1907, they were complaining to the county court and wrote letters to the Maryville Times:

"The poor man...must pay some fellow to haul his meat and flour over these bad roads, too. And you bet the merchant don't lose anything on account of bad roads. He just adds another dollar per hundred for bad roads, and the poor man just has to go down in his jeans and fork out the kale. Now who is the loser in the end?"

Feelings over the roads ran so high that it affected the choice of political party in the cove. Most of eastern Tennessee, including Cades Cove, supported the Union side during the Civil War. Although it would make sense that cove residents would support Republicans after the war, both parties remained strong in Cades Cove. In Cades Cove, Durwood Dunn says, "The most important reason, however, was the cove's conscious resentment at being shortchanged over funds for roads, schools, and other improvements common in other sections of the county."

This bad road, deeply rutted, continues up the side of Hatcher Mountain. Eventually it tops out and runs level along a ridge until it meets Beard Cane and Hatcher Mountain Trails.

4.9 Beard Cane and Hatcher Mountain trails junction. Beard Cane slopes down to the left; Hatcher Mountain continues on a ridge to the right. This intersection was one of the feeder routes by which drovers moved cattle from lowlands to the grassy balds that dot the western Smokies. In summer, these balds were favorite cattle-grazing areas. The Olivers and others maintained herders' cabins on the balds surrounding Cades Cove. In 1918, Hazel Creek's Granville Calhoun estimated the number of cattle atop the Smokies at 1,600 head.

During spring and fall, when drovers were either taking cattle up or bringing them down, the intersection of Cooper Road and Hatcher Mountain Trail must have been a pungent scene:

dozens of bawling cattle jostling each other along the ridge, hoofing up great spouts of dust as Cades Cove men drove them on.

This intersection is where Charlie Garland turned from Beard Cane onto Cooper Road in order to reach Maryville. Near the end of the nineteenth century, Charlie and Myria Garland lived a few miles down Beard Cane. Like many, Garland was primarily a farmer, but worked as a logger when the lumber companies came to the Smokies. He did a little moonshining, too.

Charlie Garland was also known as a strong man. In one of his columns for the *Knoxville News-Sentinel*, Carson Brewer tells the story of Charlie Garland's stove and how he brought it home on Cooper Road:

Charlie and Myria Garland.

"Charlie walked from his home to the Crawford-Caldwell Hardware Store in Maryville, about 20 miles, to buy a kitchen stove. He bought a step-stove. It weighed about 200 pounds. The storekeeper asked Charlie how he was going to get it home. Charlie said he'd carry it on his back. The storeowner doubted this. He doubted it so much that he told Charlie he'd give him the stove if he could carry it home without ever putting it down to rest. Charlie accepted the offer. The storeowner generously gave Charlie a heavy iron pot to carry with the stove.

"Charlie bought a rope and tied stove and pot onto his back.

The storeowner sent somebody with Charlie, just to see whether he might put down his load to rest a time or two. Charlie walked that 20 miles back to Beard Cane and never took the stove off his back, never sat down. But, according to the account handed down through the generations of Charlie's descendants, he did stop a time or two and leaned against a tree."

Beyond this junction, Cooper Road descends to cross a creek, ascends to cross a ridge, then does the same twice more. Cooper Road first crosses Wilson Branch, then climbs over the back of Stony Ridge.

8.0 Stony Ridge. Although this section of Cooper Road seems somewhat removed from even the low-key bustle that must have been Cades Cove at its height, Cooper Road here was still a better road to travel than any that could have been built on the steeper North Carolina side. And once a road emerged from the mountains on the North Carolina side, markets were still a longer way off. Waynesville and Asheville were the closest towns, but neither was on a large, navigable river. Knoxville, sited where the Holston and French Broad rivers meet to form the broad Tennessee River, was a better choice. Also, Knoxville had a railroad nearly 30 days ahead of Asheville. So, roads out of the cove headed farther into Tennessee and not toward North Carolina.

Unfortunately, like the Cataloochee Turnpike on the eastern side of the Smokies, a good through-route such as Cooper Road brought problems during the Civil War. Because Cades Cove's connections were almost all with Tennessee, the vast majority of residents stood with the Union Army, and many men enlisted. One standout Confederate in the cove was D.D. Foute.

Just before the war, an 1857 census showed only one slave in the cove, possibly belonging to Foute, who owned and housed slaves at some of his holdings outside the cove. Interestingly, the census also lists a family of free blacks living in the cove. It may be that they were among Foute's hired road builders.

As the war progressed, renegades loosely aligned with either Confederate or Union Armies began making their way into the Smokies. They came into an out-of-the-way area barely protected because most men from the Smokies were off soldiering. More outlaws than soldiers, these renegades looted and pillaged at will. Confederate renegades regularly hit Cades Cove, stealing guns, livestock, food—whatever they could get their hands on. They entered from North Carolina, but when they stole cattle, they drove them out along Cooper Road.

Cooper Road also served as an escape route for Union soldiers who had fled southern prison camps. From Cooper Road, it was only another 40 miles or so to Union-held Knoxville and safety.

After passing Stony Ridge and descending briefly to Stony Branch, Cooper Road slopes up to Arbutus Ridge. The ridge takes its name from trailing arbutus, a wildflower with leathery oval leaves. Its pink and white tubular flowers bloom as early as late February.

The trail descends again, gently. Then, Cooper Road begins curving to the right. At this point, travelers returning to the cove must have known that their goal was only a mile or so hence. Those that traversed this road the most were the mail carriers. Beginning in 1833, mail service lasted until 1947, although not all of the routes came by Cooper Road.

In 1961, Charles Myers, whose relatives arrived in the cove in the early 1800s, said, "We never were tied up in here and isolated like they might have you think. Why, we used to go to town every day sometimes for weeks. For six years and a half I carried mail over these mountains and never missed a day."

At first, mail service was only once a week, but by the late 1890s mail arrived at Cades Cove post offices three times a week. By this time, too, mail-order catalogs had become popular and cove residents could order a broad range of items, from dishes to clothing to tools.

Charlie Myers (r) and his younger brother, Sherman.

Peddlers, too, entered the cove by Cooper Road to sell their wares: needles and other sewing supplies, brooches, dozens of small items not otherwise easily obtained. Dunn says that the fate of peddlers who headed toward notorious Chestnut Flats led to chilling rumors:

"Many of these tradesmen…were never seen again after entering Chestnut Flats. Some of the flats men would subsequently be seen plowing their fields with a horse remarkably similar to that of the peddler. In a few days, the flats women would appear with innumerable ribbons and a profusion of new lace tied all around them and in their hair."

In the 1900s, residents had begun sending their children out of the cove for higher education in Maryville and beyond.

When these students returned home, they must have felt, at this point along the road, that journey's end was near.

John Oliver, who bore the same name as his great-grandfather, the first white settler in the cove, not only returned from college, but also brought everything he learned with him. He started the first home-delivery postal service and brought back new ways of farming and new breeds of livestock. But even as he educated his neighbors, the end of the Cades Cove community was near with the coming of the park in the 1930s. Many left as they entered, on Cooper Road.

As the trail approaches Cades Cove, the grade begins to slope gently downhill, past oaks, pines, tuliptrees, and Fraser magnolias. After passing the junction with Wet Bottom Trail at 10.3 miles, Cooper Road ends at Cades Cove, within sight of Elijah Oliver's place, son of the first John Oliver to live in Cades Cove and grandfather of the last.

GRAPEYARD RIDGE TRAIL

DIRECTIONS: Best hiked using a two-car shuttle. The hike begins at the Grapeyard Ridge trailhead in Greenbrier and ends at the Bales homestead along Roaring Fork Motor Nature Trail. From Gatlinburg, take Historic Nature Trail—Airport Road east to Cherokee Orchard Road and follow signs to the Roaring Fork Motor Nature Trail. (This five-mile, one-way road is open mid-March through late November.) Park one car in the parking lot at Stop 10, just above the Bales homestead where Grapeyard Ridge Trail ends.

From Roaring Fork, drive east on U.S. 321 about 5.5 miles,

turning right at the sign for the national park's Greenbrier
area. Continue past the Greenbrier ranger station and park in
one of the pullouts near the bridge where Greenbrier Road
meets Ramsey Prong Road. The trail starts on the west
(right) side of the road.

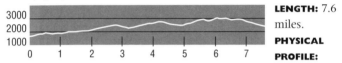

LENGTH: 7.6 miles.

PHYSICAL PROFILE:
From the Rhododendron Creek valley, this moderate trail
crosses James Gap and rambles along Grapeyard Ridge and
past a couple of drainages before descending to Roaring Fork.
The half-dozen unbridged stream crossings over generally
shallow streambeds may result in slightly wet feet—a pleasant prospect in summer.

CULTURAL PROFILE: The remains of a CCC camp, a small,
pleasant valley full of homesites, a wrecked steam engine,
and the preserved buildings of an old homestead keep this
hike culturally interesting all the way.

The first section of trail was an integral part of Big
Greenbrier back in the early 1900s when 700 people lived
in this mountain community. Now Greenbrier is a quiet, shady
forest. Then it was open to the sun and busy with human
activity. Homes, barns, farm fields, and orchards were chock-a-
block in Greenbrier Cove and along the creeks that feed the
Little Pigeon River.

What is now called Rhododendron Creek was once known
as Laurel Creek. Residents of the southern Appalachians often

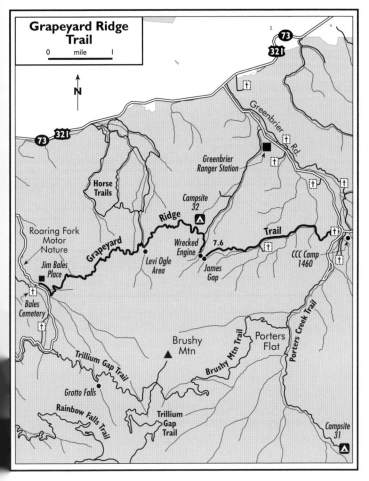

Grapeyard Ridge
Trail

0   mile   1

N

73 321

73 321

Horse
Trails

Greenbrier Rd

Greenbrier
Ranger Station

Campsite
32

Ridge

Trail

Roaring Fork
Motor
Nature

Grapeyard

Levi Ogle
Area

Wrecked
Engine

7.6

CCC Camp
1460

Jim Bales
Place

James
Gap

Bales
Cemetery

Brushy
Mtn

Porters
Flat

Porters Creek Trail

Trillium Gap Trail

Brushy Mtn Trail

Grotto Falls

Rainbow Falls Trail

Trillium
Gap
Trail

Campsite
31

call rhododendron "laurel" and speak of mountain laurel as "ivy." But so many park waterways were called "Laurel Creek" that the names of a number were changed to avoid confusion.

0.0 From Greenbrier Road, the narrow trail immediately enters woods and begins ascending through mountain laurel and hemlock with galax spreading along the forest floor.

0.05 Stone wall. Along the right side of the trail, atop a head-high bank, an impressive stone wall parallels the trail for about 60 feet. At the end of the wall, a small trail to the right arrives at a flat area above the wall scattered with red-clay pipe, blocks of concrete, and other debris from the Greenbrier Civilian Conservation Corps (CCC) Camp. Called Camp David Chapman (Company 1460), the main part of the camp lay just across from the trailhead, near the southeast corner of Greenbrier and Ramsey Prong Roads.

Like most of the Smokies' 22 CCC camps, which were started in 1933, a year before the park was established, this one had barracks, mess hall, recreation hall, officers' quarters, and other buildings. The young men who worked for the CCC made about $30 a month, most of which they sent home to families struggling to survive the Depression. Park trails, roads, walls, and bridges are among the CCC's legacy.

High stone columns bridged with a wooden arch spelling out "Timber Wolves" flanked the entrance to the camp. A tall pole topped by an electric lamp illuminated neat barracks divided by fences.

This camp was named for Colonel David C. Chapman. Called

Civilian Conservation Corps (CCC) Camp David Chapman, circa 1935.

"father of the park," Chapman was a leader of the Knoxville-based organization that fought for establishing Great Smoky Mountains National Park. When Company 1460 honored him with a program in 1935, the mess hall laid out a fine spread: fried chicken, boiled ham, June peas, potato salad, lettuce salad, rolls, lemonade, and for dessert cake and ice cream. The Greenbrier CCC quartet sang, "Ain't It a Shame" and "Quit Knocking."

0.1 Cemetery side trail. A well-worn trail on the right leads a couple of hundred feet to the Elijah Whaley Cemetery where approximately 15 graves occupy a cleared area. The Whaley family had many branches up and down this side of the Smokies, and Big Greenbrier Cove became known as the Whaley Settlement.

0.4 Up to this point, the trail has climbed a ridge separating Greenbrier Cove from the Rhododendron Creek valley. Now the trail begins its gentle descent into the valley. CCC Company 1459, which worked in this valley, recalled the "vast number of rattlesnakes they encountered." Although it is good to be alert, especially around high weeds and rock piles, snakes rarely put themselves in the way of the recreational trail walker.

0.5 First crossing of Rhododendron Creek. Just before reaching the creek crossing, a clearing to the left was probably a field. Avery Whaley's place lay on the left side of the creek, just after the first crossing, and Lewis Messer's on the right. Whaley owned 61.8 acres, about a quarter planted in apple trees. His three-room frame house was flanked by a smokehouse and a corncrib.

Around 1920, a dozen homes—maybe more—stood alongside Rhododendron Creek. The 50 children who lived in the valley had their own school. Before that, they would have walked two miles to school in Greenbrier.

The trail crosses the creek and its tributaries six times within the next two miles, after which it rises to James Gap. Unless rains have been heavy, these wet crossings are only ankle deep. Rhododendron Creek is generally about six feet wide with a level streambed—great for cooling your feet in hot weather.

After the second crossing, another flat area on the left, now filled with ferns, was once the home of George Rayfield. Farther upvalley lived George's son Andy. Born a Rayfield on then-Laurel Creek, Mrs. Isham Proffitt remembers eating well in this valley: fish, hog, squirrel, plenty of milk and butter, molasses, potatoes, and dried apples and peaches from their fruit trees.

Native vegetation has returned, with rhododendrons on the right bank shading the trail and young hemlocks on the left indicating another once-cleared area. This is a pretty little valley; settlers thought so, too. Hobart Ashley Rayfield, who grew up in this valley, entitled his short memoir "Thirteen Years in the Second Garden of Eden." Wild geranium, may-apple, trillium, and other wildflowers carpet the understory, as does plenty of poison ivy, which favors disturbed areas.

The James Whaley family lived on the left just beyond the third crossing. In Greenbrier and throughout the Smokies, people moved around: living next to their parents, moving to a nearby creek valley, trading homes with others, following the logging companies during that era, moving back to their parent's home.

The Ashley Rayfield house sat near the head of Injun Creek. 1936 photo.

At some point, the Whaleys traded a house on Porters Creek with the Sam Ownby family, who lived near what is now Ramsey Prong Road. Rather than arduously haul household goods over streams and bad roads, they simply exchanged houses, fully equipped.

In her memoirs, Evolena Ownby tells that after her parents

moved to Porters Creek, Mark Naugher of Rhododendron Creek began courting her older sister, Ezalee. Eventually they were married by Reverend Bradford Whaley, who lived near the upper end of Rhododendron Creek. Then the couple moved to Rhododendron Creek themselves, where his family lived.

Evolena remembered when a cousin died she and a friend came up the creek to sit with the body, as was the custom. They ate apples all night to keep from falling asleep.

1.8 Just after the fourth crossing, fence posts line the right side of the trail. A fifth crossing, then a sixth that leads into a small flat area filled with ferns and berry bushes. The creek now lies to the left of the trail. A few hundred feet to the left, beyond the creek, the small Dodgen-Rayfield Cemetery sits atop a knoll overlooking the creek. A small side trail near a striped maple tree leads toward there, but it can be difficult to locate. A bit beyond, 40 feet of rock wall lines the far side of the creek. This may be a wall associated with Isaac Stinnett's place.

South of Stinnett's place lived Reverend Bradford Whaley. Granny College, which stood along Porters Creek, was named for his wife, Granny Catherine Brown Whaley. When the Whaleys became too old to care for themselves, Reverend Bradford's son, Vander Bill Whaley, moved them from Rhododendron Creek to a house next to his on Porters Creek. After they died, Vander Bill donated their house on Porters Creek for an elementary school. He named it after his step-mother, Granny Catherine.

Now the trail leaves Rhododendron Creek and crosses a couple of seeps. Look for more fence posts, a thicket of sweet-shrub, and, among ferns on the right side of the trail, large pink lady's slippers. Posts continue sporadically as the trail climbs toward James Gap.

On the left, just below the gap, lived the Andy Rayfield family. Around 1900, Andy and his brother Jim roamed nearby peaks looking for Fraser firs. They would tap the resin-filled blisters under the tree's thin bark and sell it to medicine companies for 75 cents a pint. The companies bottled the fir resin and sold it as a remedy for burns and cuts. It was also taken internally as a kidney medicine. Rayfield said, "It took about a day to collect a pint, but by working extra hard as much as a quart of sap could be gathered."

Andy collected other plants to sell: ginseng, may-apple, and lobelia. His father caught, fattened, and slaughtered bears, then sold the meat for $1 a pound in Knoxville. The Rayfields grazed cattle on Silers Bald, farmed in summer, and worked for logging companies in winter. They found ways to make it in these difficult mountains.

In 1915, Andy and Caledonia Rayfield's eighth child, Hobart, was born in a log cabin on their 293-acre farm. The Rayfields had 500 apple trees and made many trips to Knoxville to sell the apples. The trip became a special treat for Hobart after his father bought a Model-T Ford truck whose speed could reach 15 miles per hour.

In the fall they gathered chestnuts. Among their crops were corn, beans, and sweet potatoes, which his mother turned into seasoned beans and sweet potato butter, as part of memorable meals. Hobart, who became a minister, remembered his parents as resourceful, industrious, and religious. He remembered, especially, his father singing hymns as he worked.

2.8 James Gap. A path to the right reveals a rock pile about 20 feet off the trail. Perhaps this is from the homesite of Ish Whaley who also lived near the top of James Gap. The gap was named for either Dallas James or his father, who lived near Rayfield, Tennessee.

2.9 Injun Creek engine. Injun Creek, a new watershed, begins just over the crest of James Gap. The creek's name most likely derives from a corruption of the word "engine."

    The trail crosses the creek; immediately to the right lie the

remains of a wrecked steam engine: boiler, gear wheel, and large metal-rimmed wheels. Stamped into the engine is the following: "Nichols & Shepard Co., Battle Creek, Michigan, 4246."

The wrecked steam engine on Injun Creek.

    Here's the story. About 1920 people in Big Greenbrier Cove needed a new school. Residents of Laurel Creek contributed the lumber. A logger drove this tractor-mounted steam engine into the valley to saw the wood. When the job was done, the driver decided to bring the engine down the creek valley now known as Injun Creek. Unfortunately, the driver got too close to the edge of the road and the vehicle tumbled toward the creek. No one was injured, but the engine was too heavy to move, so here it lies. The new schoolhouse was built, yet only a year later it was destroyed by fire.

Injun Creek continues to be heard, but not seen, toward the right. The trail passes a relatively open and flat site on the right, possibly an old homesite since a number of people lived along Injun Creek.

3.2 Backcountry Campsite Number 32. Campsite 32 is about 100 yards to the right of the trail, veering off where a sign points ahead toward the direction of Roaring Fork and Big Dudley Trail. A two-foot-high, moss-covered rock wall lines the right side of the path leading to the camp, probably a wall surrounding a former farm field. The flat areas around Campsite 32 add to the sense of former habitation.

From the junction with Campsite 32, the trail heads uphill, passing an old fence post as well as striped maple, Fraser magnolia, and white violets. After crossing a small branch, the trail switchbacks up past mountain laurel, then into a hemlock grove and past rhododendron.

Here, at about 4 miles, is Grapeyard Ridge. The trail winds below the ridge, from cove to cove, past beds of wildflowers: Solomon's seal, bloodroot, rue-anemone, blue cohosh, and others. Big trees reign—oaks and maples—and the thick, twisted ropes of grapevines tell how the area got its name. The Cherokee named the place winnesoka, for "grapevine," and white settlers adopted the name. Nearby rises Mount Winnesoka.

Eventually the trail begins to descend toward Grapeyard Branch and Dudley Creek. Squawroot and pipsissewa dot the oak-leaf litter on the forest floor. In season, a brilliant orange flame azalea blooms amid tuliptrees and other deciduous trees.

Old fence posts appear as well as a low section of rock wall along a slightly sloping former clearing. You will pass a hemlock grove, patches of crested dwarf iris, then descend past Grapeyard Branch to Dudley Creek.

4.8 Dudley Creek. A section of rockwork runs perpendicular to the far side of the creek. Step across the creek, and a low rock wall lies along the right side of the trail near rusted remains of what looks like an old stove. A piece of enameled pan hangs from the branch of a hemlock. On the right side of the trail, a flat area reveals the former Ogle homesite, bought by Levi Ogle in the early 1880s. The teacher for the school down along Dudley Creek boarded at the Ogle place. Another Ogle, Preacher Noah Ogle, lived in the Grapeyard Ridge area.

Here, a tub mill stood along the branch. A two-room log cabin, a barn, an apple orchard, and crops spread over this hundred-plus acre property, which the Ogles sold to the park for $1,900 in 1929. Still visible in the former clearing are hints of a road and what look like the remains of a chimney at the base of a yellow buckeye tree. Always a clue to human habitation are the black walnut trees, which most settlers planted for its nuts, for dye obtained from its shells, for its comfortable shade, and for its fine wood.

4.9 Big Dudley Trail junction. Big Dudley Trail veers right, leading to the Smoky Mountains Riding Stables on U.S. 321. The main trail veers left and rises. As the park has returned to its natural state, grouse, too, have returned. In season, you may hear them drumming in this area. Just beyond where the trails levels out, a rock pile and rose bushes on the right are signs of former habitation. A few small streams flow down from the left, the water breaking over 2.5-foot-high rock walls that run downslope from the trail. These walls may have been part of splash dams from the logging era.

The Levi and Julia Ogle family in 1912.

The trail rises again: rough, rocky, and deeply rutted by horse traffic. This part would not be a pleasant ascent in wet weather. In about 0.2 mile, look for a half-dozen fence posts on the right; these continue sporadically to a flattish area that was probably a former field.

The trail continues upward under trees that include a sprinkling of silverbell and sourwood. Mountain laurel and crested dwarf iris crowd a low gap just before the next trail sign.

6.1 A sign announces Roaring Fork 1.5 miles ahead. (The path to the right leads back to the riding stables.) A half-mile ahead, past a few more posts, is the highest point on the Grapeyard Ridge Trail at 3,000 feet. From Grapeyard Ridge, the trail has climbed into the steep heights of Roaring Fork and, now, the last mile plunges through cathedral forests full of tall tuliptrees and dense rhododendron slicks. The deep red blooms of Vasey's trillium and other wildflowers brighten the shaded understory as the sound of Roaring Fork begins to match its name.

7.3 A sign points to Roaring Fork 0.1 mile ahead. (The trail to the left intersects with the Trillium Gap Trail.) Just past the sign, rock outcrops and huge boulders make a dramatic end-of-the-trail farewell. Almost immediately the Cole place comes into view. The trail passes through an opening in a squat rock wall, then into the homesite clearing. The barn, with its low sloping roof and dirt floor, holds four stalls with rough-cut troughs. Nearby stands a good-sized corncrib with two 4- by 10-foot bins and a "dogtrot" between. Closest to Roaring Fork

The Jim Bales corncrib (foreground) and barn after restoration in 1962.

Motor Nature Trail is the cabin, approximately 17 feet square, sitting atop stone pilings.

The cabin originally stood in the Sugarlands. It belonged to Alex Cole, a logger and later a well-known guide who led visitors up to Mount Le Conte and elsewhere in the Smokies. After the park was established and that part of Sugarlands began returning to its natural state, the Cole cabin was moved here.

The corncrib and barn, part of the Jim Bales place, have stood here since they were built. Just across Roaring Fork

Road, near the end of Baskins Creek Trail, lies Bales Cemetery. The Ephraim Bales home is at Stop 11 on the Roaring Fork Motor Nature Trail. Jim and Ephraim Bales were brothers, two of seven children born to Caleb and Elizabeth Reagan Bales, who once lived in this section of the park.

JAKES CREEK TRAIL

DIRECTIONS: From Sugarlands Visitor Center, go west on Little River Road 4.9 miles and turn left into Elkmont. From the turn it is about 2.2 miles to the trailhead. Bear left at the campground, which lies about 1.5 miles from Little River Road. About 0.5 mile farther, bear right where the road forks and follow signs for Jakes Creek Trail for another 0.2 mile. The road ends at a gate marking the trailhead. Parking is available in a defined parking area off the road.

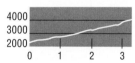

LENGTH: 6.6 miles. This hike goes from the Jakes Creek trailhead to Jakes Gap and back (3.3 miles, one way).

PHYSICAL PROFILE: The trail climbs at a moderate and fairly steady grade over its length, topping out at Jakes Gap. Water crossings include a couple of railed footlogs and some easy rock-hops.

CULTURAL PROFILE: The restored Avent Cabin, near the trail's beginning, is the most obvious evidence of habitation on Jakes Creek. In addition, scattered railroad detritus hints at the extensive logging that occurred here.

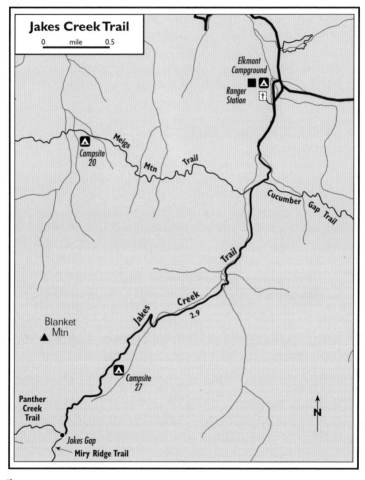

Jakes Creek Trail

0   mile   0.5

Elkmont
Campground

Ranger
Station

Meigs

Mtn

Trail

Cucumber Gap Trail

Creek

Trail

Jakes

2.9

Campsite
20

Blanket
Mtn

Campsite
27

Panther
Creek
Trail

N

Jakes Gap

Miry Ridge Trail

*D*uring the late 1800s and early 1900s, two billion board feet of lumber were stripped from the Smokies. About ten major lumber companies were involved, but Little River Lumber Company took the most, by far.

From 1901 to 1939, its years of operation in the Smokies, Little River Lumber Company cut approximately three-quarters of a billion board feet from the Tennessee side of the mountains. In order to haul logs to mills at Townsend, the company built a railroad along the Little River.

In his book *Last Train to Elkmont*, Vic Weals reports that Little River Lumber Company employed 600 people at its peak, and thousands over its three-plus decades of operation. Weals says: "[Little River Lumber Company] wore out 10 locomotives, three log loaders, several incline machines, two steam shovels, one ditcher, five steam-powered overhead skidders, and about 75 railroad flatcars."

A Little River Company log loader, circa 1911-1918.

Elkmont was a center for Little River Lumber Company operations. Logging trains came down from the mountains with their loads of logs; 1909 saw the start of daily passenger train service from Knoxville; Elkmont became a lumber town with a commissary, church, school, and houses. After the passenger train began operating, people from Knoxville and farther began vacationing in the Elkmont area.

Little River Company encouraged tourism development by selling lands it had stripped. Members of Knoxville's Appalachian Club began building rustic vacation homes at Elkmont. The original Wonderland Hotel was built, attracting more vacationers and more vacation homes. By 1934, when the park was established, more than 70 vacation homes and other structures stood cheek-by-jowl on the slopes near Elkmont. These moldering cottages continue to be a source of controversy.

Little River Company chose Jakes Creek as one of the first Elkmont drainages to log. But the company was not the first to arrive at Jakes Creek. Although Jakes Creek and Jakes Gap could have been named after any of a number of Jakes, they probably bear the name of Jake Houser. Houser, who moved here from Pennsylvania, built the first cabin in this drainage

The Elks and the Rebeccas on their annual picnic at Elkmont.

between 1840 and 1850.

Jakes Creek Trail begins as a broad former railroad bed. After Elkmont logging ended in the mid-1920s, automobiles used the railroad bed. When the National Park Service bought out landowners in the early 1930s, at least 17 families lived on Jakes Creek, on properties ranging from 1.5 acres to farms of 30 to 70 acres. As it did in the immediate Elkmont area, Little River Lumber Company sold off plots after all the saleable timber had been cut.

The first logging in Jakes Creek began in the late nineteenth century, when Swaggerty and Eubanks formed a partnership and selectively cut tuliptrees (yellow poplars) and ash, hauling the huge logs out with ox teams. It was not until 1901, when Little River Lumber Company came into the Elkmont area, buying land at $3 an acre, that serious treestripping began.

By 1909, a narrow-gauge rail line probed Jakes Creek. During the second cutting of the creek in the early 1920s, the rail line extended deep into the drainage, and the logs were hauled down the mountain by train. As one small tributary after another was clear-cut, the tracks would be lifted and transported down to Elkmont to be set up in another drainage. By 1926, all the tracks were removed and logging operations were switched to the Middle Prong (Tremont) area. But, by then, a major fire had swept Jakes Creek and, in another incident, three men had died in a train wreck.

0.0 By the 1930s, logging had shorn the slopes around Elkmont of their forest cover. Although now shaded by second-growth forest, Jakes Creek Trail, too, was once open to the sun.

0.03 In its moderate ascent, the trail passes over Tulip Branch, formerly known as Poplar Branch. In 1909, when Little River Lumber Company started logging the Jakes Creek drainage, Poplar Branch was cut. In *Last Train to Elkmont,* Weals reports that Pharis Trentham with John and Otha Ownby cut down what was reputed to be the largest tuliptree in the Smokies: 32 feet in circumference. They found the tree in the lower reaches of Poplar Branch and had to take a handle off Trentham's 11-foot crosscut saw in order to span the tree's girth while cutting. It was so big that, even after it was felled, they had to

The Avent cabin in July, 1938.

blast the tree into sections in order to load the monster on flatcars bound for the mill in Townsend.

0.3 Cucumber Gap Trail junction. Veering off to the left, Cucumber Gap Trail leads 2.3 miles to Little River Trail. Here, the smooth, lilylike leaves of Fraser's sedge arch over a bank beneath a canopy of northern red oaks, maples, tuliptrees, and Fraser magnolia. Continue on Jakes Creek Trail.

0.4 Meigs Mountain Trail junction. Dropping down to the right, Meigs Mountain Trail leads six miles to Buckhorn Gap.

Although people lived all the way into the upper reaches of Meigs Mountain, those who lived near this junction mingled with residents of Jakes Creek. The area from the trailhead to approximately Newt Prong Bridge, at 1.2 miles, used to be crowded with small farms, loggers' homes, and mining detritus. Now the slopes are crowded with dog-hobble, yellow birch, and tuliptrees, as they originally were.

0.7 Avent Cabin. The trail continues to rise gently, with Jakes Creek running parallel below. Look for a rocky, somewhat ill-defined path on the right leading down to the creek and crossing via a footlog. The narrow trail on the other side of the creek is much more obvious and leads upward, about 200 feet, to the restored Avent Cabin.

Built in the 1850s, the cabin originally belonged to Sam and Minnie Cook. Florence Cope Bush, who wrote *Dorie, Woman of the Mountains,* the lively and insightful story of her mother's life in the Smokies, tells that Sam Cook had an apple orchard between lower Jakes Creek and the Elkmont school. One day, while passing the orchard on his way home from school, Dorie's son Paul admired the apples. Cook had a hard time keeping youngsters from helping themselves to his apples, so the Cope family was pleased if surprised when Cook appeared with a box of apples for the boy.

The Cooks gave the cabin to their daughter and son-in-law, Eva and Steve Ownby, who sold the cabin and 18.5 acres to Mayna and Frank Avent in 1918. The next year, Mayna Treanor Avent began using the cabin as a studio and continued spending summers there, painting, until 1940.

Frank Avent was a Murfreesboro attorney who served for many years as state railroad commissioner. He died in 1941. Mayna, a nationally recognized artist, taught painting in Nashville for many years and exhibited throughout the United States until her death in 1959. The Smithsonian Institution's National Portrait Gallery contains her work. "The Brown Madonna" and "Tennessee Wheatfield" are two of her best-known paintings. "The Log," a painting flamboyant with color, is Avent's rendition of this cabin.

The Avents added a fireplace and the broad southwest-facing window. When a bear destroyed the old outbuilding that served as the kitchen, they added a kitchen shed to the main building. The mantle was painted Chinese red and on it stood candlesticks that the Avent's son Jim, an official with Standard Oil Company, brought back from China. When Mayna used the cabin, bright orange curtains fluttered at the big window and the main room was decorated with antiques, including a tall spinning wheel. The Avents encouraged friends and travelers to stay and record their experiences in a journal.

In 1932, the National Park Service (NPS) bought the cabin and leased it back to the Avents. In 1993, the cabin reverted to the NPS, and it is now on the National Register of Historic Places. In 1980 the last farm on Jakes Creek ceased operations. Now, Avent Cabin is the only original log home that remains along what was once a busy if rustic thoroughfare.

1.2 Newt Prong Bridge. Beyond Avent Cabin, the trail continues to rise through rhododendron thickets shaded by tall hemlocks. The creekbed, too, becomes steeper. At a particularly scenic spot, a path leads down to a small pool fed by a modest waterfall. Loops of rusting logging cable rest at the top of the path. These are probably the remains of an overhead skidder cable. The most efficient way to transport logs from steep slopes to railroad sidings was by fastening the logs to cables suspended above the ground. These steam-powered cable systems carried clusters of logs to sidings as much as a half-mile downslope.

Just below the railed footlog that crosses Newt Prong, a piece of rusting rail lies along the trail. Just above the bridge, where two tiny streams merge, lies another piece of rail. After the bridge, the road becomes more a trail, narrower and rockier.

It was in this vicinity that one of the Smokies' worst logging accidents occurred. Now the forest is a mix of red mulberry, maples, Fraser magnolia, beech, and other trees. Mossy rock pools lie between stretches of tumbling stream. And the edges of the trail are thick with wildflowers, including squirrel corn, rue-anemone, foamflower, and toothwort.

On June 30, 1909, the scenery looked much different. A railroad scored the forest. Back from the railbed's bare edges lay stumps and a clutter of branches. Gordon ("Daddy") Bryson was ready to take down a load of logs. At 55, stocky Daddy Bryson was an experienced engineer who was a favorite with Elkmont children. He took time to wave at them from the cab of the locomotive and, at ice-cream socials, provided dinner for children who might go without. With Bryson that day were brakeman Charles Jenkins, log loader Robert Headrick, conductor Aaron Jones, and fireman "Hoot" Foster.

It had rained the night before and the tracks were still wet.

The train wreck that killed Gordon "Daddy" Bryson and Charlie Jenkins on Jakes Creek.

Behind the Shay locomotive five flatcars were heavily loaded—overloaded—with stacks of huge logs. As an aid to braking on steep slopes, locomotives were fitted with sand reservoirs that sprinkled sand on the tracks while the train descended. Perhaps the sand reservoir was blocked that day. Whatever the reason, the train picked up speed and, when it hit the main line junction at a siding, it jumped the track.

The five men jumped, too. Three of them jumped clear, but Daddy Bryson was caught, crushed by his engine as it tumbled into the ravine along Jakes Creek. Vic Weals reported that Lem Ownby, the "Honey Man" who lived nearby on Meigs Mountain Trail, "was felling trees when he heard a 'thunderous rumble' of logs cascading from the wrecked train and saw the pall of steam and smoke and dust" rising from the overturned locomotive.

Charlie Jenkins almost made it, but a falling log pinned him to the rail and he died on the way to the doctor at Townsend. Six years later, Charlie's brother Tom died in a similar incident along Hazel Creek on the North Carolina side of the Smokies. The brothers had married two sisters. Widowed with small children, neither married again.

The next week, on July 5, daily passenger service from Knoxville to Elkmont began, and many came out to see the scene of the wreck. That day, the commissary at Elkmont sold out all 30 gallons of ice cream it had in stock. Someone composed "The Song of Daddy Bryson." Someone else wrote a song called "Daddy Bryson's Last Ride." Bryson's son Bose, also a railroad man, once threatened a man singing "Daddy Bryson's Last Ride," feeling that the song showed a lack of respect.

2.6 Backcountry Campsite Number 27. Mountain laurel mixes with rhododendron under a canopy that includes generous numbers of Fraser magnolia as the trail continues to rise. The sound of Jakes Creek fades as the trail moves toward the ridge. In a flat area on the left of the trail is Campsite 27. Probably this area served as a logging camp in the 1920s.

Flatcars would haul up lumber company-built houses and, using cranes, would deposit these cheap houses alongside the railroad tracks: instant camp, instant home. At about 8 by 14 feet, the houses were the size of flatcars and known as box-cars, cracker boxes, car shacks, and shotgun houses because they were scattered in camps along railroad tracks. When a lumber company was done logging a particular area, workers would hoist the houses back on flatcars and move them to the next logging site.

The five Ownby brothers, accompanied by wives and children, worked together up Jakes Creek in such a camp, 10 hours a day, six days a week. In the 1930s, a few of the Ownbys accompanied the last flatcar of logs to the mill at Townsend. During their logging years, the brothers had each saved enough to buy a farm in Sevier County.

Fred and Dorie Cope and their children lived in a boxcar house up Jakes Creek. Because of her husband's work with Little River Lumber Company, Dorie lived in camps all over the mountains, sometimes running boarding houses for single men.

Life in the lumber camps could be interrupted any time by accident or fire. One day in June, 1917, the cry went out: "Fire on the mountain!" Dorie and others in the camp watched as fire ate piles of brush and other logging debris. Set by sparks flying from a skidder cable, the fire climbed the ridge and burned along the ridgetops through the night. They evacuated camp and the fire continued to burn, charring huge portions of the Jakes Creek drainage over the next two months before it burned itself out.

3.3 Jakes Gap. The trail winds upward, the forest cover thinning toward the gap. At the gap (4,055 feet), Jakes Creek Trail meets Miry Ridge and Panther Creek Trails. Joe Barnes, who made 25 cents a day as a logger, remembered cutting huge hemlocks in the Panther Creek area near Jakes Gap. What lives at the top of the gap now are young, thinly scattered trees. From here, turn and retrace the trail down to the parking lot.

LITTLE BRIER GAP TRAIL

DIRECTIONS: From Sugarlands Visitor Center, travel west on
Little River Road 9.8 miles and turn right into the Metcalf
Bottoms Picnic Area. Go straight across the bridge and continue on Wear Cove Gap Road. The road swings left and, soon
after, a one-lane gravel road turns right off the main road.
Take this road as it winds up 0.5-plus mile, but watch for
oncoming cars at blind corners. The road ends at a small
parking lot at Little Greenbrier School.

   The gravel road is closed in winter, so during that season
and for those who like more natural approaches, park in the
Metcalf Bottoms Picnic Area and take the Metcalf Bottoms
Trail 0.75 mile to the schoolhouse, adding 1.5 miles,
roundtrip, to the hike.

LENGTH: 2.6 miles. This hike goes from Little Brier
Gap trailhead at Little Greenbrier School to the
Walker sisters cabin and back (1.3 miles one way).
PHYSICAL PROFILE: A short, country-lane walk on
a broad old roadbed that ascends, but only slightly.

CULTURAL PROFILE: Little Greenbrier School and Cemetery
introduce the hike. At the end of this short walk is the
Walker sisters' cabin, springhouse, and corncrib, one of the
most complete homesites left in the Smokies.

*A*lthough the Walker sisters' home now seems to sit in
splendid isolation, it was once part of the larger Little
Greenbrier community. Alexander McKenzie and Arthur
"Brice" McFalls were among the earliest arrivals in Little

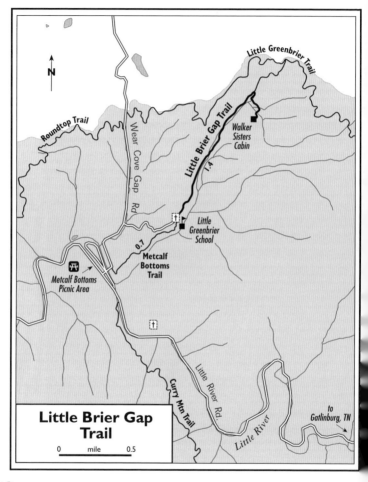

Little Brier Gap Trail

0   mile   0.5

Greenbrier. They were friends and neighbors in South Carolina, and came over the mountains to settle here in the 1830s. Little Greenbrier was at its height from the late 1800s to the early 1930s, when Great Smoky Mountains National Park was established.

Metcalf Bottoms, now the site of a park picnic area, was the entrance to the Little Greenbrier community. This low, level area is named for two Cherokee brothers, Ridley and William Metcalf, who came from North Carolina to settle here in the late 1800s. The Metcalf family had bean and corn fields near Little River Road, which overlays the route of the old Little River Railroad. When crews were constructing Little River Road, in the 1930s, the Metcalfs brought dippers of water to the workers.

Just beyond the bridge at the back of the picnic area, Dave Moore's orchards spread. Moore owned 28.3 acres with 100 apple trees, two acres of cultivated fields, a four-room frame house, a barn, and a woodshop.

During the logging era of the late 1800s and early 1900s, lumber became so affordable that, when the park was established, the majority of the buildings in Little Greenbrier were of frame construction. In fact, many of the houses that once dotted the Smokies were framed, but when the park was established, frame houses hardly seemed historical. As a result, the majority of preserved structures in the park are log structures.

Approaching from the gravel road, the view of a picket fence with a log building behind gives the impression of approaching a neighbor's home from some long-ago period. It sets the right mood. Just off the small parking lot at the end of Little Brier

Gap Road lies a small cemetery and, next to it, stands Little Greenbrier School. As with most Smokies communities, school and church were central gathering places.

Recess at Little Greenbrier school, March 2, 1936.

The school first opened in 1882, built on land donated by Gilbert Abbott, a resident of the cove. The tulip-tree (yellow poplar) logs used to build the school are so broad that each side is only five logs high. The roof was made with white oak shingles. About 20 feet by 30 feet, the school held sets of double desks flanking a center aisle. At the front of the one-room school are a long bench and a teacher's desk. On the wall behind the teacher's desk is a blackboard—literally, black-painted boards.

A cookstove warmed the room in winter and, undoubtedly, a bucket of water with a dipper used by all sat in one corner. The school lasted from 1882 until the 1935-36 school year, but was in session only a couple of months a year, some years as few as six weeks.

In 1952, Harrison Moore, a former pupil, recalled that school was held only during the coldest winter months. "…too cold for the boys to be needed in the fields." Another former pupil, George Milton, said that most students arrived at school barefoot, even in winter. "I've come here barefooted, frost on the ground," said Milton. "Our toes would be as red as turkey snouts when we got here." Some students walked as much as nine miles.

In 1929, Myrtle Perry drove her Model-T Ford over from Wears Valley to serve as the school's last teacher. She began the year with 50 students. Like other teachers in the one-room schoolhouses that were standard in the Smokies, Perry managed to teach a broad range of ages, generally from first through sixth grades. She was paid $85 a month, but $15 of that

Teacher Herman Matthews and the Little Greenbrier school class of 1935. Matthews was the first Little Greenbrier instructor with a college degree.

went to John Walker, brother of the Walker sisters, at whose home she boarded. The frame Walker house and barn stood within view of the school.

As families began moving to make way for the national park, her students dwindled to 30 by 1930, at the end of the school year. The students cried on the last day of school, Perry said, "but back then they always cried when school was out."

The school is flanked by a cemetery because, for most of its years, the building also served as a Primitive Baptist Church.

Once a year the old schoolhouse still rings with the sounds of voices, as it must have when churchgoers met on Sundays or for revivals in the summer. At the annual Little Greenbrier School homecoming, shaped-note singing is a musically evocative event.

The cemetery, which holds some 59 marked and unmarked graves, reflects the surnames of those who lived in Little Greenbrier: Jennings, Moore, Heaton, and many Walkers. A row of gravestones, many with doves etched at the top, memorializes Walker children, some who lived a few years, some only a few months. The inscription on one, a boy who lived only one and a half months in 1933, reads: "budded on earth to bloom in Heaven."

0.0 From the schoolhouse, pass the steel gate at the beginning of Little Brier Gap Trail. The old gravel roadbed ascends easily through a young, airy forest full of sourwood, hemlock, pine, oak, and tuliptrees. Mountain laurel leans from the banks at the side of the road. On the right, banks of dog-hobble slope down to Little Brier Branch. Beyond stretches a fine view of Rocky Ridge.

1.1 Here, Little Brier Gap Trail and road part company. The trail narrows and continues another half-mile to the park boundary, where it meets Little Greenbrier Trail at Little Brier Gap. Take the road, which swings in a broad U toward the right and downward, looking exactly like the country lane it once was. It leads into Five Sisters Cove, named for the five sisters who were among the last to live in the Smokies.

1.3 Walker sisters' house. Entering the clearing, the first visible structure is the springhouse. The rock-lined spring is not far from the springhouse. Its water flows down through the bottom of the small springhouse, where milk, butter, and other perishables were stored on flat rocks and shelves to keep cool during the hottest of days.

Beyond stands the house, with its low-slung front porch fronting a squat room. The room is attached to a tall, two-story structure whose back wall centers on a huge stone chimney. Behind the house, a corncrib is overhung with eaves wide enough to shelter the Walkers' tools and other gear.

The Walker sisters' home in May, 1936.

Even if no buildings stood in the clearing, it would be obvious that people had once lived here. The glossy green leaves of non-native vinca drift over the ground. Daffodils bloom here in spring. Lilac and other shrubs dot the landscape. Tall privet punctuates the area around the cabin, which is fronted by clumps of yucca planted long ago. When the Walker sisters lived here, more than 30 varieties of roses rambled over fences and other structures. Chrysanthemum and cosmos bloomed in the front yard, and who knows how many other flowers colored this clearing.

The house itself is actually a pairing of two houses: the smaller one married to the larger one. The smaller structure was built by Brice McFalls in the 1840s and originally stood about 400 yards from its present location. When Wylie and Mary Jane King acquired the land not long afterward, they lived in the small cabin until Wylie decided to build a larger house for his wife and children. In the 1860s, their youngest child, Margaret Jane, attracted the attention of a young man from Wear Cove, just over Little Brier Gap.

John N. Walker courted Margaret Jane, but the Civil War intervened. Walker, an ardent Unionist, was captured and spent time in a Confederate prison where he might have starved were it not for the kindness of a farmer who brought a load of pumpkins to the prison. In 1866, after he returned home, he and Margaret Jane married. A few years later, Wylie King died. All of the older children had left home, so the Walkers moved in with his widow to help her run the farm.

Eventually, the King cabin become too small for the Walker family, which grew to 11 children. So, in the late 1870s, John Walker dismantled the small McBride/King cabin and moved it piece by piece, joining it to the larger, two-story house. The small cabin, with its own fireplace, became the kitchen. The large cabin, with its fireplace, was both living room and bedroom for the Walker sisters. When they and their siblings were small, however, the upper level was the children's bedroom. At the same time, Walker added the railed and covered front porch.

John Walker shared the same name as many other area men, so he was called Hairy John for the full beard that distinguished him from the others. He was a skilled craftsman. All mountain farmers had to be remarkably self-sufficient, but John was good at more than most. He was a blacksmith, a leather craftsman, and ran a little gristmill that had a wood-turning lathe where he worked his carpentry skills. Walker built tables, chairs, looms, spinning wheels, wagons, and the sturdy beds the Walker sisters used all of their lives. He also built the numerous other structures that dotted this property.

The Walkers sisters' place showing row crops and orchard. 1936 photo.

In addition to the three structures remaining, the Walker farm had an apple house, a blacksmith shop, a gristmill, a pig-pen, and a smokehouse hung with salted and smoked pork and mutton. The barn, which had an attached, open-sided wagon shed, housed a mule, dairy cows, and sheep during the harsh months of winter. The one structure missing was an out-house. Margaret Jane found the odor of an outhouse embarrassing, so men relieved themselves in the woods above the house, and women in the woods below.

Besides wood and stone structures, the clearing also held drying racks, tar kiln, charcoal-making pit, and an ash hopper. To make soap, Margaret Jane ran water through ashes saved in the hopper, leaching out chemically caustic lye. The lye was cooked with lard in a big kettle to produce the lye soap found in all mountain homes. Elsewhere in the clearing stood sections of hollowed-out black gum trunks—bee gums—where bees made gallons of honey that fed their own broods as well as the Walkers.

The garden was full of peas, beans, tomatoes, beets, potatoes, turnips, pumpkins, and other vegetables. Large heads of cabbage were made into sauerkraut packed in crocks and stored in the springhouse. Often the sisters interplanted rows of vegetables with rows of flowers. And there were always plots for herbs. The sisters learned herbal uses from their mother, who was known for her skills as an herb doctor and a midwife.

The fact that Margaret Jane Walker raised all 11 children to adulthood was a feat in itself. Her husband bragged that he spent no more than 50 cents for a medical doctor in his whole life, and that was for two sons who contracted measles while away at school.

Margaret Jane was as self-reliant as she was knowledgeable. Once, when she heard the chickens squawking, she ran out to find that a weasel had seized one. She grabbed the weasel, but it bit her and would not let go. With great composure, she walked to the washtub and submerged her hand with the weasel dangling from it. She held her hand deep in the tub until the weasel drowned.

She taught her daughters everything she knew about herbal remedies; throughout their lives, they grew boneset, catnip, peppermint, and dozens of other herbs. Beyond the herb and vegetable garden lay cornfields as well as fenced pastures for the livestock. Although early farmers allowed their livestock to roam free, fence laws were instituted in 1947 in Tennessee. Some earlier laws were just the opposite, requiring farmers to fence cultivated crops to keep free-ranging livestock out. Many of the fenced fields in the Smokies were of the latter sort.

In the orchard, dozens of apple trees, including red Milam, limbertwig, sour John, Abraham, and other old varieties, produced apples from summer through fall. Some were carefully wrapped in straw and stored in the apple house. Some were dried for baking in stack cakes. Some were boiled, spiced, and put up as apple butter. The orchard included plum, peach, chestnut, and cherry trees. An arbor of blue concord grapes provided fruit to eat off the vine and for jellies and jams.

This was how the farm appeared when John Walker died in 1921, about a decade after the death of his wife. By then

From l to r, Margaret, Polly, Martha, Louisa, and Hettie Walker. Photo circa 1933-1935.

the Walker boys were gone. All of the Walker children had attended the Little Greenbrier School, but the first two sons had gone on to graduate high school and spent a short time at

Murphy College in Sevierville. The sons had married and moved to their own homes, one of them traveling as far as Idaho. Margaret Jane, Mary Elizabeth (Polly), Martha Ann, Nancy Melinda, Louisa Susan, and Hettie Rebecca remained at home.

Sarah Caroline, the only sister to marry, lived nearby with her husband, Jim Shelton. Shelton worked for the Little River Lumber Company, which employed a majority of area farmers in the early 1900s.

From l to r, the Shelton family: Caroline, John, Leona, Effie, and Hazel. The giant chestnut tree was eventually cut by Jim Shelton. Photo circa 1920.

Shelton also took his spinster sisters-in-law for outings to church conferences in towns around east Tennessee. This was not the only contact they had with the world beyond Little Greenbrier. Martha was occasionally employed in domestic work, spending two to three weeks at a time away from home. Hettie worked in a Knoxville hosiery mill for a year or two.

Shelton's work with Little River Lumber was building and maintaining the company's railroad tracks. When he had free time, however, Shelton was out photographing Smokies life with his boxy bellows camera. He documented the logging era, its people, what was left of its soaring forests, and—most of all—logging trains, crews, boxcar camps, and treeless, devastated slopes. It was the scraped-off, ruined, and eroding slopes with heaps of brush and trash in the creek valleys that convinced people to push for a national park.

By the time the park was established, in 1934, the five sisters remaining on the Walker farm had committed themselves to their situation as spinsters. (Nancy Melinda died in 1931.) Martha and Polly had been engaged, but both of their fiancés had met accidental deaths. The experience so affected Polly that she remained mentally unsettled the rest of her life. Her sisters and life on the Walker farm succored her, but they were all threatened by the coming of the park. Everyone around them had sold their land and moved away.

The National Park Service, realizing the position of these aging, unmarried women, offered them a life lease, allowing them to live out their lives on the Walker farm. After their father's death, the Walker sisters also committed themselves to keeping the farm and their way of life exactly as it was in the 1920s.

Although they adhered to their parents' restrained Primitive Baptist beliefs, their house was anything but the austere, empty place it looks now. It was packed full of possessions. Four sturdy beds anchored the corners of the large room, with a fifth bed and trundle bed beneath it against the back wall. Chairs, two chests, and a treadle sewing machine (a concession to modernity) rounded out the large pieces of furniture in the downstairs room. A sweet potato cellar opened in front of the fireplace. Accessible by ladder, the upper floor held three beds and chests.

Beds were piled with soft wool blankets, wool the sisters sheared from their sheep, then carded, spun, and wove themselves. In the summer, a spinning wheel and loom stood on the porch.

From the rafters and from wall pegs hung peppers and onions, bags of flower seed, corn seed, and other seeds, bundles of herbs, hats, clothing, baskets, walking sticks, kerosene lamps, kitchen utensils, and dozens of other items. The walls were papered with magazines and newspapers. Newspapers were a favorite wall covering in log homes because the white paper brightened the inside of wood-darkened cabins. Papering also cut down on drafts.

The kitchen was crowded with a dining table, chairs, benches, two wood stoves, a cupboard, a worktable, and a flour bin made from a hollow black gum log. In front of the kitchen fireplace was the opening to another cellar, this one for white potatoes.

No one ever went away from the Walker house hungry. The sisters fixed sumptuous meals that might include warm corn-bread baked in their Dutch oven and slathered with home-made butter, seasoned greens, mutton, pickled beans, sweet potatoes, and pie for dessert.

In a 1946 issue of *The Saturday Evening Post* featuring the Walker sisters, the unmarried sisters were aged enough to be able to laugh with the Post reporter about growing bachelor's buttons in their garden. Their brother-in-law answered the question of why five of the Walker sisters never married: "Reckon I'm about the only man that had courage to bust into that family," he joked, "or else the rest of them gals got discouraged when they couldn't get me and jus' quit."

The article brought them so much national attention that

the sisters themselves became a Smokies tourist attraction for a while. One by one, however, the sisters died. During that time, National Park Service rangers cleared the road to their house and checked on them, until the last sister, Louisa, died in 1964. To the end, the sisters honored the code of the Smokies: make do or do without. Although they did without a lot compared to the world just beyond the borders of their farm, the Walker sisters had as much—or more—in their own way.

Louisa Susan Walker, the poet of the family, spoke for all of them in "My Mountain Home":

There is an old weather bettion house
That stands near a wood
With an orchared near by it
For all most one hundred
years it has stood

It was my home in infency
It sheltered me in youth
When I tell you I love it
I tell you the truth

The Walker sisters' house in 1936.

MEIGS MOUNTAIN/CURRY MOUNTAIN TRAILS

DIRECTIONS: Best hiked using a two-car shuttle. The hike begins at the Jakes Creek trailhead in Elkmont and ends near the Metcalf Bottoms Picnic Area parking lot. From Sugarlands Visitor Center, go west on Little River Road 9.8 miles and turn right into the Metcalf Bottoms Picnic Area.

Leave one car in the southeast corner of the parking lot.

Drive the second car back toward Sugarlands about 5 miles and turn right into Elkmont. From the turn it is about 2.5 miles to the trailhead. Bear left at the campground, which lies about 1.5 miles from Little River Road. About 0.5 mile farther, bear right where the road forks and follow signs for Jakes Creek Trail for another 0.5 mile. The road ends at a gate marking the trailhead. Parking is available alongside the last section of road.

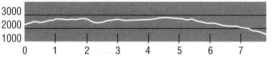

LENGTH: 7.8 miles. Jakes Creek Trail to Meigs Mountain Trail, 0.4 mile; Meigs Mountain Trail to Curry Mountain Trail, 4.1 miles; Curry Mountain Trail to Little River Road, 3.3 miles. Optional 0.8 mile (0.4 mile one-way) farther down Meigs Mountain Trail from the junction of Meigs Mountain and Curry Mountain trails for a total of 8.6 miles.

PHYSICAL PROFILE: Meigs Mountain Trail wends its way along the lower slopes of Meigs Mountain at a fairly level elevation. From its junction with Meigs Mountain Trail, Curry Mountain Trail descends steadily to Little River Road. Along the way are a few easy rock-hops over creeks.

CULTURAL PROFILE: Rock walls, springhouse foundations, and other evidence of homesites lie near the bottom and top of Meigs Mountain Trail. A small cemetery lies at the farthest point of the hike. Curry Mountain Trail exhibits the markings of old fields.

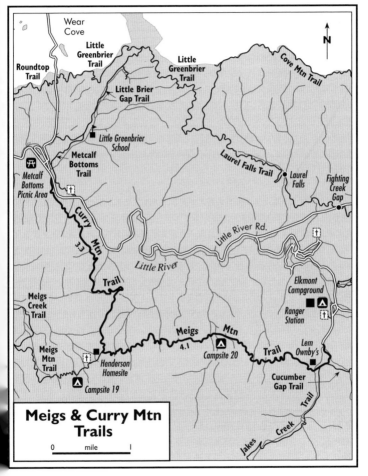

Meigs & Curry Mtn Trails

0   mile   1

*T*he name "Meigs" refers to Colonel Return Jonathan Meigs, a Revolutionary War hero who was appointed to survey boundary lines set by government treaty with the Cherokee. In 1802, Meigs hoisted a colorful blanket atop the mountain that lies just behind Meigs Mountain. The blanket served as a line-of-sight guide for a member of the survey party atop a neighboring peak. That mountain, near the top of Jakes Gap, became known as Blanket Mountain.

Meigs received his unusual first name from his parents' unusual courtship. His mother, a Quaker who did not feel ready to take marriage vows, put off his father each time he asked for her hand. But she must have known that the right moment would eventually come, because at last she urged him to "Return, Jonathan, return." He did, they married, and to celebrate his reward for steadfast courtship, he named their first child Return Jonathan Meigs.

Like those who lived along nearby Jakes Creek, the Meigs Mountain community started in the mid-1800s with a core of subsistence farmers. As that century closed, logging gained ground in the Smokies. By the early 1900s, many of those who lived along Meigs Mountain Trail made their living, both directly and indirectly, from Little River Lumber Company.

Jakes Creek Trail

0.0 From its start at the Jakes Creek trailhead, this hike travels less than a half-mile to the junction with Meigs Mountain Trail, passing a left-hand intersection with Cucumber Gap Trail at 0.3 mile.

Meigs Mountain Trail

0.4/0.0 Meigs Mountain Trail junction. Meigs Mountain Trail veers right from Jakes Creek Trail and descends to Jakes Creek, where a footlog crosses the creek.

0.2 On the other side of the creek, the trail skirts Lem Ownby's former homesite, a broad, weedy apron of land full of may-apples. Little remains of Ownby's farm: a low section of rock wall, a few fence posts still strung with wire, some cinderblock, pipe, and the spring that fed his property. Slightly downslope was Ownby's pasture, which the National Park Service used as a horse corral after his death. Ownby, who died in 1984 at age 94, was the last permanent resident of the Smokies outside of Cades Cove.

In 1902, at age 13, Lem Ownby helped his father build the cabin Lem would live in for the rest of his life. Family and homeplace were ever important in the lives of those who lived in the mountains. One incident Lem remembered hearing when he was a child made an especially big impression. On a Sunday, toward the end of the Civil War, his mother knelt in the kitchen corner of her family's home, praying for the safe return of her seven brothers. Union soldiers all, the brothers met in Elkmont by chance that very day. Her prayers were answered when they walked in together to greet their sister.

Lem and Jemima, his wife of 43 years, lived in a cabin that had a tin roof, a wood stove, and a fireplace. He used gravity to pipe water into the house from the spring. They even had electricity and a telephone in later years. Marigolds and poppies bordered the house, clothes fluttered on the line, chickens scratched in the yard, and peach and plum trees stood nearby. Although the Ownbys did not have children, as they grew older they were helped by Lem's nephew Roy Ownby, who lived in a mobile home about a hundred feet away.

During his long life, Ownby was well known in the Smokies, part of a family that was scattered over a broad section of what is now parkland. His relatives were among Elkmont's original families. Some came to Elkmont seeking gold; most of the Ownbys came to farm. They grew corn and potatoes, cultivated apple orchards, and kept bees.

Ownby was proud of the quality of the tobacco he grew, although he said, "The land was so steep, you had to plow with one hand and hold on with the other." He was best known for the quality of the honey his bees produced: sourwood, tuliptree, basswood, and locust. Basswood honey was his personal favorite. Before he became old and totally blind, Lem Ownby had as many as 145 bee gums on his 44 acres of land. His biggest hives produced up to 60 pounds. People hiked up to his cabin to buy his honey when Ownby was well into his later years. At that point, he could no longer see and had to make change from bills and coins kept separate in various vest pockets.

Then-Governor Lamar Alexander issued the following statement upon Ownby's death: "Everyone who loves the Great Smoky Mountains should have had the chance to meet him." But, in the 1970s, when U.S. Supreme Court Justices Potter Stewart and Harry Blackmun did pay Ownby a visit, Lem refused to see them, saying he had no use for those fellows.

Continuing up the trail, foamflower, blue phlox, violets, trillium, and other wildflowers decorate the trail's edges.

Although little is left, other old homesites are also apparent. The lower portion of Meigs Mountain Trail was well populated. **0.5** Boxwood and cultivated flowers that have naturalized are always tip-offs of old homesites. Here a large patch of daffodils on the right of the trail indicates a former residence. On the left, the stone foundation of a springhouse lies adjacent to the trail. Nearby are the remains of an old washtub, other containers, and rusting metal parts. A cavity in a flat piece of ground is all that remains of a former building.

Past this point, signs of habitation cease for a time. The trail heads gradually uphill, then curves around the end of a cove crowded with wildflowers and big trees. Beyond a small hemlock grove, the trail levels off, winding below the ridgeline, following the land's sinuous contours from cove to cove, crossing over a couple of small branches. Altogether pleasant.

1.5 The trail crests an unnamed gap. Then it descends.

1.9 Backcountry Campsite Number 20. The descent ends at an easy crossing of King Branch. On the other side of the branch, in a broad area with a nearly bare forest floor canopied by trees, lies Campsite 20, which was once a homesite. Just beyond Campsite 20, Kiver Branch plus some smaller branches join Blanket Creek in this well-watered area.

In the late 1880s, the slopes of Blanket Creek were logged by the J.L. English Company, which removed some 3,300 board feet of cherry and basswood. In the early 1900s, a small logging and milling company selectively logged ash and tuliptree in the Blanket Creek area, sawing it on portable mills.

Past Campsite 20, a low rock wall parallels the trail on the left, which is all that remains of the garden and orchard that once filled these flats. Near the end of the 100-foot-long wall there is a quick crossing of Kiver Branch, which is edged by Michaux's saxifrage. On the other side of the branch, earthen banks frame the trail, pointing to its use as a road that has become eroded.

The rock wall continues on the left to Blanket Creek. Downstream, low rock walls flank the creek, hinting that logging companies may have built splash dams here. Splash dams were constructed across creeks and the resulting head of water was allowed to build up. When enough water and logs were

Loggers and their team on a skid road on Blanket Mountain.

piled up, a logger would open the dam gates, and a rush of water would carry the ponderous logs downstream.

Within sight of the creek is a collection of detritus: a blue enamel dishpan, a rusted tub next to the rusted remains of some mechanical equipment. Stamped into the metal is "TY-SA-MAN Machine Co., Knoxville, Tenn."

TY-SA-MAN was the stamp of the Tyson, Savage, Manning Company, which started business in the 1880s making water-wheels and other parts for gristmills and sawmills. Lying near water, this piece of metal may have had something to do with a gristmill or a sawmill. Cornmeal was the staff of life in the Smokies and most every populated waterway had at least one gristmill alongside. Or, it could have been part of one of the portable sawmills used in this drainage.

2.1 At another flattish area lie an old tub and some corrugated metal, perhaps roofing remains. A few posts stand here as well. Pieces of rusting machinery are propped against a huge maple. The forest around is full of sourwood trees and Fraser magnolias.

Within the next 0.1 mile, two parallel lines of fence posts march downslope to the right. Between the lines of posts, the outline of an old road runs down to Blanket Creek. A spur of the Little River Railroad ran along this roadbed. In the early 1900s, the railroad served Little River Lumber Company, which logged most of the slopes on this side of the Smokies.

Ahead near the trail lie other signs of human involvement: a rocked spring, a rock pile, a washtub hanging in a tree. Only a few of the trees are large, telling that this area was once cleared.

As the trail ascends, other fence posts line yet another old roadbed below. Tuliptrees tower above and silverbell trees line the branch. Another old road meets the trail a few hundred feet farther on, then the trail levels and leaves this area. Now Meigs Mountain Trail is a quiet, shaded place, but the criss-cross of roads, the second-growth forests, and the shards of human endeavor mark it as a place that was once open and busy with activity.

Striped maples, dogwoods, blue cohosh, wild hydrangea, and wildflowers of every sort—from bloodroot and hepatica to trout-lily and Solomon's seal—fill the understory as the trail winds from one small cove to another. The trail parallels both the ridge of Meigs Mountain above and Little River Road far below.

4.1 Curry Mountain Trail junction. Signs point ahead 5.4 miles to the Sinks and 3.3 miles to the right down Curry Mountain Trail to Little River Road. Two building sites once lay on the right of Meigs Mountain Trail just before its junction with Curry Mountain Trail. Neither is discernible. One was John Huskey's homesite. Members of the Huskey clan once lived all over the Tennessee side of what is now the park. Many still live in communities adjacent to the park. A quarter-mile beyond the trail junction, a small cemetery filled with the graves of Huskeys lies off Meigs Mountain Trail.

The second site belonged to the Meigs Mountain school-house. The schoolhouse served the families who lived near this junction and along Curry Mountain Trail, which used to be an old farm road. The road connected the upper Meigs Mountain community with the wider world 3.3 miles down the trail.

At the trail junction are oil-nut bushes. Settlers used the oil from the nuts to stabilize candle tallow. Past the junction are the homesites of four families that probably used nuts from these bushes. Two of their family names are memorialized by waterways in the vicinity: Henderson Prong and Bunch Prong. Before turning onto Curry Mountain Trail, take a few minutes to explore historic sites another 0.4 mile along Meigs Mountain Trail.

4.2 Henderson homesite. The near-flat area that lies below the northwest corner of the trail junction was the old Henderson place: two cabins, a barn, and a chicken house. An old, degraded road veers down to the homesite, a small stream, and a spring where the rock remains of a springhouse are set into the slope. A line of posts parallels a stream that is interrupted by a large, rusting cookstove. Just upstream, rotting timbers mark the doorframe of one of the Henderson's cabins, which faces a bit of road running alongside the stream. More fence posts and rusting debris dot the site.

The Henderson place in February, 1936.

4.4 Cemetery. A path to the right of Meigs Mountain Trail leads less than 100 feet to a small cemetery perched on a sunny prow of land. Of the dozen or so graves, most bear low, unmarked stones. Of the few engraved stones, the tallest belongs to Polly Huskey (1866-1909). A square block set into the ground marks the burial place of L.M. and Lillie Huskey's infant son.

4.6 Backcountry Campsite Number 19. This campsite, adorned with silverbell trees and a broad patch of may-apples, was once the property of Andy Brackin, who had a home, barn, and smokehouse here. The sloping campsite is smaller and less accommodating than Campsite 20, but the spring that rises here shows signs of once having supported a springhouse. A few fence posts, still strung with barbed wire, parallel the waterway.

Andy Brackin was brought up with two brothers and a sister in the Sugarlands section of the Smokies just below the Chimneys. His sister Mary married a neighbor boy, H. Marshall Whaley, and they eventually ran a boarding house for lumberjacks in the Sugarlands. Mary was famous for her skills with rifle, pistol, and shotgun, skills she learned from Andy and her two other brothers.

Although the Bunch place and the Smith Jennings place, which included a house, barn, and springhouse, lie farther down Meigs Mountain Trail, this is a good place to turn back and take a left onto Curry Mountain Trail.

Curry Mountain Trail

0.0 Curry Mountain Trail. From its junction with Meigs Mountain Trail, Curry Mountain Trail descends to Little River Road. Except for a slight rise at Curry Gap, and a smaller rise beyond that, the descent is steady. Although homesites are not as obvious along this somewhat broad, former road, signs of field fences abound on either side. This used to be a well-traveled road into the Meigs Mountain communities.

0.2 An old road meets the trail from the left.

0.3 Fence posts parallel the trail on the right, marking the boundaries of former fields. Oaks, pines, and mountain laurel are plentiful on dry Long Arm, a ridge that extends down from Curry She Mountain. The trail affords fine views of the coves that reach down toward Little River Road, some of them coves that you have recently traversed along Meigs Mountain Trail.

1.3 Curry Gap. The name "curry" has nothing to do with spices from Asia. It is a muddled version of a Cherokee term: gura-hi. Gura refers to a spring salad green and hi indicated it grows "here." Settlers, thinking the Cherokee were referring to the name of the nearby mountain, anglicized the term to Curry He and, for balance, named the adjacent mountain Curry She. Fence posts continue to spot the road sporadically as it descends through hemlock into denser, moister forest.

3.0 Near its end, the trail descends through a tunnel of rhodo-dendron, then crosses two small streams before arriving at Little River Road.

3.3 Little River Road. The Metcalf Bottoms Picnic Area parking lot is a couple of hundred feet to the left and across the road.

MOUNT CAMMERER TRAIL
& Connecting Trails

DIRECTIONS: From Gatlinburg, go east on U.S. 321 19 miles to the intersection with Route 32. Or take U.S. 321 from Interstate 40. At Cosby, go south on Route 32 1.5 miles to the

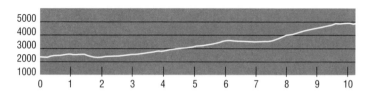

Cosby entrance to the national park and turn right. Go 2 miles and park in hiker parking near the campground entrance. To reach the trailhead, walk approximately 0.5 mile through Cosby Campground. At the fork in the park road, continue straight—not right—then stay to the left. Just beyond the group camp, a graveled, gated entry and a sign for Lower Mount Cammerer Trail marks the trailhead.

LENGTH: 15.6 miles. This hike makes a large loop: Lower Mount Cammerer Trail to Appalachian Trail (A.T.), 7.5 miles; A.T. to Mount Cammerer Trail, 2.3 miles; Mount Cammerer Trail, 1.2 miles (0.6 mile one-way) in and back to A.T.; A.T. to Low Gap Trail, 2.1 miles; Low Gap Trail to Cosby Campground, 2.6 miles.

PHYSICAL PROFILE: For sheer panoramic splendor, this is one of the best hikes in the park, especially in autumn when leaf color is at its height. This broad loop is a full-day hike, but a satisfying one. The 2.3 miles from the Appalachian Trail to the Mount Cammerer Trail are rigorous but not daunting. The hike begins and ends at Cosby Campground.

CULTURAL PROFILE: Cosby Campground was once the center of a thriving community, which spread along what is now Lower Mount Cammerer Trail. Farther up, the Civilian Conservation Corps (CCC) built fine stone walls and overlooks. The fire

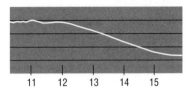

lookout atop Mount Cammerer not only affords remarkable views of the Smokies, it is itself picturesque and historical.

$\mathcal{C}$ocke County, at the northeastern edge of the park, has a reputation as a haven for moonshiners, marijuana growers, and general scofflaws. National magazines have helped burnish this outlaw image. Yet, the drive into Cosby Campground passes the birthplace of Ella Costner (1894-1982), a nationally recognized writer whom the Tennessee legislature designated as the poet laureate of the Smokies.

Twenty-five years after Costner was born in what is now the Cosby district of the park, Mary Bell Smith was born nearby. She, too, became a writer. She and her sister attained master's degrees when that level of learning was unusual for women anywhere. And her relatives included three generals and an admiral. In her book, *In the Shadow of White Rock,* Smith tells of life in the Smokies before the park came. White Rock was the Indian name for what is now called Mount Cammerer, and white settlers adopted the Cherokee term.

Between outlaws and authors lies the history of most who settled here. Most were farmers working hard to get by, trying to improve life for their children, mixing field work with logging when the timber industry was at its height in the late 1800s and early 1900s. Smith's family raised corn, apple trees, and farm animals, including some of the first Holsteins in Cocke County. Her mother made their clothes, lye soap, what-

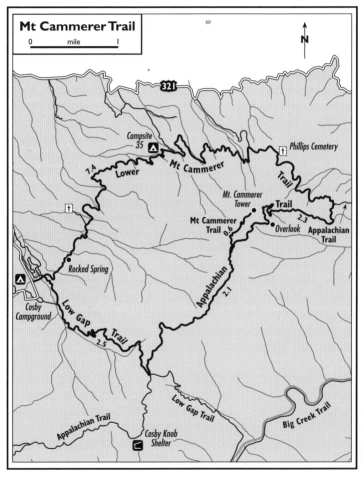

Mt Cammerer Trail

0   mile   1

N

321

Campsite 35

7.4   Lower   Mt Cammerer

Phillips Cemetery

Mt. Cammerer Tower

Trail

Mt Cammerer Trail 0.6

Overlook

Appalachian Trail

2.3

Rocked Spring

Appalachian

2.1

Cosby Campground

Low Gap   Trail

2.5

Appalachian Trail

Low Gap Trail

Cosby Knob Shelter

Big Creek Trail

ever was needed. In terms of amenity, it was a narrow life. During the Depression, Smith went to school wearing a dress made from a flour sack and decorated with red piping, plus her brother's hand-me-down high-top shoes.

Even earlier, what is now Cosby Campground was the heart of a thriving community whose branches spread along Snake Den, Low Gap, Lower Mount Cammerer, and other trails. After the park was established in 1934, the Civilian Conservation Corps built one of the park's 22 CCC camps near the head of Low Gap Trail and constructed the trails, bridges, and overlooks in this part of the park.

Beginning about 1940, Perry Audley Whaley became the Cosby District's first park ranger. He was one of the many Whaleys who populated Greenbrier, just down the road, but Cosby people did not know him. In one of his columns for the *Knoxville Journal*, Vic Weals reported what Whaley was told when he came into Cosby: "Now we make whisky for a living here, and that's all we have to make a living. So don't you be messing in our business."

Perry Audley Whaley in 1946.

Whaley served for 25 years, leaving notes when he found a still, telling the culprits to move. He remembered "revenuers"—officers from the Internal Revenue Service—making raids as often as once a week.

Although it was hard to make a living in the Smokies, the coming of the park brought tourism and a whole new focal point for the local economy.

Lower Mount Cammerer Trail

0.0 Lower Mount Cammerer Trail begins on an old graveled road in dense second-growth woods and, in less than 0.1 mile, crosses Cosby Creek on a footbridge. On the other side, in an open area, Lower Mount Cammerer Trail, a horse trail, and a spur to Low Gap Trail (to the right) all meet.

Ella Costner, who grew up a short walk across Cosby Campground, trained as a Red Cross nurse, served in World War II, and began writing as a war correspondent. Her book *Song of Life in the Smokies* gives a taste of the early 1900s:

"While I roasted the coffee, at intervals I would run out the door to cool from the heat of the oven, and throw my head back to better feel the cool breeze from the south, the delicious lazy caressing breeze, laden with fragrant aroma of the roasting coffee. And as twilight faded, and the stars came out and the moon showed an orange glow through the tree tops, I would forget the tasks of the day, the long day in the field, I would forget my bruised and briar-torn feet and the discomfort of a sweaty grimy body burned by the sun. I would forget that the rattler's fangs had missed me just by a hair's breadth. I would forget that life was ever difficult or hard here in this place, this my world was so filled with beauty that nothing else mattered."

0.3 In pre-park days this trail was a road lined with homes and fields. A moss-covered rock pile just before this point signals one of the upcoming old homesites. In the open, weedy areas along both sides of the trail, look for homesites for the next 0.2 mile.

In autumn, after harvesting potatoes, stringing beans, cribbing the corn, drying apples, making kraut, smoking side meat, people had enough food to last the winter, but just barely. By late winter, farm families often faced hunger. Costner remembers her sister's trip to a neighbor to borrow a cup of milk for their ailing baby brother. On the way home, her sister noticed a young girl facing the wall of a mud-chinked log cabin. The girl's face and dress were streaked with clay. She had been eating the wall.

0.4 Look for a rocked spring on the right side of the trail. About 2.5 feet high and nearly as wide, the stonework served as a "dipping pool" for people coming to draw water.

0.7 Follow the sign at the fork, which points right to Sutton Ridge, a high point of Lower Mount Cammerer Trail. The gravel berm at the fork is a clue to this spot's former use as a traffic circle.

0.8 Just after an easy step across a small creek, the trail seems to divide. But the low road and high road, divided by an "island" of trees, converge in a few hundred feet. Just beyond, a footlog crosses a branch of Toms Creek.

1.0 At a small bend to the left near the creek, the drainage leads to more former clearings, a tiny cemetery, maybe even a former still site. But these are hard to find, so continue on the main trail as it starts winding upward toward Sutton Ridge.

1.4 Sutton Ridge Overlook. A short but steep side trail leads 200 yards up to the overlook, passing black gum, mountain laurel, and chestnut oak on the dry, rocky ridge. Some hikers make Sutton Ridge the goal of a late afternoon hike to see the sun set from the overlook.

This expansive view takes in Cosby Cove, with Gabes Mountain to the west. Directly ahead, Green Mountain rises just outside the park boundary. Stewart Ramsey, who was born in what is now the park, was one of the first rangers in the Cosby District. When park employees were called to fight a fire on Green Mountain, Ramsey was among them. In what must be a highly unusual circumstance, Ramsey was said to have inhaled excessive fumes from burning mountain laurel. The fumes from this toxic shrub apparently overcame him and he died less than a week later at a Knoxville hospital.

From Sutton Ridge Overlook, the trail descends to Riding Fork and a view of its gentle cascade. It then climbs to Gilliland Ridge and descends to Gilliland Fork and Campsite 35.

3.3 Backcountry Campsite Number 35. A short spur trail leads down to Campsite 35, which lies in a flat area of the hollow and was probably a former homesite. The campsite is supplied with horse hitches, as the trail also accommodates horseback riders.

As it swings out toward the next ridge, the main trail passes drifts of wildflowers: stonecrop, rue-anemone, goldenrod, aster, rattlesnakeroot, white baneberry, and others. The trail continues to wind in and out, from shaded creek hollow to ridge front, along the lower slopes of Mount Cammerer. The forest mix includes tuliptrees, chestnut oak, northern red oak, and Fraser magnolia with a thick understory of rhododendron. Clusters of dwarf crested iris hug the trail. Other low plants include jewelweed, mountain gentian, galax, wintergreen, and Dutchman's britches.

5.3 Phillips Cemetery. At the top of Turkey Knob, a small path leads left about 25 feet to Phillips Cemetery. There, in a tiny clearing, stand eight low gravestones, crumbling slabs with no inscriptions. The only one that is inscribed is at the back of the cemetery: "G. Estes, son of S.D. & Minnie Phillips, 1910-1912, Asleep in Jesus." Smokies cemeteries, like all old cemeteries, are filled with a high proportion of youngsters under two years old.

A number of Phillips once lived just below here, on the eastern flanks of Turkey Knob. Jonas and Sarah Phillips, the ancestors of one part of the Phillips clan, are buried not far from here, above the headwaters of Tobes Creek. Sarah, a midwife, was so large when she died that the family had to tear out part of the wall of her house in order to remove the body.

Tobes Creek, which begins its flow on the eastern side of Turkey Knob, was named for Tobias Phillips. "Tobe" Phillips kept the tollgate on the turnpike that ran from Cosby to Cataloochee around the time of the Civil War. He was also a famed bear hunter.

Over the next two miles, from Phillips Cemetery to the A.T. junction, the trail follows its previous pattern: winding in and out, from hollow to ridge front.

Appalachian Trail

7.5/0.0 Appalachian Trail junction. At a somewhat broad clearing, centered on a huge tree, trails meet. Take the right fork onto the A.T. at the sign that says: Mount Cammerer Trail 2.3 miles. From here to the Mount Cammerer spur, the trail is somewhat steep, but so full of character that the miles pass quickly. The trail switchbacks up through deep, old forest and moist shade, wending its way past rhododendron and dog-hobble.

At the first switchback, see evidence of an old rockslide and vines with the large, heart-shaped leaves of Dutchman's pipe. After the second switchback, look for a low, fern-topped remnant of a rock retaining wall, built by the Civilian Conservation Corps. Tall and massive rock outcrops begin to appear.

1.6 CCC wall and overlook. On the left, a finely worked rock retaining wall curves around the nose of a huge outcrop. The base of the wall plunges 10 feet below the level of the trail. Just past the wall is a terrific, 180-degree view of the Smokies and beyond. The trail passes mountain laurel, Fraser magnolia, maples, black gum, and galax. As the trail climbs ever higher, yellow birch appears.

Between the CCC overlook and the Mount Cammerer Trail junction, look for a couple of small, live chestnut trees growing from the roots of old stumps. Before 1904, these slopes were covered with chestnuts. In the early 1900s, an Asian fungus inadvertently introduced to North America began killing the trees. By 1940, 3.5 billion trees were killed nationwide, and the American chestnut had all but vanished.

Mount Cammerer Trail

2.3/0.0 Mount Cammerer Trail junction. From here, the side trail on the right follows a narrow ridgeline 0.6 mile to the Mount Cammerer fire lookout. At 0.4 mile, hitching posts and a sign tell riders that horses are not allowed past this point.

0.6 Mount Cammerer fire lookout. Atop Mount Cammerer, it is easy to see why the peak was called White Rock: the peak's granite outcrops shine white in the sun. The peak was renamed Mount Cammerer to honor Arno Cammerer, who joined the National Park Service at its beginning. Cammerer served as assistant director under Stephen T. Mather and Horace Albright, the first and second NPS directors. Cammerer became the third director of the Park Service (1933-1940), but he is especially remembered in the Smokies because he was a resolute champion

Arno Cammerer explores the Smokies on muleback in August, 1925.

for establishing the park. He spent many days on its trails, walking with Horace Kephart, David Chapman, and other local park supporters.

The fire lookout perches atop Mount Cammerer, picturesquely set amid rocks and mountain ash. With its wrap-around windows encircled by a narrow wooden catwalk, the octagonal lookout seems transported from some rocky Maine precipice overlooking the Atlantic Ocean. Not quite a tower, this is one of only two such designed lookouts in the eastern United States.

The Cosby Creek CCC began building the fire lookout in 1937 and finished two years later. The stone was quarried nearby and shaped by masons. The timber, too, was cut close at hand. All the rest—from window glass to furnishings—had to be hauled up the mountain. The lookout was used to detect fires until the 1960s, when more modern methods replaced rangers with binoculars. Over the next 20 years, the lookout deteriorated until a crusade to restore it ensued. The rebuilt lookout reopened in 1996.

The fire lookout tower atop Mt. Cammerer.

Historically, the Smokies have two fire seasons: mid-February through April and mid-October into December. Lennie Garver, who was born in what is now the park, served six seasons in the lookout, from 1959 through 1964, accompanied by his wife Vigi. Although he was paid for an eight-hour day, Garver was on duty 24 hours. A dispatcher called him every hour to make sure Garver had a look at the surrounding forests.

Groceries, clean linens, and other supplies were driven up

by jeep every ten days or so. But they had to haul supplies by foot the last quarter-mile. Their water supply came from rainwater funneled to a cistern in the basement of the lookout and pumped up by hand. The Mount Cammerer lookout ranger communicated with the park dispatcher via a radio with a 90-volt battery bank. When the batteries died, as they occasionally did, the ranger used mirrors to communicate with the lookout ranger on Mount Sterling. At night they communicated with flashlights.

Long days and weeks of watching were punctuated by fires and a few more unusual events. One rainy night a stranger approached the lookout. Garver and his wife offered him supper, but something about the man made them uneasy. Vigi kept a piece of firewood in her hand and Lennie held his gun under a piece of newspaper. The stranger eventually departed, but the Garvers later learned that police had tracked down the man for murdering a gas station attendant in Asheville.

The lookout is a fine place for lunch and the views cannot be bested. From Mount Cammerer, a full 360 degrees showcases the breadth of the Smokies, plus range upon range stretching to the horizon. When autumn turns leaves a fireworks display of gold, red, purple, and orange, the views are exceptional.

Return to the junction with the A.T. and head straight across from the Mount Cammerer Trail. Follow the A.T. 2.1 miles to the junction with Low Gap Trail.

Low Gap Trail

2.1/0.0 Appalachian Trail junction with Low Gap Trail. Turn right onto Low Gap Trail and descend 2.9 miles back to Cosby

Campground. The trail passes big oaks and tuliptrees. The first switchback, marked by a huge hemlock, signals the halfway point.

1.7 Rocked spring. Look for a small rocked spring on the right next to the trail, the first sign of habitation on lower Low Gap. After passing the spring, the sounds of Cosby Creek become audible. A few hundred yards farther, low rockwork lies near the trail just before a lovely view of Cosby Creek cascading over mossy boulders.

The Lucinda Benson house in 1937.

2.1 Low Gap Trail spur junction. This spur leads back to where the hike began, at the bridge over Cosby Creek. From that bridge, retrace your steps to the gated entrance near the top of Cosby Campground.

Cosby Campground was once the site of the Cosby Creek CCC Camp, in operation for five years during the 1930s. The 212 young men of Company 1462 constructed Low Gap, Hen Wallow, and Snake Den trails. They also landscaped the area, planted trees, and constructed the barracks they lived in. By all reports they ate well: three squares a day, during the Depression.

The CCC camp offered courses in arithmetic, English, auto mechanics, and other subjects. Boxing teams challenged CCC teams in other parts of the Smokies. When rain forced a work break, some would walk up nearby hollows and help local moonshiners cut firewood for their stills. They could buy a half-gallon jar of whiskey for 50 cents, fruit jar included.

Before the CCC occupied Cosby Campground, the camp-ground area was the center of the Upper Cosby community. The site was dotted with the homes of Vergil Messer, Lucinda Benson, and William Proffitt, as well as the Mountain Grove School.

Poet Ella Costner remembered Bill Proffitt and his wife Telie Ann as good people. Of their five sons, some served in World War II, some later became businessmen. Of their seven daughters she said, "All of these women were the finest that ever came out of the mountains."

OLD SETTLERS TRAIL

DIRECTIONS: Best hiked using a two-car shuttle. The hike begins at the Maddron Bald trailhead, off U.S. 321 between Cosby and the Greenbrier entrance to the park, and ends at the Old Settlers trailhead where it meets Ramsey Prong Road in the Greenbrier District.

From Gatlinburg, drive east on U.S. 321 6 miles and turn right (south) at the sign for the Greenbrier entrance to the national park. Continue past the Greenbrier ranger station. The paved road will change to gravel. At 2.3 miles past the ranger station, turn left and cross the first bridges on the road to Ramsey Cascades trailhead. After 0.2 mile, look for the Old Settlers trailhead and a small parking area on the left. Park one car here.

Go back to the Greenbrier entrance and continue driving east on U.S. 321 about 9 miles. Turn right on Baxter Road, just past Yogi's Campground. Keep to the right until you reach the signed trailhead. The small parking area at the trailhead lies about 0.25 from the highway. Maddron Bald Trail begins just beyond the gated entrance. Because this three- to five-car lot is somewhat secluded, cars parked here have occasionally been stolen or vandalized. A couple of alternatives exist. Pay a small fee to park in the lot of a business along U.S. 321. Or use only one car, park it in Greenbrier, and hire a Gatlinburg taxi to drop you off at

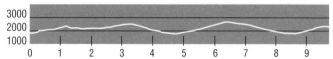

Maddron Bald trailhead.

LENGTH: 17.0 miles: Maddron Bald Trail to Old Settlers Trail,
1.2 miles; Old Settlers Trail to Ramsey Prong Road, 15.8
miles. This hike can be accomplished in one long day, or
divide it in two and stay overnight at Backcountry Campsite
Number 33.

PHYSICAL PROFILE: Although Old Settlers Trail never attains
much in elevation, it continually rises and falls, winding
from one watershed to another. The numerous creek crossings are by footlogs or rock-hops; the rock-hops are fairly
easy except during high water periods. The Dunn Creek
crossing is potentially the most dangerous. You may want to
check at a ranger station before your trip.

CULTURAL PROFILE: This trail traverses an area that was once
the most heavily populated in the Smokies. The numerous
small communities along the trail each clustered around a
creek. Baxter Cabin, Tyson McCarter barn and outbuildings,
numerous rock walls, homesites, chimneys, and cemeteries
make this one of the most historically rich trails in the park.

Old Settlers Trail runs parallel to U.S. 321 and, for most of
its length, runs only a mile or two in from the road.
Hidden within the forests that have reclaimed this former
farming area, however, it is hard to imagine that a busy highway lined with businesses lies just beyond. Once the commu-

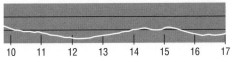

nities along
what is now Old
Settlers Trail
were the nine-

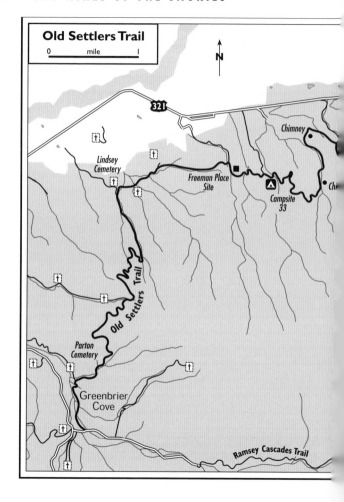

Old Settlers Trail

0   mile   1

N

321

Chimney

Lindsey
Cemetery

Freeman Place
Site

Campsite
33

Ch

Old Settlers Trail

Parton
Cemetery

Greenbrier
Cove

Ramsey Cascades Trail

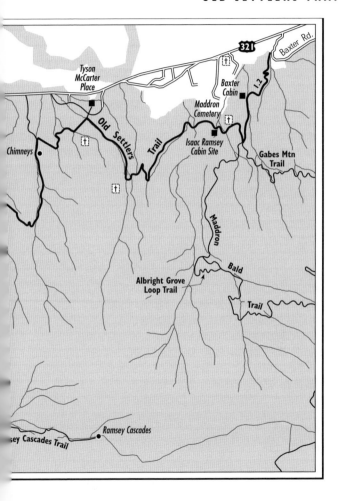

teenth-century equivalent of U.S. 321.

From Maddron Bald Trail to Big Greenbrier Cove, the trail crosses about a dozen creeks and numerous small tributaries. Settlers cleared the creek bottoms and the lower slopes, and along each of these creeks a community sprang up. Each community formed a long, narrow strand running up its creek valley. A road connected the families in each community, ending at the home farthest up the valley.

To make Old Settlers Trail, the National Park Service linked these old roads by building connecting trails over the backs of the intervening ridges. Because the ridges are narrow and the creek valleys are so numerous, much of this hike is stippled with the sight of old chimneys, remnants of outbuildings, and rock walls.

By the 1850s, the land was well settled. From the mid-1800s through the early 1900s, the land along Old Settlers Trail was bright and busy with cornfields and orchards; barns and bee gums; pigpens and corncribs, and log and frame homes surrounded by flower-filled yards. Beginning in the early 1800s, the first settlers began clearing land, planting crops, and building gristmills along the creeks. Their descendants, plus numerous newcomers, continued the process of wrestling a living from slopes so steep they can cause a farmer with a plow to fall off his field. The average farm here was about 40 acres, acres so tough and rocky that 40 was about all a family could manage.

These communities eventually began to converge toward the bottom of the creek valleys, as they all needed links to nearby markets. Stretches of road connected communities with

Cosby and populous Big Greenbrier Cove. Cosby was a gateway to Newport, an important market town for settlers on the east side of the Smokies. From Greenbrier, farmers could connect with White Oak Flats (later renamed Gatlinburg), a gateway for Sevierville and Knoxville, the most important market town for the Tennessee side of the mountains.

Logging came to the Smokies in the late 1800s. Although the Old Settlers area was not commercially logged, the logging industry affected those communities. Newcomers came to the Smokies looking for logging jobs, and farmers supplemented their income with cash from logging work. Some moved often, following logging jobs around the mountains.

As the twentieth century progressed, more stores began popping up in the communities along what is now the Old Settlers route. People interested in the latest technology brought in cars. But 1934, the year the national park was established, saw an end to commercial growth along this particular route. Those living within park boundaries received payment for their property, then moved.

Most did not move far, and they built new businesses, many related to the new national park. The businesses along U.S. 321 bear the names of "Old Settlers" descendants. Families with ties to those communities live all along the way, from Cosby and Pittman Center to Gatlinburg. "Old Settlers" descendants can be counted among Park Service personnel.

As tourism to Great Smoky Mountains National Park grew, hikers sought out trails, even in winter. For a long hike, the Appalachian Trail was the obvious place to head, but severe weather on the heights often threatened hikers. In the 1970s, then-superintendent Boyd Evison decided a long trail at a lower altitude would make a safer option. The Park Service began building connecting trails between the "Old Settlers" communities where old roads did not already exist. The result was called the Lower Elevation Trail—not an inviting name. Happily, the name was changed to Old Settlers Trail, reflecting the wealth of historical sights along its length.

Maddron Bald Trail

0.0 The Maddron Bald Trail begins at the gate at the small parking area off Baxter and Laurel Springs roads. The trail, which rises at a gentle rate, is level and broad, hinting at the road it once was. Park Service vehicles still use the road to provide maintenance at Baxter Cabin, which lies about halfway between the trailhead and Maddron Bald Trail's junction with Old Settlers Trail.

Just west of the trailhead, the Civilian Conservation Corps (CCC) established their County Line Camp. Between 1933 and 1935 the young men of this camp built many of the trails, bridges, and other structures in this part of the national park. It was one of 22 CCC camps in the Smokies.

0.7 Baxter Cabin. On the right, in a small clearing, stands Baxter Cabin. This is often called the Chandler Jenkins Cabin because he was the last to own the place before the Park Service bought it. In 1937 the site contained two cabins, barn, corncrib, smokehouse, blacksmith shop, pigpen, and chicken house. Except for the chicken house, which was moved to the Mountain Farm Museum near the Oconaluftee Visitor Center, all outbuildings were removed.

Unusual among most log cabins that remain in the national park, Baxter Cabin was made almost entirely of chestnut. The walls, ceiling, joists, and rafters are the original chestnut from which the cabin was constructed. Until the early 1900s, about the time the park was established, the slopes of the Smokies were covered with magnificent chestnut trees. They were some of the most numerous deciduous trees in the mountains. In 1904, an Asian fungus was inadvertently introduced in New York. It began killing chestnuts and, by the time the park was established, the fungus had worked its way down the Appalachians, destroying nearly every chestnut tree in its path.

The Baxter cabin in April, 1937.

Not only did the tree's nuts provide good and plentiful eating for black bears and other native species, but also for people and their livestock. The Cherokees made meal and dumplings from chestnuts. Settlers roasted them, made bread from chestnut meal, and gathered them to sell for cash in Knoxville and other markets. Smokies farmers allowed their hogs to run free knowing they would fatten up on chestnuts before being rounded up for market and the family's dinner table. Chestnuts attracted Wild Turkeys, another source of meat. The trees provided shade and virtually rot-proof lumber that was used in all sorts of construction.

Willis Baxter built this chestnut dwelling for his son and

daughter-in-law, William and Nan Baxter. Willis and his wife Via Webb Baxter had settled on Indian Camp Creek after they married and they built their first house a short way up the creek from this spot. They had four children; the oldest, William, married in 1889. Father and son worked together so that William and Nan could move into their own home.

Nan, however, inherited two properties on Cosby Creek, one above the site of the CCC camp on Cosby Creek and one outside what is now the park boundary. When they left, the Baxter's second-oldest son, Alex, moved into the chestnut cabin with his wife Sara (Sally) Sutton Baxter. Their four children were born in the cabin. Eventually, Chandler Jenkins came to own the place.

Not too many years ago, an old man approached a park maintenance supervisor, who was repairing Baxter Cabin. "I was born in this cabin," the man said. "Look here," he said, and took the supervisor to the end of the cabin opposite the chimney. There, on the outside wall, was a rectangular pattern of nail holes, about 5 by 12 inches, all the nail holes evenly spaced. "When I was about 11," the man continued, "my father told me to make a corn grater." So, many years earlier, that young boy had punched holes in a piece of tin and succeeded in fashioning a usable grater.

The cabin is 16-by-18 feet: one large room with a loft above where children slept. The loft floor, however, is gone. The fieldstone chimney was mortared in with mud. The cabin had a "universal" layout for a one-room Smokies dwelling, with the chimney at one end and a door in either sidewall. What is unusual is that the cabin has no other opening: no windows, not even a granny hole, those one-foot-square wall openings, usually near the fireplace, that allowed grannies to stay warm yet have a small window on the world.

The floors are wide puncheons: halves of split logs laid as flooring, with the rounded side below. The top side was planed smooth, using hand tools. A hole in the ground near the fireplace served as a root cellar for sweet potatoes. The cabin's furniture consisted of three beds, a cupboard, a small center table, and chairs. It also held a sewing machine, but this was a more recent addition. Quilts, blankets, feather beds, pillows, pots, pans, and dishes rounded out the remainder of the cabin's contents. Mrs. Baxter did not have a spinning wheel or loom. She used her mother's.

Once there was a lean-to on the west side of the cabin, approximately 8-by-18 feet. The lean-to, which was used as a kitchen, was furnished with a worktable, dining table, chairs, corner cupboard, and step stove.

In the woods behind the cabin stand remnants of a rock wall. The wall bordered a field, now filled in with trees. As the forest returned, so did grouse. Red-tailed hawks can be seen here, too.

Just beyond the cabin, the trail crosses Cole Creek, the source of the Baxters' water. The woods that line Old Settlers Trail are full of large buckeyes, northern red oaks, and other deciduous trees with thick stands of rhododendron in the understory. At about 0.75 mile, a side road on the right once led to someone's home.

Old Settlers Trail

1.2/0.0 Junction with Old Settlers Trail and Gabes Mountain

Trail. At the junction, turn right onto Old Settlers. (Gabes
Mountain Trail bears left.) Old Settlers begins as a narrow
path through the woods, edged by plenty of groundnuts, low
leguminous plants with light green leaves whose nuts were
eaten by both people and hogs. A black cherry grows from the
base of an old chestnut stump, and partridgeberry, glowing
with small red berries, creeps along the ground. Hemlocks mix
with the deciduous trees. Near where an old roadbed parallels
the trail, rectangular holes made by Pileated Woodpeckers
score a few of the trees.

Soon after turning onto Old Settlers Trail, a crumbled chimney appears to the right of the trail. A cornerstone of the house
remains, as does the root cellar. A path leads past the chimney
about 200 feet to small Maddron Cemetery. A dozen graves
with both headstones and footstones all face east. Most graves
in the Smokies are so positioned, anticipating resurrection.
These gravestones are so weathered that any inscriptions they
may have borne are no longer legible. Once a fence surrounded
the cemetery. Now it is edged by dogwoods and maples.

Back on the trail, a canopy of mixed hardwoods, including
Fraser magnolia and large tuliptrees, serviceberry, holly, golden-
rod, and white wood aster in the understory. The trail crosses
Maddron Creek; immediately, on the left, stands a large rock pile.

As settlers found out, the Smokies seem to grow rocks. To
make fields, farmers had to clear as many rocks as trees. They
used rocks for building walls around their corn and potato
fields. They used rocks as foundations for their homes, springhouses, and other buildings. They used rocks for everything
they could think of and still had rocks left over. So they piled

them up; rock piles dot Old Settlers Trail and many other low-lying trails where farms once spread. Sometimes communities competed to see whose rock piles were the largest and neatest.

Holidays, such as the Fourth of July, were always good times for communities to meet and compete: baseball, horse-shoes, and sack races, whatever was at hand to make a game. Farm families were generally too busy to spend a lot of time socializing. When they did, their socializing centered on practical events. Bean-stringing, corn-husking, molasses-making, and taffy-pulling were all anticipated social occasions. Fiddle and banjo music often followed the work, and people danced fourhanded reels. These get-togethers provided young people with a chance to look each other over, with an eye toward marriage. Back in the late 1800s and early 1900s, 15 was a fairly typical age for a girl to marry.

Perhaps this is how Eda and Oliver Whaley met in Greenbrier. They fell in love, but Eda did not think she would receive her father's permission to marry, so she and Oliver road horses all night to Newport. They waited for the courthouse to open, got married, ate breakfast, and returned to Greenbrier by nightfall. When they broke the news to Eda's father, he did not object, but allowed that if his son-in-law was going to be sleeping in his house, he might as well get busy and help out with the work. Despite its impromptu beginning, Eda and Oliver Whaley's marriage lasted 63 years.

The road to marriage in the Smokies included other types of obstacles. Ernest Ogle apparently had met Lucinda Oakley. (Lucinda's father was Wiley Oakley, renowned as the "Roamin' Man of the Mountains" and the "Will Rogers of the Smokies.")

They lived far enough apart that Ogle began sending letters to Lucinda, but she never wrote back. When the postmaster asked, "Why not write that boy?" she answered that she could not afford the stamps.

So she would not need stamps, the postmaster told Lucinda he would hand-deliver her letters himself. Thus he made the marriage match. Pleased with his work, he gave them a crabapple sapling. Offspring of that sapling exist to this day.

0.6 Indian Camp Creek. A huge, gray-barked beech tree stands sentinel next to the footlog crossing the creek. Directly across the creek and at the top of a bank on the left side, stand the rock foundations and the crumbling chimney of an old cabin. Although rocks were plentiful, most log cabins did not have fully rocked foundations but stood on stone footings, as did this one.

The 16-by-20 foot cabin was a typical size for a beginning home. When more room was needed, most people built side-by-side matching structures, the two separated by a floored "dogtrot" breezeway.

This was probably Isaac Ramsey's cabin. Many members of the Ramsey clan lived along Old Settlers. A creek bearing their name bisects the trail about halfway along its length, and the far trailhead lies near broad Ramsey Prong. Just downstream, where Maddron Creek meets Indian Camp Creek, Sam Bales had a home. Bales is another common surname in this part of the Smokies. In fact, some of the preserved historical buildings along Roaring Fork Motor Nature Trail belonged to the Bales.

Patches of oil-nut shrubs line the trail. This vase-shaped

shrub, about five feet high, is a parasite, obtaining nourishment from the roots of nearby deciduous trees. Because it produces no chlorophyll of its own, when the trees it feeds from become dormant, the oil-nut's leaves all fall off at once.

Glenn Cardwell, who grew up in Greenbrier and served as supervisor of the park's Sugarlands Visitor Center for 20 years, can trace his family back seven generations in the Smokies. Cardwell says youngsters used to play with oil-nuts, using them like marbles. Before kerosene was available, his mother extracted oil from the nuts, boiling the oil as a stabilizing ingredient in candle-making.

Look for a low rock wall on the right. A bit farther, an old roadbed coming from the direction of U.S. 321 meets the trail on the right. Along the trail are patches of galax as well as old chestnut stumps and fallen chestnut logs. What is left of the chestnuts have been here a while and will remain a while longer because it may take a century for downed chestnut to rot.

0.9 Dunn Creek crossing. On the far side of Dunn Creek a long section of rock wall, about 2 1/2 feet wide and 3-4 feet high, runs perpendicular to the creek. Rock piles speckle what were once fields. Multiflora rose, a nonnative, grows here—always a clue to former habitation. To beautify and tame their wild Smokies farms, settlers planted roses, yucca, daffodil, boxwood, privet, and many other types of ornamental plants. Where the forest has regained its ground, only the shade-tolerant ornamentals remain.

Native plants, too, were planted close to the house. Spicebush was used to make a spicy, lemon-tasting tea. Walnut trees provided shade, wood, and nuts.

Plants that now line the trail are typical natives: mountain gentian, goldenrod, witch-hazel. On the left, New York fern grows near the base of a neatly stacked rock wall 1 1/2 feet wide, 4-5 feet high, and about 100 feet long with a squared corner at the far end. Beyond lie Solomon's seal, ferns, and sweetpepper shrubs, which settlers used as a pepper substitute.

The trail crosses a small creek where cinnamon fern grows with whorls of clubmoss covering the ground nearby. An old clearing appears, full of blue lobelia. Because gardens and fields were fertilized, grasses and other sun-loving perennial plants created a dense root matrix that often proved hard for tree saplings to penetrate. Although the forest will overcome in the end, relatively weedy, open areas are signs of former clearings.

The Sam Ramsey barn.

Old Settlers Trail begins a gentle climb to Snag Mountain, one of the highest points along the trail. About halfway between Dunn Creek and the top of Snag Mountain two Ramsey homes stood near each other. One, a frame house, belonged to George Ramsey. The other, a log cabin, belonged to Mrs. Sam Ramsey.

2.3 Snag Mountain. The trail switchbacks up Snag Mountain, where settlers used to come to log trees and gather chestnuts. By about 1933, the deadly chestnut blight had already killed 75 percent of the chestnut trees in the Smokies. Once this hillside and many others throughout the park were white with chestnut flowers in late June and early July.

At the top of the ridge grows a mix of black gum, sourwood, mountain laurel, and pines. Wintergreen spreads across the ground at the feet of the trees. All are species commonly found on sunny, dry sites in the Smokies. The view is a treat.

Now into the Webb Creek watershed, the trail crosses a small tributary edged by pink turtlehead wildflowers. A small bit of wall on the left is a cue: a homesite with its crumbling chimney lies just beyond. Polly Duggan had a log cabin, barn, and shed just about here. Near a trail sign, an old roadbed wanders off toward the north.

The trail now follows a fairly level roadbed that runs along the narrow ridge leading down to Webb Creek. The road along Webb Creek was a major route between Cosby and the Greenbrier-Gatlinburg roads.

After crossing another small Webb Creek tributary as the trail descends, look for chestnut fence posts on the right. Where Webb Creek becomes visible below, on the left, other fence posts edge the trail. The forests here are obviously second growth, filling what were once fields on both sides. As Old Settlers nears Webb Creek, a rock wall—about four feet high and wide—appears on the far side, meeting the trail at a right angle. Soon, rock walls and a number of large rock piles stand on both sides of the trail, the walls decorated with ferns.

In these narrow valleys, residents did not have the luxury of building homes far from the "flood plain," although some built rock walls to protect their homes from floods. In the early hours of August 5, 1938, five cloudbursts, coming one on top of another, dumped 11 inches of rain on the area. The Balls, their four children, and two guests were sleeping in their beds in the Ball home next to Webb Creek. Swollen with rainwater, the creek topped its banks, and the flash flood swept away the Balls' home and everyone in it. None survived.

3.2 Webb Creek crossing, side trail to Tyson McCarter barn. In terms of historical sites, this is the richest section of the hike. Nearly a dozen farms lined Webb Creek on both sides of this crossing. Upstream, Howard Brannam had a house, barn, out-buildings, and a gristmill, a focal point for every Smokies community. Lucinda Ogle, who grew up in the Smokies, said, "It was sorta prestige if you had a mill...like a man buys a Cadillac now, you had you a mill built then." Mitchell Ramsey, who lived adjacent, had a mill and a forge. Downstream lived other members of the Brannam family as well as Huskeys, McCarters, and others.

The dry-laid rock walls near Webb Creek are among the finest in the Smokies: broad, high, and well formed. The McCarters, whose homeplace lies nearby, built these walls. During his tenure as Sugarlands supervisor, Glenn Cardwell spoke with Olive McCarter Ramsey, who was born in 1904. He admired the rock walls that "her father and brothers built." Ollie pointed out that she had no brothers, that she and her four sisters had helped build those walls.

Near the trail sign at the creek crossing, a path to the right leads to the Tyson McCarter place. After approximately 100 feet, the path meets a dirt road. Take a left onto the road and, almost immediately, turn right onto a smaller roadbed. Within a few hundred feet, the road arrives at the Tyson McCarter barn. This is as close to U.S. 321 as the hike gets, and traffic noise is audible.

Built around 1876, the earthen-floored barn is a delightfully rambling hodgepodge of enclosures: a lean-to corncrib; a gabled-roof smokehouse; two stalls flanking a wagon drive-through. The broad overhangs protected equipment from the elements. The good-sized stalls indicate that McCarter raised livestock. The livestock that they slaughtered would be preserved in the smokehouse. The McCarters kept a couple of mules, cows, hogs, plus chickens, ducks, and geese. They had a peach orchard and a large apple orchard. They grew corn, wheat, rye, and tobacco.

In his book, *Hiking in the Great Smokies,* Carson Brewer records a conversation with Ollie McCarter Ramsey. "She said the men 'chewed tobacco like worms.'"

"All the people around us were poor," Ollie said, "But they got along better than we do now. They loved each other then." At that point Ollie and her husband, Perry Ramsey, who grew up nearby, had been married 66 years. Had they ever thought about divorcing? No. "However, she joked, 'I've felt like whipping him.'"

The Ramseys raised nine children to adulthood, a significant accomplishment for those times. The twins looked just like Ollie, who lived to be 95 years old. Perry Ramsey, who outlived his wife, was 98 when Ollie died.

Tyson McCarter, whose ancestors were among the area's original settlers, laid out his farmstead in an unusual manner. The buildings formed a circle around the farmyard. Perhaps

The Tyson McCarter place showing a springhouse on the left and log and frame home in the center. 1936 photo.

this was to protect against wild animals or potential thieves, or maybe it was just a creative way to fit into the landscape.

The old road passes the barn and, 100-200 feet beyond, arrives at a clearing with the remains of the McCarter home and springhouse. What remains of the clearing is softly greened by grasses and the trees that are beginning to creep in.

Remnants of two fieldstone chimneys, each about nine feet high, are spaced 30 feet apart, giving an idea of the size of the McCarters' frame house. The springhouse door is held shut with a handmade fastener and, inside, a shelf sits above the water. The springhouse was a standard structure on every Smokies farm because it served as the family refrigerator.

Return to Old Settlers Trail, make a right onto the trail, and continue west toward Greenbrier. The tall, well-made McCarter sisters' walls continue to parallel the trail. The wall running along the left side of the trail is nearly six feet high and more than 200 feet long.

At the end of the wall, the trail turns right and heads uphill through rhododendron and hemlock. This area was once filled with homes and farms, and some homesites are still visible, but barely. On the right, a former clearing is now a stand of young hemlocks, all leaning from the weight of snow during a particularly heavy snowstorm in 1993. In the early days, Smokies children would play on young, pliable saplings such as hemlocks.

Glenn Cardwell remembers "riding" the trees with his friends, swinging from them, seeing how far they could propel themselves into the snow. When Cardwell retired from the Park Service, he became mayor of Pittman Center, a small community dedicated to preserving its gracious, semi-rural character at the edge of Gatlinburg's exurban sprawl. Webb Creek Road was the center of the Old Settlers community back then, and it continues as the "main street" of Pittman Center today. The small community includes Emerts Cove, but most of the Emerts moved to Texas in the late 1800s.

As the trail climbs, it passes into the Texas Creek watershed, crossing small tributaries of Texas Creek. At one tributary, where the trail bends toward the right, lies a rusted car fender. The trail follows an old roadbed. A low rock wall appears on the right. When the clearing behind this wall was a field, planted with crops, Cardwell's grandmother might have passed it on her way to the Maddron Bald area.

The Cardwells lived in Greenbrier Cove and, back then, the trip to the Maddron Bald area took about nine hours by horse. Often travelers would opt to take the high road. Although it was longer and rougher, the high road presented fewer creek crossings. Not only were creek crossings more numerous the lower one traveled, the water was broader and more powerful. Lowland crossings could be especially treacherous for those driving wagons.

4.1 Texas Creek and trail sign. At an intersection with an old pathway stands a sign for Old Settlers Trail, which makes a distinct turn to the left. As the 1800s drew to a close, many people left the Smokies. The best lands of a difficult terrain had already been claimed, and jobs were hard to come by. People left mainly to seek opportunity. Like the Emerts, many from this area traveled to Texas. One young man started off with his new bride, headed for a new life in Texas. His wife, however, became so homesick that he agreed to return. They settled on this creek, which the young man began calling Texas Creek so that he could feel like he attained some measure of his dream.

After the left turn, a wall and old homesite appear on the left of the trail, which is gullied in this section. As the trail rises, it passes the remains of two fine chimneys (at mile 4.2), which stand just to the left of the trail. One has a distinctive "V"-shaped lintel over the fireplace. With its two chimneys, the Lunsford place was larger than usual. Like Tyson McCarter, they had a frame house; theirs had four rooms. They owned 35 acres here, including an orchard of apple, peach, and cherry trees. Little else is left to see of Fletcher and Ada Lunsford's home and barn, except the chimneys, a few shards of window glass, and pieces from an old fruit jar.

The trail continues to ascend, passing rock walls on the right, crossing a second branch of Texas Creek, passing an indistinct rock wall on the left, then a third branch of the creek. All the rock walls tell of former fields and, indirectly, of former homes. A spicebush on the left hints at a homesite. Wild hydrangeas and jewelweed edge the trail, as does another rock wall on the left. Texas Creek was heavily populated.

The main course of Texas Creek now lies below on the right, as the trail climbs toward Chestnut Ridge and the last branch of the creek. Yellow buckeye shells litter the ground, and Dutchman's pipe vine, with its large, heart-shaped leaves, twines through the trees. Roy McCarter had a log cabin, barn, and smokehouse somewhere in this section. At the last branch crossing, wall remnants run parallel to both branch and trail. On the far side of the trail the presence of walnut trees indicates an overgrown homesite.

The Roy McCarter cabin sat in the vicinity of Texas Creek. 1935 photo.

What was a roadbed now narrows as the trail pushes upward, switchbacking through hemlocks. Huge chestnut stumps and fallen chestnut logs come into view. Chestnut Ridge is a virtual chestnut graveyard. The trees fell long ago to the fungus, but the wood is so rot-proof that their remains still testify to the chestnut groves that once filled this ridge. One of the CCC's jobs was to clear dead chestnuts from the Smokies. Bears, which had depended on chestnut mast, soon switched to acorns as oak trees helped fill the niche left open by the chestnut's demise.

Before chestnuts fell prey to disease, settlers would come up to the ridge and selectively log out tuliptrees, maples, and other types of trees. The area along Old Settlers Trail was never commercially logged. People simply cut what they needed for building materials. At first, homes were all log cabins. In the 1880s, when commercial logging came to the Smokies, water-powered sawmills were built on Webb Creek and people began building frame homes.

As settlers removed other species from this ridge, chestnuts naturally filled out the canopy. Families came up to the "chestnut orchard" on the ridge to collect chestnuts for their own larders and to sell in Sevierville and Knoxville. In addition, the bountiful chestnuts that once littered the ground went a long way toward fattening up farmers' hogs.

After topping a rise, the trail dips for about a half-mile or so before reaching the ridgecrest. Just beyond this rise, the trail passes what look like a sinkhole or two. These are the result of the infamous 1938 cloudburst that killed eight people on Webb Creek. The water pummeled the earth fiercely, filling up underground aquifers so fast that the water gushed out of weak points on the slope. As they gushed, these instant geysers created soil pits around them that look similar to sinkholes.

Besides dead chestnuts, Chestnut Ridge is dense with rhododendron punctuated with huge, live old-growth trees: hemlocks, maples, tuliptrees, and oaks. Although this section of trail exhibits few historical sites, it is full of natural glory. Look for a cluster of standing dead chestnuts. Such trees provide "apartment" dwellings for numerous animals. Rectangular holes signal the presence of Pileated Woodpeckers, which prefer drilling nests in dead trees among old-growth forests.

One tall chestnut snag is marked by a hole much larger than a woodpecker's. About 40 feet up and bigger than a basketball is a cavity whose bottom edge is scarred with claw marks. Here some mother bear bore young, protecting them at this height from potential enemies.

At 5.2 miles, Old Settlers crests Chestnut Ridge. Your elevation here is nearly 2,500 feet, the highest point on the trail. Then begins a steady descent toward Tumbling Branch, a tributary of Noisy Creek. Not far from the ridgecrest, look for fence posts on the right, a clearing, and rock piles.

.Beyond Tumbling Branch, Noisy Creek comes into view below on the left. A rock wall, 3-4 feet high and about 100 feet long parallels the trail on the right. More rock walls appear just before the first crossing of Noisy Creek, a name that fits the sound of this exuberantly tumbling waterway.

Carson Brewer wrote that Civil War veteran Sam Ramsey and his family lived here. Sam Ramsey was the grandfather of Perry Ramsey, who married Ollie McCarter.

Some of the largest Timber Rattlesnakes in the world live in this area, too. In fact, the robust rattlers in this section have been featured on a television wildlife program. Glenn Cardwell saw one of the largest timber rattlers he had ever seen in the vicinity of Noisy Creek. Thick as a forearm, the snake was coiled to strike. It had recently sloughed its old skin and its new skin was still delicate, a lovely pale green with a golden sheen.

Unlike Northern Copperheads, rattlesnakes come equipped with an early-warning defense system, but you can't absolutely depend on getting a rattling alert. Fortunately, they are not particularly aggressive and are as happy to avoid you, as you are to avoid them. But, as one hiker put it, "The difference between a good snake story and a trip to the hospital is about six feet."

Less than a quarter-mile farther, the trail crosses Noisy Creek a second time, and a mossy rock wall parallels the trail on the right. Less than another quarter-mile farther is the third crossing of Noisy and another mossy wall. Behind the wall rises what is left of a chimney, about seven feet high. Like many fireplaces along Old Settlers Trail, this one has a "V"-shaped stone lintel, a bit of artistic presentation.

Records suggest W. Anson ("Anse") and Elvira ("Vira") Whaley Ramsey and their children lived in a frame house at this site. Foundation stones and old timbers from the barn lie on the site as well. Spicebush and walnut trees, planted near-by, are in better condition than the buildings. Besides a house and barn, the Ramseys owned nearly 80 acres of farmland and orchards between here and U.S. 321. The highway did not exist then; it was built around 1953.

6.8 Pathway junction. Noisy Creek now parallels the trail below and to the right. Not long after the third Noisy Creek crossing, an old pathway intersects with Old Settlers Trail, and a sign indicates that Old Settlers makes a sharp left toward Greenbrier. The trail continues its gentle descent flanked by thick banks of rhododendron. A rock wall appears on the right. It ends, but soon another, shorter wall lines the trail. The trail bends left, becoming gullied between low banks. Yet another section of wall lines the right, joined on the left by a wall that is almost six feet high.

Soon, a short path on the left leads to chimney so tall that it looks imposing even from the trail. Imposing, yet alone in a shaded, enfolding forest, the chimney reminds one of poet William Wordsworth's sense of imagined landscape on view-ing, again, the ruins of Tintern Abbey.

About 25 feet high with a five-foot-wide fireplace on either side, the chimney was carefully fitted with fieldstone. It is the finest chimney along Old Settlers. The fireplace, of course, dis-plays a "V"-shaped lintel. Such a tall, double-sided chimney implies a two-story house with at least two rooms on the ground floor—larger than the usual house along this trail. Homer Reagan lived here. Although the forest is closing in, the trees are still young enough to say that this was once cleared land.

The trail has entered a new watershed, this one centered on Ramsey Creek. The homes and farms of the Ramsey family were scattered all over this part of the Smokies. The Ramseys first settled in the Smokies in the mid-1800s. Just recently, descendents of these Ramseys convinced the U.S. Geological Survey that they had been misspelling their family name on maps for some 70 years. Consequently, the park's "Ramsay" place names are being changed to "Ramsey."

As it descends, Old Settlers Trail crosses Ramsey Creek five times, all in little more than a half-mile. Between the first and second crossing, the trail becomes narrow and rocky. Between the second and third crossing, look for a wide, crumbling chimney about 20 feet to the left of the trail. A piece from the top of a rusted cookstove lies at its base.

Just before the fifth crossing, a seven-foot remnant chimney rises on the right of the trail, with foundation stones outlining part of the floor plan. A rosebush, planted long ago, grows at the trail's edge. After crossing Ramsey Creek for the last time, the trail angles left up a steep, 0.2-mile ascent. Look for an old road coming in from the left and, just up the trail on the left, what remains of a home hunkers under a gloomy canopy of hemlocks and hardwoods. Anchored by the 10-foot-tall chimney, undoubtedly this spot was sunnier when people lived here.

Not far past a trail sign, at about 8.4 miles, the trail crests the gap dividing the watersheds of Ramsey Creek and Redwine Creek. Patches of wintergreen carpet the sunny area. Black gum, sourwood, mountain laurel—typical gap species—spread themselves around. The trail begins a descent through hemlocks, then a mixed forest of hickory, oak, maple, and tuliptree. A few low cairns edge the trail in this section.

The trail crosses Redwine Creek, which is also known as Brandywine Creek. The first name comes from James Redwine, a circuit-riding minister who settled in the area. The second comes from the native wild grapes that were used to make wine and brandy.

9.2 Redwine Creek and Backcountry Campsite Number 33. Nearby is Camp 33, which is an old homesite. Perry Ramsey, who married Ollie McCarter, was born here and was the last owner before the park bought the property in the 1930s. A house and barn stood here. About 50 feet off the trail to the right are the remains of the chimney. Segments of low rock wall, former clearings, what looks like the remnants of a springhouse all help tell the story of this spot. Campsite 33 is the only campsite on Old Settlers and, at roughly halfway, it is the place to stop on a two-day Old Settlers backpacking trip.

The Perry Ramsey home surrounded by tobacco in September, 1935.

Return to the trail, which now winds below a ridge, rounding the back of one cove, then another, passing from hemlock groves into mixed hardwoods, then back again through hemlocks. Eventually, Old Settlers descends through rhododendron, hemlocks, and chestnut oaks to Darky Creek, a narrow strip of a stream.

Beyond the stream, a bit of wall lines the left side of the trail as it ascends. More hemlocks and then, on the left side of the trail, begins the trail's longest segment of rock wall. About 3 1/2 feet high, the wall stretches more than 300 feet. Partway along, a perpendicular wall meets the trail on the right.

These walls may have been part of the Freeman place,

which lies a few hundred feet beyond. Clumps of yuccas on the left mark the spot. Settlers often planted yuccas at the edge of their yards. Flowers usually bordered the house, and vegetable and herb gardens were always close. Yet, settlers' yards were cleared, packed earth. A clean space kept snakes, rodents, and other undesirables from lurking, hidden in the grass. Settlers packed the earth so that they would not track dirt into their homes.

Below the yuccas, a segment of rock wall lines a short piece of roadbed that ends at an old corncrib or pigpen, a rectangular structure about 7-by-15 feet. Six layers of notched hand-hewn timbers remain, but the roof is long gone. After allowing their hogs to roam freely in the forest, fattening up on mast, mountain dwellers drove them home and further fattened them in pigpens. Charlie Hedricks, a blacksmith in Cades Cove, said he would fatten a pig until flesh caused its eyes to close and the animal could barely stand up.

Although some call this the Freeman place, others say it was Elmer Proffitt's place. Maps showing structures at the time the park was established list Proffitt as the last owner. Both answers may be right because, like today, people passed their houses down to relatives, moved, sold their houses, and rented to tenant farmers. Any number of families might have lived in any given house in the Smokies.

On the right side of the trail stands a well-preserved chimney, about 12 feet high. The rock walls bordering former fields at Joe Freeman's farm look as though they were built as terracing. To prevent soil erosion, some farmers in this area terraced their fields.

Past the Freeman place, Old Settlers Trail turns left, on its way toward Timothy Creek. Just before the creek, Old Settlers passes an old path on the right. On the far side of Timothy Creek, a rock wall lines the trail with another well-preserved wall angling off into the woods. Soon the trail begins a short but steep descent, passing yellow birch, beech, and mountain laurel.

Evans Creek flows along the left side of the trail. Also on the left, angelica, sunflower, blue lobelia, Joe-Pye-weed, other wildflowers, and saplings have taken over former clearings. Everett Sherrick, whose descriptions of Old Settlers Trail have appeared in Sevier County's *Mountain Press* newspaper and in his book, *Trails of Invitation,* says one of these homesites belonged to Sam McGaha.

10.7 Another path comes in from the right to meet Old Settlers Trail. Here and there, throughout the park, former pathways intersect official Smokies trails. In order to protect nature and avoid getting lost, always stick to official trails. No need to pull a Wiley Oakley. Follow the Old Settlers Trail sign pointing the way onward.

Wiley Oakley, circa 1935.

Wiley Oakley, who grew up in the Smokies, guided visitors into the mountains even before the park was established. He was known as the area's number-one guide as well as a popular raconteur. Once, when asked by one of his travelers, "Have you ever been lost?"

the intrepid Oakley answered, "No, but I spent three days pretty bewildered."

The trail now passes through the relatively low-lying Soak Ash watershed, crossing Soak Ash Creek and its branches about four times. Near the first crossing, a small clearing lies on the left. Unlike most of the terrain through which the trail has passed, the Soak Ash area is bottomland. Instead of boisterous, bubbling streams, the water here runs lazily through broad, flat areas. Because they are easier to plant than slopes, one would imagine that settlers chose to clear these bottomlands first.

The name Soak Ash comes from the common method of making soap in these parts, before commercial soap was widely available. Each family emptied their fireplace ashes into hoppers. When enough ashes had collected, they soaked the ashes with water, leaching out lye. Most families killed a hog or two each autumn, then preserved the meat to feed them over the winter. They used the animals' lard for many purposes. To make soap, they cooked lard with lye, which produces the jelly-like soap once found in all mountain homes. (Some, such as Lucinda Oakley Ogle's mother, made a Sunday soap using butter and crushed rose petals.)

The Conley Huskey store.

Conley Huskey grew up in the Soak Ash area. His family

was one of the first to settle this side of the Smokies, in the mid-1800s, and the Huskey name is still widespread on the Tennessee side of the national park. At the time the park was established, Conley Huskey owned a frame house and five out-buildings along Soak Ash. It probably included his parents' property, because Leonard and Lora Huskey had lived here, too. A civic-minded man, Conley Huskey served as mayor of Pittman Center. To his west, in the broadest part of the valley, lived Partons, Whaleys, and another member of the Huskey family. More than a half-dozen families lived along Soak Ash Creek. A frame church stood nearby.

During the growing season, the trail can become overgrown and weedy near the second crossing. The third crossing passes through a pretty valley, once cleared and still fairly open. Hearts-a-bustin' are common in the Soak Ash valley. The fruits of these shrubs are magnificent in fall, when the hard red berries "bust" open to reveal bright orange seeds. A walnut tree close to the trail hints that someone once lived here. It is easy to imagine farms filling the lowlands that spread across this part of the hike.

A rock wall, about 4 1/2 feet high and thick with moss and dirt, appears on the left, paralleling the trail. The trail now fol-lows Snakefeeder Branch. Where a path comes in from the right, look for an Old Settlers Trail sign.

11.3 Lindsey Cemetery side trail junction. Where sign and path intersect is an optional short side trip to Lindsey Cemetery. The path descends to Snakefeeder Branch on the right, then con-tinues on the other side. Although Snakefeeder is deeply gullied at this point and the banks are steep, it is usually an easy rock-hop over the branch to see Lindsey Cemetery.

In about 0.2 miles, the path enters a broad grassy clearing, where a dirt road coming from the direction of U.S. 321 seems to terminate. Cross this clearing and continue uphill to the right. The path ends soon at Lindsey Cemetery, a clearing surrounded by oaks and sourwoods that dapple sunlight onto this peaceful place. The cemetery contains nearly 60 graves. Reverend John Lindsey, who once lived nearby, is buried here. His relative, Jesse Lindsey, received a land grant in this area in 1841.

Conley Huskey's father, Leonard, is buried here, as are other members of the Huskey family. Dr. R. C. Wright, who lived along Lindsey Creek, lies here, too. On decoration days, descendents come to the cemetery to clean the graves and brighten them with pots of flowers.

Return to Old Settlers Trail, turning right toward the direction of Greenbrier. The trail begins a long, gradual ascent toward Copeland Divide, nearly three miles up the trail. Snakefeeder Branch still flows along on the right and walls of rhododendron flank the left. Where the trail passes through a damp area, cardinal flowers bloom red in season. Where a huge-leaved umbrella magnolia rises on the far side of the branch, look for a remnant chimney, about seven feet high and six feet wide.

In the next three-quarter's mile, Old Settlers crosses small forks of Snakefeeder Branch as the trail slowly ascends. A few hundred feet beyond the last chimney, a nailed post stands next to the trail, near holly, witch-hazel, and an umbrella magnolia. With oval leaves two feet long and half as broad, umbrella magnolias are hard to miss. They prefer low elevations and streambanks, such as adjacent Snakefeeder Branch.

On the far side of the stream stands a two-foot-high segment of rock wall. Just beyond a fork crossing, a wildflower-filled clearing on the right reveals another chimney, with the foundation stones of the house on the downhill side. As the trail rises, it crosses back and forth across Snakefeeder forks, passing a crumbled wall on the far bank and some pretty, silver-splotched little brown jugs, low groundcover related to wild ginger. Settlers brewed tea from the roots of this plant and used it to treat whooping cough and other ailments. They also collected and sold the roots for 34 cents a pound.

Just before the last crossing of Snakefeeder, look for a rusted tub hanging from a tree on the right. Not far past Snakefeeder Branch, a couple of fence posts hide among massed mountain laurel, with wildflowers such as Solomon's seal and sundrops nearby.

Old Settlers Trail begins climbing a series of switchbacks, passing striped maple, rhododendron, and, on the forest floor, trailing arbutus and galax. Farmers used to collect galax to earn money, selling the plants to florists who use galax's coppery evergreen leaves in arrangements. Although the white flower spikes are pretty, their odor is not; sometimes people unloved by their neighbors would find wreaths of smelly galax tacked to their door.

Below the divide, the trail crosses the upper reaches of Copeland Creek. Between here and the present park boundary far below, more than a dozen families lived and farmed along the creek. The next couple of miles were too rough for habitation, but are full of natural pleasures as the trail crosses the divide and continues down the other side toward Greenbrier.

14.1 Copeland Divide. To the left rises Greenbrier Pinnacle, the long, tall ridge that has given rise to the folded watersheds that etch the length of Old Settlers Trail. Rivulets start high on the ridge, cut paths down the broad face of the ridge, then gather into streams. All along the face of Greenbrier Pinnacle, these streams form a series of sloping valleys divided by their own low ridges. The lower slopes of these vertical valleys each attracted a community of settlers.

In the spring, when mountain families were hungry for anything fresh and green after the winter's supply of preserved foods had dwindled, members of the Parton family hiked up coves on the Pinnacle to find ramps. The Partons lived in Greenbrier, along the Little Bird Branch section of Old Settlers Trail. Often they hiked as much as seven miles seeking these wild, pungent relatives of the onion that are a treat scrambled with eggs and potatoes. They brought along lunches of cornbread and bacon and stuffed their sacks full of ramps.

Later in the season they traveled up the mountain in search of blueberries to preserve and bake

The Dan Parton log cabin, 1936.

in pies, and ginseng to sell. They took along their dogs to keep the copperheads and rattlers at bay.

On its way down, the trail passes pine and laurel, with gray deer moss scattered on the ground. Steadily descending, Old Settlers winds around the back of four or more coves, then switchbacks down through stands of hickories and oaks. Hemlocks and rhododendron take over, as the elevation becomes lower and moisture retention higher.

A rocked-lined spring—perhaps a former springhouse—announces that the trail has reached civilization again. The trail now weaves alongside Little Bird Branch, which was home to so many members of the Parton family that it was called Parton-town, much as Big Greenbrier Cove was called the Whaley Settlement. The most famous member of the Parton family is, of course, Dolly Parton. A singer, business-woman, and film star, Dolly Parton is as much an institution as the national park.

In 1979, Beverly Parton Bowen told something of Parton family history in the Mountain Historical Society newsletter. "The family had a saying," she wrote, "'mean as old Moses.'" Moses R. Parton, that is. He purchased land in the Smokies in 1866, 150 acres in Sugarlands, probably the first area in which the Partons lived.

By the time Bowen's great-grandfather William H. Parton died, at 47, the family had moved to Parton Hollow. Parton's oldest son, Joseph, helped his mother raise the other seven children. But Joseph was a wild one, with a bootleg business. He stayed out of jail only because he delivered his goods to the judge and sheriff.

Bowen's grandfather, another of William Parton's sons, was one of those who left the Smokies in the late 1890s, he to Kansas. His brother George went, too, but returned soon after. George said of the notorious midwestern winds, "Any place you can throw your hat up against the barn wall and it stays all day, ain't the place for me."

Former clearings appear to the right and left, and a crumbling two-foot high section of wall parallels the right side of the trail. Ahead are more old homesites, spicebushes (a favorite planting), and a higher, finer wall on the left.

Little Bird Branch flows along on the right as the trail continues to descend. A walnut tree stands at the beginning of a low wall about 75 feet long. Walnut trees were often planted next to homes, to provide both nuts and shade in the days when all the lower slopes and bottomlands were cleared for vegetable gardens, cornfields, and orchards.

Past the wall, on the right, a path leads to Parton Cemetery, where Chris Parton's house once stood. Chris and Margaret Evans Parton married in 1853 and raised 10 children here. They were country singer Dolly Parton's great-great-grandparents. In her memoirs, *Reflections of the Pinnacle,* Lona Parton Tyson remembers her grandmother carrying sweet chestnuts in her apron pocket, gathered from the large chestnut tree on the hill above the house. Tyson wrote that her grandfather's forehead was scarred by a bullet that hit him while fighting in the Civil War. Although many men left the Smokies to join one side or the other, the Civil War also came to the Smokies as small numbers of troops crossed the mountains, and deserters and raiders from both sides sought refuge in them.

Lona's mother was Tennessee ("Tennie") Russell Parton, named for the state. Her father, Albert Huston Parton, trapped mink and muskrat for the money the furs brought. The family hunted and fished, but most of what they had they made themselves: pickled beans, tomatoes, beets, cucumbers, barrels of sauerkraut, cabbages holed up for the winter. Her father also had a little gristmill so they could grind their corn.

Sarah Parton, age 74, taken in 1936.

Dinner might be a kettle of beans and fresh potatoes, green onions, radishes, and apple pie. They would rest for a half-hour, then go back up the hollow to hoe corn or cut tops and pull fodder to feed the cows and horse.

She remembered her mother as fair and honest, someone who made quilts and meals for those less fortunate than they. She could spin, weave, knit, sew, and quilt. Her mother knew herbs and raised ducks so they could pick feathers for feather beds. She made vinegar, soap, dye, sour dough, whatever life required.

Lona Parton Tyson's parents raised nine children. Their oldest son was Dolly Parton's grandfather. Church was a touchstone of their lives, and this is where Dolly began singing. "We are proud of her and her talent," Lona said. "God has blessed most of the Parton family with talent. Some preach and some pick and sing for the glory of God, and some pick and sing in other places, but we are proud of them all."

Return to Old Settlers Trail, rounding the back of a cove, then descending to Bird Branch and the woods beyond, which are filled with blue aster, white wood aster, ferns, and mossy logs. This flat footpath through low-lying woods with the sound of the Little Pigeon River to the right suggests that the hike is almost over. It ends in Greenbrier, which was once a center of the Smokies, filled with nearly a hundred families as well as churches, schools, stores, mills, and a hotel. Soon Old Settlers Trail emerges at Ramsey Prong Road.

15.8 Ramsey Prong Road junction.

OLD SUGARLANDS TRAIL

DIRECTIONS: Best hiked using a two-car shuttle. The hike begins at Old Sugarlands trailhead off Cherokee Orchard Road and ends at Newfound Gap Road (U.S. 441) near Sugarlands Visitor Center. Leave one car at the Sugarlands Visitor Center parking lot. Then, from Gatlinburg, take Historic Nature Trail—Airport Road east to Cherokee Orchard Road and park in the Rainbow Falls parking lot. The trailhead lies a few hundred feet before the parking lot, just behind a gate barring automobiles.

LENGTH: 3.9 miles, plus optional 1.3-mile roundtrip visit to cemetery.

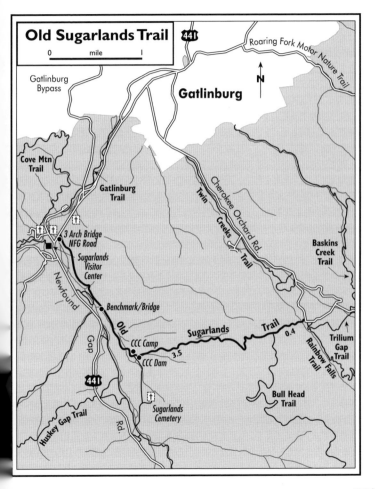

Old Sugarlands Trail

0   mile   1

Gatlinburg Bypass

Gatlinburg

441

Roaring Fork Motor Nature Trail

N

Cove Mtn Trail

Gatlinburg Trail

Cherokee Orchard Rd

Twin Creeks Trail

Baskins Creek Trail

3 Arch Bridge NFG Road

Sugarlands Visitor Center

Newfound Gap

Benchmark/Bridge

Old Sugarlands Trail

CCC Camp

3.5

CCC Dam

0.4

Rainbow Falls Trail

Trilium Gap Trail

441

Sugarlands Cemetery

Bull Head Trail

Huskey Gap Trail

Rd.

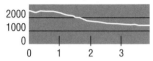

PHYSICAL PROFILE: An easy walk, Old Sugarlands Trail descends gradually through the park's lowlands. One caveat: watch for directional signs because a number of unmarked trails and old roads intersect with Old Sugarlands. Although it ends near busy Sugarlands Visitor Center, the trail itself is lightly used, a delightful get-away at the heart of the park.

CULTURAL PROFILE: Old homesites with standing chimneys, a cemetery, a former quarry, and a major CCC camp with remains of officers' quarters, parade grounds, and more. Old Sugarlands Trail offers a rich stroll through history.

*W*hen settlers started moving west from North Carolina into Tennessee during the early 1800s, one of the best-known routes, Indian Gap Trail, led directly into Sugarlands. Road Prong Trail overlays the upper reaches of this ancient Cherokee way over the Smokies. Old Sugarlands Trail lies at the lower reaches.

The Sugarlands area generally follows the course of the West Prong of the Little Pigeon River, spreading into a fertile valley in the lowlands. Sugarlands is bounded on the west by long, narrow Sugarland Mountain and on the east by Mount Le Conte and Grapeyard Ridge.

Newfound Gap Road now parallels the West Prong of the Little Pigeon River. Before the park was established, small communities and individual farms dotted the sloping river valley and its tributaries. Because it afforded the best and most level land for farming, the center of Sugarlands was between where Sugarlands Visitor Center now stands and Cherokee Orchard Road. Old Sugarlands Trail traverses this area.

In the days before cane sugar became widely available, settlers could satisfy a sweet tooth by growing sorghum and extracting molasses, raising bees for honey, or tapping maple trees. Sugarlands got its name from the many sugar maple trees that grew here.

The first settlers into Sugarlands were Martha Huskey Ogle, a 40-year-old widow, and her seven children. They came from Edgefield County, South Carolina, in 1795. Soon after came Richard and Julia Shults Reagan, whose son Daniel Wesley Reagan was born in 1802—the first white child born in the White Oak Flats settlement (later renamed Gatlinburg).

Maples, Bohannons, Trenthams, and Oakleys were among the surnames of Sugarlands' first families. They are still associated with old homesites along Old Sugarlands Trail.

0.0 Past the gate at the trailhead, Old Sugarlands Trail almost immediately crosses Le Conte Creek via a railed footlog. The first English name for this creek was Mill Creek, because its edges were dotted with 25 mills. When the national park was established in 1934, 35 creeks in the Smokies were called Mill Creek. Special nomenclature committees had to reduce that confusion and parcel out new names.

Of Sugarlands' first families, Richard Reagan and two of Martha Huskey Ogle's sons, William ("Black Bill") and Isaac, owned land along this creek in the early 1800s. They passed the land on to their children. From a rough beginning of hunting, fishing, gathering berries and nuts, and planting subsistence crops, successive generations of Sugarlands farmers added cash-producing crops and orchards. Cherokee Orchard Road, for instance, was full of orchards, especially apple orchards. Among the last to live here, Lucinda Ogle said they grew old-time varieties such as green pippin, sour John, and sweetnose.

Apple trees still mark old homesites, but in this section Old Sugarlands Trail has reverted to a quiet forest of oak, sourwood, tuliptree, and maple. Deciduous trees give way to a hemlock grove, which in turn gives way to hardwoods.

0.4 Bull Head Trail junction. Bull Head Trail heads left, up to Mount Le Conte, and Old Sugarlands continues through rhododendrons.

0.7 Twomile Lead Trail junction. At the fork, Twomile Lead Trail goes right, and is an alternate way to Sugarlands Visitor Center. Take the left-hand fork to continue on Old Sugarlands, passing oaks and hickories.

At about 1.5 miles, signs of former habitation appear. A small creek on the left has been rock-lined. Soon afterward, giant rock piles loom on the left, like the cairns of giants. When settlers cleared land for fields, they used the rocks they dug out to build walls around their fields. When they had more than they could use, they simply made rock piles such as these.

At 1.75 miles or so, a section of rock wall, about four feet high, parallels the far side of the creek. Here, too, holly, pipsissewa, and Adam-and-Eve orchid grow among the understory.

1.9 Civilian Conservation Corps (CCC) dam. On the left, a low

The Burton Ogle Place on Old Sugarlands Road. Alex Cole and Aunt Moll Cary lived nearby. 1931 photo.

concrete dam about 20 feet across spans the creek. Affixed to the dam is a brass plaque: "Lt. Edward E. Hunt, April 1935." Here, CCC workers built a gravity-fed water system, complete with chlorinator, for the camp and the National Park Service. Proud of their work, they put up this plaque.

2.1 Homesite. The trail, which has been gently descending, passes a broad, flat bench of land on the left where clumps of yucca grow. Like boxwood, roses, walnut trees, and daffodils, nonnative yucca are a sign that former homeowners have embellished the land around their house.

On the right, across from this former homesite, is a former park dumpsite, or "midden." Although little is left, all historical sites and artifacts are protected by law and should not be disturbed.

2.2 Burton Ogle homeplace. The trail curves to the left and almost immediately reaches a junction where a sign says Newfound Gap Road, 1.5 miles. From Cherokee Orchard Road to a bit beyond this point, this was known as the Cherokee Road or Bullhead Road. The trail at the sign once led to Burton Ogle's place. Although forest is once again enfolding it, enough open areas still exist to hint at a time when all was open to the sun.

Immediately on the left stand the remains of a chimney. Nearby rock walls once fenced fields. A path led to the Ogle's front door. The chimney once anchored a two-story frame house that was surrounded on three sides by a neat, fenced garden. Burton and his wife Isophine Newman Ogle had six children here. One died young and another died as an infant, soon after his mother's death.

Burton Ogle was the grandson of William "Black Bill" Ogle, who came into Sugarlands as a boy with his mother and siblings, bound from South Carolina. Burton's mother, Jane "Jennie" Conner Ogle was the "granny woman" (midwife) for Sugarlands in the mid to late 1800s. The Ogles lived here from the late 1800s until the park was established. From the 1880s on, his mother lived with them as well. Both mother and son are buried in Sugarlands Cemetery, along with many others who once lived in Sugarlands.

2.3 CCC Camp. Companies 1458 and 1459 had barracks, offi-

The men of the Sugarlands (NP-10) Civilian Conservation Corps (CCC) camp. 1934 photo.

cers' quarters, mess hall, recreation hall, supply building, baseball field, and parade grounds here. Where the trail comes to an intersection at the heart of the CCC camp, the main trail curves to the right. Look for a perfectly straight line of hemlocks on the right that marked one end of the CCC parade grounds. Across the trail on the left were the mess hall and barracks that housed 200-plus men.

The Sugarlands CCC camp operated from 1933 to 1942, providing young men with jobs during the Depression. The men of the 22 CCC camps in the Smokies basically built the park's infrastructure: roads, trails, bridges, fire towers, whatever was needed. In their spare time the men here could take classes in bee culture, gardening, and high school basics. They also played baseball and had two championship teams.

Bob Owensby came north from near Chattanooga to work at the Sugarlands CCC camp. He helped build restrooms and the original tower on Clingmans Dome, driving up every day by truck on the recently paved Newfound Gap Road.

Of his $30 per month pay, Owensby sent home $25 to his family, as did the other men. The CCC took care of room and board. Although CCC literature cautioned that "broiled lobster and squab are not regular items on CCC menus…few homes serve meals as scientifically selected as those served in CCC camps." Some of the cooks went on to become chefs in the up-and-coming Gatlinburg tourist trade.

Owensby used his remaining money for movies in Gatlinburg: they cost 10 cents and CCC'ers could go every night. He met his future wife as he passed the nearby Pi Beta Phi School one day. Mary Alice and her friends were sitting along the rail fence that fronted the school. She was raised in upper Sugarlands, the site of the present Chimney Tops Picnic Area. In fact, the CCC planted the trees that now grow in the picnic area.

During World War II, the Sugarlands camp was used to house conscientious objectors. From the late 1940s to the late 1950s, the site was used for park vehicle maintenance. After the Park Service moved vehicle maintenance closer to park headquarters, squatters moved into the old maintenance garages, so the Park Service destroyed the garages in the winter of 1968-69.

On the right side of the trail, a broad grassy area marks the CCC parade grounds. A chimney with mantle belonged to the recreation hall. A low stone circle may have been a flagpole base or a fire pit. Nearby stands a tall light pole with a rusted shade. The foundations of the officers' quarters spread along the rise just beyond. And the large concrete conduits are from park maintenance yard days.

2.3 Old Sugarlands/West Prong junction. In the 1930s, this junction was a busy place with the large CCC camp, Pi Beta Phi school for women on the southbound West Prong road, and homes with barns and other outbuildings on the main road. At the intersection, the main trail turns right. But for a quick side trip to Sugarlands Cemetery, turn left on the West Prong section.

About 0.5 mile from the junction, look for a weedy path to the left. This path continues for about 600 feet atop a bench of land to the fairly large Sugarlands Cemetery, where Ogles, Carrs, and other members of Sugarlands extended families are buried.

Near the road stood the Pi Beta Phi Settlement School. The national women's college organization, Pi Beta Phi, had been looking for a community whose women needed skills to help themselves economically. They chose the Smokies, sent college-educated women as teachers, and established a settlement school in the Sugarlands in 1912.

By this time, the old crafts were dying out as mail-order goods became available and affordable. The Pi Beta Phi

Teachers and pupils of Pi Beta Phi school. 1921 photo.

Settlement School educated young women of the Smokies in everything from traditional subjects such as arithmetic and English to quilting, basket-making, and weaving. The crafts were taught by long-time Smokies craftswomen from their own community, and the resulting craftworks were sold to tourists looking to purchase authentic mountain products. Return to the main trail.

Walking north toward Sugarlands Visitor Center, the trail now overlays what was once the highway through this area: Tennessee State Highway 71. That early paved road—one of the first over the mountains—has been replaced by Newfound Gap Road, which runs parallel just to the west. Between the two roads flows the West Prong of the Little Pigeon River, which is audible from here.

2.9 Bullhead Branch bridge. The 15-foot concrete span over Bullhead Branch is marked with a "U.S. Coast & Geodetic Survey" benchmark from 1934. Although it is now a quiet trail, the old telephone pole farther down the trail reminds hikers that this once was a major thoroughfare in the heart of Sugarlands. Along its sides lived dozens of families: Newmans, Maples, and others.

Alie Newman Maples remembered her grandfather's black-smith shop in the Sugarlands. Along with gristmills—and a number of small gristmills dotted streams flowing through Sugarlands—blacksmith shops were a community necessity. Her grandfather, a small man barely five feet tall, forged tools and wagon parts, and occasionally let her pump the bellows.

Maples' father, Fred Newman, had a store in the Sugarlands where he sold salt, coffee, kerosene, shoes, cloth, canned goods, and other products. Farmers who could not buy with cash could barter with their chickens and produce. Almost everyone in the Smokies grew corn, beans, and both sweet and white potatoes. And almost everyone had a few fruit trees. For early farmers, especially, these were among the basic foods that fed them through the winter. The corn was kept in cribs to be ground for meal; the beans and fruit were dried, and the potatoes were kept in root cellars. From the late 1800s, however, a cash economy began to enter the Smokies.

In the early 1900s, the Smokies tourist trade began to blossom. Fred Newman saw an opportunity and, in 1927, he put up the first gasoline pump in the Smokies, along Highway 71. Of his farming, Fred Newman said, "We could work that corn in one day, and it'd be about three weeks before we'd have to hoe it again." He said it was a good life "because I didn't expect much."

Leaving the bed of Highway 71, the trail narrows, following the river, passing a connector trail on the right that leads to Twomile Lead Trail (a local riding stable trail).

3.2 Old Sugarlands Trail sign: Newfound Gap Road 0.6 mile; Cherokee Orchard Road 3.3 miles. Below, the sparsely treed floodplain tells that this spot was once cleared and filled with crops. Where the trail curves toward the right stands a sheer, 70-foot-high cliff. Approaching trail's end, Old Sugarlands ascends slightly, curves to the left, and passes Twomile Branch Trail, a bridle path used by the local stable-horse concession. A quarry site which supplied gravel for the construction of Newfound Gap Road lies at trail's end.

At the end of the trail, turn left at Newfound Gap Road to reach Sugarlands Visitor Center. The three-arch stone bridge on Newfound Gap Road was built by the CCC, the stonework

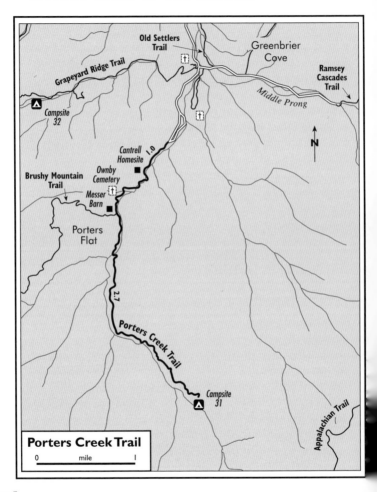

Porters Creek Trail

0   mile   1

Old Settlers Trail

Greenbrier Cove

Grapeyard Ridge Trail

Ramsey Cascades Trail

Middle Prong

Campsite 32

Cantrell Homesite

1.0

Ownby Cemetery

Brushy Mountain Trail

Messer Barn

Porters Flat

N

2.7

Porters Creek Trail

Campsite 31

Appalachian Trail

supervised by an Italian stonemason. Sugarlands Visitor Center lies a few hundred feet to the south. To avoid the busy highway, cross over to park headquarters and take the short, paved trail connecting headquarters and the visitor center.

PORTERS CREEK TRAIL

DIRECTIONS: From Gatlinburg take U.S. 321 5.9 miles east and turn right at the sign for the Greenbrier entrance to Great Smoky Mountains National Park. Continue on Greenbrier Road past the ranger station. The paved road will change to gravel and pass the turnoff for Ramsey Prong Road. About 4 miles from U.S. 321, the road ends at a gate. Park near here. The trail starts on the other side of the gate.

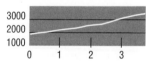

LENGTH: 7.3 miles. This hike goes from the Porters Creek trailhead to Campsite 31 and back (3.6 miles, one way).

PHYSICAL PROFILE: A fairly easy trail that follows an old roadbed for the first mile, Porters Creek Trail rises at a steady grade. This is one of the park's best trails for spring wildflowers.

CULTURAL PROFILE: A cemetery, old homesites, the remains of an old vehicle, a large, well-preserved barn, and the old Smoky Mountain Hiking Club cabin all lie within the first mile or so. Beyond, the trail reveals little of human history, outside of gold- and silver-mining stories. It does provide riches of another sort: waterfalls and spring wildflowers.

Hotel LeConte (located in Greenbrier) in 1927.

*B*ig Greenbrier Cove was one of the most heavily populated parts of what is now Great Smoky Mountains National Park. Every creek valley leading into Greenbrier Cove was eventually dotted with homes and farms. In the early 1900s, just before the park was established, approximately 800 people lived in and around Greenbrier Cove. Approximately 75 families lived here and the number of children totaled about 575.

Greenbrier Cove was also called the Whaley Settlement because so many Whaleys lived here. The Whaleys came to this country from England in the 1700s and settled in North Carolina. Around 1800, brothers William and Middleton Whaley crossed over Dry Sluice Gap, bound for Sevier County, Tennessee. From the gap, they descended along Porters Creek, arrived at Big Greenbrier Cove, and decided to stay. Soon they were joined by Ownbys, Proffitts, and others whose surnames are integrally linked with the Smokies. Through the late 1800s and early 1900s, Greenbrier expanded with schools, churches, mills, stores, even a hotel.

Hotel LeConte (also known as the Greenbrier Hotel) stood about 150 yards past the bridge at Ramsey Prong Road, in the broad "V" formed between Porters Creek and Middle Prong. Built by Kimsey Whaley and James West Whaley in 1925, the two-story hotel served visitors until 1935, when it was removed to accommodate the newly established national park.

Porches bordered three sides of each floor, and each floor had a bath with water piped in from the stream. The women took the downstairs bath, the men the upstairs. Coal-oil lamps lighted the small rooms and the screened dining room. Rates averaged $1.75 per day, and visitors came from all over the nation to hike, fish, and relax. During the 1930s, when Civilian Conservation Corps (CCC) Camp David Chapman was situated in the same area, CCC officials stayed at the hotel.

If Greenbrier Cove was once a center of the Smokies, Porters Creek—from its confluence with the Middle Prong of the Pigeon River up to Porters Flat—was Greenbrier's heart.

0.0 Gate. Just before the gate, William Whaley had a home on the far side of the creek. But there were so many Whaleys and so many William Whaleys—three on Porters Creek alone— that nicknames were attached so people knew which Whaley, Ownby, or Parton they were talking about.

The Whaley Family.

This William Whaley was called Whitehead Bill Whaley. Farther up Porters Creek lived Vander Bill Whaley and Booger Bill Whaley. "Vander Bill" is a play on the name Vanderbilt, because that particular Bill Whaley had left Greenbrier for a

period and returned with money to spend. "Booger Bill" got his
nickname because "he laid around and wouldn't shave."

Mary and David Proffitt, buried in the Ownby Cemetery on
Porters Creek, lived opposite Whitehead Bill on this side of the
creek. Proffitt, who had one of the best farms in Greenbrier,
also had a sawmill on Porters Creek that he owned with
Pinkney Whaley.

From the gate up to the hiking cabin and barn, a mile away,
the trail is broad and level, still used by the Park Service as a
road to maintain the historic structures. Along the way, it is
easy to see why Greenbrier settlers felt they lived in paradise.
Shaded by hemlock and rhododendron, Porters Creek tumbles
over boulders greened by moss. Witch-hazel and dog-hobble
fill the steep bank, which is dotted with trillium, geranium,
daisies, ferns, violets, may-apple, and other wildflowers.
Farther up, dogwoods hang over the bank where toothwort
and squirrel corn nod delicately. Along this stretch of creek
Vander Bill Whaley had a gristmill.

0.4 Elbert Cantrell homesite. Remnants of rock wall appear on
the right. Soon, a four-foot-high wall is breached by a set of
well-made stone steps, now flanked by clumps of Solomon's
seal. The steps lead to a path through the flat, former clearing
where the Elbert Cantrell family lived. The remains of a chimney as well as building foundations lie next to the path.
Beyond the farthest part of the rock wall runs a spring, which
must have provided easy access to water.

Cantrell, who lived here in the early 1900s, was a photographer as well as a farmer. Evolena Ownby, who lived farther up

Porters Creek, said in her memoirs, "You might go into any home of anyone who lived in Big Greenbrier and find a picture that Elbert Cantrell made."

The trail continues its gentle ascent past rock walls both parallel and perpendicular. Just before the bridge, Vander Bill and Sally Jane Whaley lived with their ten children. The Whaley children—both girls and boys—built some of the walls that remain. This homesite was their second place on Porters Creek, and it was known for its quality workmanship and its fine views. Their first, just above Ownby Cemetery, became a one-room school known as Granny College.

0.7 Vehicular bridge across Long Branch.

0.8 Ownby Cemetery. A set of stone and concrete steps—not as fine as the Cantrell's—leads up to Ownby Cemetery, which contains 23 graves. David Proffitt (1846-1909), a veteran of the Civil War whose farm and mill stood near the trailhead gate, lies here. Joel Ownby, who owned the Granny College property just above the cemetery, lies here, too.

Across the creek from Ownby Cemetery lived Sam and Sarah Ownby. In 1912, they had moved from Ramsey Prong to a one-room house with a lean-to kitchen on 85 acres along Porters Creek. Here, they raised a large family. They also raised most of their food, said Evolena, the second oldest. In her memoirs, she says:

"There were other things our family did to bring in a few pennies. In the fall we would pick up bushels of chestnuts and sell them…. I have picked up chestnuts on my way to school and taken them to the store and bought my pencils and paper; sometimes candy and crackers. Wherever Daddy lived he wanted an orchard. We had apples, peaches, plums, and grapes."

The Ownbys had the first "turning plow" in the area and were proud that their children never lacked shoes in winter. Even though Evolena was admonished for her flapper haircut in the 1920s, she, like most who lived in the mountains, cleaved to her religion. From Granny College in Greenbrier, she went on to earn a degree from New Orleans Theological Seminary.

0.9 A stand of young hemlocks indicates that this area was once cleared, probably part of the former homesite that included Granny College. Before the Civil War, "Humpy" John Ownby built two large, one-room log houses here, the houses joined by a rock chimney and a porch that spanned the front of both. During the Civil War some Confederates, who were run out of Gatlinburg, destroyed all of Ownby's bees and honey on their way south.

Ownby also saw two of his sons die of typhoid in the house that stood here. Although typhoid was often a threat, it and other infectious diseases always struck Smokies' communities particularly hard after wars, when soldiers returned home, bringing in disease.

The house was passed down, eventually, to Vander Bill Whaley. He bought the house and 80 acres for $600 and made the first half of his payment by barter: a team of mules and a new wagon.

Vander Bill moved his family to the new house he built just below Ownby Cemetery, then moved his aging father and step-mother, Reverend Bradford Whaley and "Granny" Catherine Brown Whaley, into the old house here. After they died, he successfully petitioned Sevier County to provide a teacher if he provided the house. Porters Creek parents said the school down in Greenbrier was too crowded and too far for children to walk. The school became known as Granny College, after Granny Catherine. The first teacher was a high school student who taught first through eighth grades.

A footpath on the right leads to the remains of an old, rusting car. Although cars were not common, they came into the cove in the 1920s. Evolena Ownby said that her brother-in-law, Mark Naugher, was the first to have a car in Greenbrier. In 1922, he drove it back from Sevierville over 21 miles of bad road.

0.95 A footlog crosses Sand Branch on the right edge of the maintenance road.

The John Messer cantilever barn in 1935.

1.0 Porters Flat. The maintenance road ends here in a broad turn-around. Bear right toward the sign: "Historic Farm Site, 200 Yards." This path leads to the Messer barn and the historic hiking club cabin. Following the turn-around less than a quarter-turn beyond, Brushy Mountain Trail intersects on the right. At the back of the turn-around, Porters Creek Trail continues up the mountain.

Historic Farm Site. The land originally belonged to the Cherokee and some accounts say that Cherokees lived here well into the 1800s. Perhaps that is why settlers called the Porters Flat area "Indian Nation." This property passed from Ownby to Whaley to Messer and, finally, to the park in 1929. Pinkney Whaley built the barn about 1875.

Pinkney Whaley, a first cousin to Vander Bill Whaley, was a blacksmith, wagon-maker, and logger, as well as a farmer. He logged the big tuliptrees from Porters Flat for one of the early logging companies: Scottish Lumber and Land Company, which cut mostly tuliptrees and white pine between 1890 and 1900. John W. Messer owned the property after Pinkney, so the barn bears his name.

Measuring about 25-by-45 feet, the barn is a cantilevered structure, a classy type of barn. Few are found outside eastern Tennessee, yet a large number of the older barns in eastern

The Smoky Mountain Hiking Club cabin shortly after restoration in 1935.

Tennessee's Sevier and Blount counties are cantilevered. Plenty of hay could be stored on the overhanging upper floor. Below, cribs sheltered horses and milk cows. The deep eaves and drive-through allowed farmers to protect vehicles and equipment and to shelter cattle in particularly bad weather.

On the far side of the barn, the path passes a spring and springhouse decorated by daffodils, which are always a sign of human habitation in the Smokies. When the Whaley clan lived at Porters Flat, cabins, barns, orchards, cornfields, vegetable gardens, livestock, small gristmills, and other signs of rural life were part of the picture.

About 50 feet from the springhouse stands the former Smoky Mountain Hiking Club cabin, whose entrance is announced by boxwoods, another type of ornamental planted by settlers. During the late 1920s, the Smoky Mountain Hiking Club had been looking for the perfect place for a club cabin. Members asked the National Park Service if they could restore a cabin at Porters Flat, and they were granted a lease to 1981.

When they set to work, all that was left of the Messer cabin was the chimney. So, between 1934 and 1935, working on weekends and vacations, club members used logs from other Whaley cabins to build this two-room cabin on either side of the original chimney. For about 50 years, club members used the "Cabin in the Brier" as a central point for club hikes.

Return to the main trail, which passes the junction for Brushy Mountain Trail. Continue in the direction of the sign that says 2.7 miles to Campsite 31. From this point on, Porters Creek Trail does not exhibit any historic sites, but the natural beauties are bountiful.

1.5 Porters Creek footbridge. Between the historic farm and the footbridge, the trail is flanked by forest, deep and tall. Rhododendron and violets crowd banks along the path. The long footbridge allows a close-up view of Porters Creek, which tumbles exuberantly, spraying whitewater over huge boulders.

In the spring, masses of fringed phacelia mantle the forest floor like white lace. Squirrel corn and delicate bishop's cap add their flowers to this study in white. As the trail switch-backs upward, hepatica, geranium, stonecrop, speckled wood lily, and several types of trillium are just some of the wildflowers that fill this part of the hike with delight.

It is hard to imagine that, like most of the Smokies, Porters Creek was heavily logged. By the early 1900s, the best hardwoods had been cut and, by 1916, 738 acres of this drainage looked like a wasteland, the results of repeated fires fueled by tinder-dry piles of brush. After World War I, Champion Fibre Company bought these tracts to hold as part of a forest reserve, which they planned to log later. When it became parkland, the area was permanently protected.

1.8 Fern Branch Falls. From a bluff 50 feet above, Fern Branch Falls gracefully cascades down a dark rock wall. A steep path on the left of the trail approaches the base of the falls, which are named for relatively rare walking ferns, whose long green blades stretch out like fingers. Wherever a "fingertip" touches down, a new fern becomes rooted. Beyond the falls, the trail continues to ascend through cove hardwoods. Eventually, Porters Creek rises to meet the trail.

3.6 Backcountry Campsite Number 31. Under a canopy of hemlocks, the flat area of the campground suggests this was once inhabited, perhaps by a logging camp. This is the end of the hike. But, in the mid-1800s, near the headwaters of Porters Creek above, Perry Shults is said to have had a hidden mine.

"A lot of people back then would see him coming out of the mountains with silver and gold," said Nadine Oakley, Shults's great-granddaughter. "He always had silver dollars in his pocket."

In 1867, Sevier County issued Perry Shults a 99-year lease on mineral rights around the headwaters of Porters Creek. Every year, Perry Shults and his wife traveled from their home near Pittman Center up Porters Creek, taking a different route each time to keep his mine location hidden. Just below the mine he made his wife sit on a rock and wait for him.

Former park historian Ed Trout said that the Tennessee side of the Smokies holds no appreciable mineral wealth. Some say Shults found a cache of coins from the Civil War. Whatever his source of silver, Shults made counterfeit half-dollars with a higher silver content than the real thing. The Secret Service set out to investigate, but when he heard they were coming, Shults headed west and disappeared. He died without leaving a map to his mine.

While plowing their garden, later owners of his Pittman Center property purported to uncover a cache of coins worth $37,000. To this day, the Shults mine and the source of Shults's silver are still a mystery.

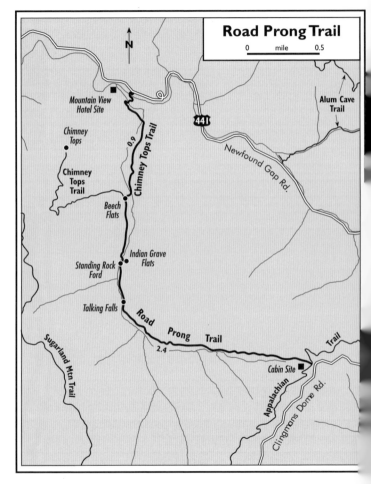

Road Prong Trail

0   mile   0.5

N

Mountain View Hotel Site

Chimney Tops

Chimney Tops Trail

Chimney Tops Trail

0.9

Beech Flats

Indian Grave Flats

Standing Rock Ford

Talking Falls

Road Prong Trail

2.4

Alum Cave Trail

441

Newfound Gap Rd.

Sugarland Mtn Trail

Cabin Site

Appalachian Trail

Clingmans Dome Rd.

ROAD PRONG TRAIL

DIRECTIONS: From Sugarlands Visitor Center, take Newfound
Gap Road (U.S. 441) 6.7 miles south. Or, from Newfound
Gap, take Newfound Gap Road 6.3 miles north. Park in the
Chimney Tops parking area. The first 0.9 mile will be on the
Chimney Tops Trail.

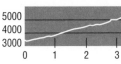

LENGTH: 6.5 miles. This hike goes
from the Chimney Tops trailhead to
Indian Gap on Clingmans Dome
Road and back (3.3 miles, one way):
Chimney Tops trailhead to Road Prong Trail junction, 0.9 mile;
Road Prong Trail to Indian Gap, 2.4 miles. (Road Prong Trail
also can be a one-way hike by parking a car at each end.)

PHYSICAL PROFILE: Near the top of the Smokies, Road Prong
Trail rises steadily, sometimes steeply, passing a range of
exquisite scenery. The hike includes a number of easy rock-
hops over the stream, plus one challenging stream crossing,
which might equal wet feet. This trail makes a good choice for
summer into autumn, when water levels are generally lower.

CULTURAL PROFILE: This trail was old when the Cherokee used
it. Although it is one of the oldest trails in the park and a
number of dramatic incidents occurred here, no historic artifacts remain and hikers will have to use their imaginations
for Road Prong's cultural history.

*R*outes over these rugged and jumbled mountains have
always been few. Even today, only one road, Newfound
Gap Road, crests the range. Before settlers of European descent
came to the Smokies, Indians wore a route over the back of the

mountains. Perhaps they were following an old game trail. Most early roads in the United States began as game trails, became well worn with Indian use, were widened to accommodate wagons, and, finally, were paved in the age of automobiles.

Road Prong was part of the ancient Indian Gap Trail, which perhaps pre-dated the Cherokee. But the Cherokee defined the route. Hiram C. Wilburn, the first park historian, said that it is the oldest known Indian trail in the Smokies. And it remained the only road over the Smokies until the 1920s, when Newfound Gap Road was built.

Indian Gap Trail connected the Great Indian War Path with the Rutherford War Trace. The first trail traversed the great valley of east Tennessee; the second traversed the basin between the Blue Ridge and Balsam mountains in western North Carolina. From Sevierville, Tennessee, the trail connecting the two followed the West Prong of the Little Pigeon River up to Indian Gap. On the North Carolina side, it followed the Oconaluftee River down to Whittier.

As early as 1765, white traders lived among the Cherokee at Nununyi, a town along Indian Gap Trail. Then the Cherokee allied themselves with the English during the Revolutionary War. In 1776, a detachment from General Griffith Rutherford's army headed up toward Indian Gap and destroyed the old Cherokee town.

In 1832, North Carolina gave the go-ahead to build a road from Indian Gap down to what became known as Smokemont. When the road was finished, in 1839, the Oconaluftee Turnpike Company charged road tolls: 75 cents for a six-horse wagon, 6.25 cents for a horse and rider, 2 cents for each head

Veterans of the Thomas Legion.

of cattle, and 1 cent for each hog or sheep. Many of the travelers were drovers from Tennessee and Kentucky driving livestock down to markets in the cotton-growing lowlands of
North and South Carolina.

In the mid-1850s, Arnold Guyot, the Swiss geographer
assigned by the Smithsonian to explore the Smokies, saw the
road and had this to say: It was the "only one tolerable road,
or rather mule path, connecting Sevierville, Tennessee, with
Webster in Jackson County, North Carolina." He did note that
the mountain pass could be of strategic value. And it was, during the Civil War.

Chimney Tops Trail

0.0 Chimney Tops Trail. In ascending the first 0.9 mile, the trail crosses four bridges, the first over Walker Camp Prong, the rest over Road Prong. The two streams meet here to form the West Prong of the Little Pigeon River. Mountain laurel, bursting with pink-and-white blooms in late spring, overhangs the boulder-tumbled, rushing waters. Rhododendron, dog-hobble, and a wealth of wildflowers crowd together under the forest canopy.

During the Civil War, about 1863, soldiers were encamped just below the confluence of Walker Camp Prong and Road Prong. Here, Colonel William H. Thomas commanded a group of North Carolina Confederates, 300 to 400 Cherokees, and about 500 Tennesseans who enlisted in the cause, although most of east Tennessee sympathized with the Union. Their job was to improve Oconaluftee Turnpike, which paralleled Road Prong down from Indian Gap, so that Confederates could make incursions. As protection against Union forces, they built breastworks and posted guards as they worked on the road. In 1916, the Mountain View Hotel, which accommodated mostly loggers and hunters, was built on the site of Thomas's camp.

During the Civil War, Colonel Thomas was in charge of a regiment that included two companies of Cherokees. He not only led Cherokee soldiers, he was also one of them. A white man, Thomas was raised by Chief Yonaguska as the chief's only son. Thomas lived with the Cherokee from 1820 to 1870, becoming their chief. After attaining a law degree, he fought for their land rights, one of the few who were successful in preserving some vestige of Cherokee land.

0.9 Road Prong Trail junction. Chimney Tops and Road Prong trails meet at Beech Flats.

Road Prong Trail

0.0 Road Prong Trail: Beech Flats. The open understory is full of grasses, which soften the edges of the trail. High above, yellow buckeye, yellow birch, and beech filter the light. In June, purple-fringed orchids put on a show among the grasses, ferns, and New York ironweed, which waits for its purple moment of beauty later in the summer.

Beech Flats' open aspect suggests past use. In the early 1900s, Three M Lumber Company logged this section of the Smokies and Beech Flats was the site of their original mill. Later, the company transferred operations to the Smokemont area in North Carolina. Until the 1930s, fenced meadows on the flats held grazing cattle. In not too many years, it will be hard to tell any human activity happened here at all.

From Beech Flats, the trail parallels Road Prong upward.

0.3 Indian Grave Flats. Benign, peaceful, with rhododendron shaded by hemlocks and a view of Mount Le Conte, this spot was once the scene of a murder. In the last days of the Civil War, Colonel George W. Kirk, a Confederate who joined the Union, led a band of renegades from Tennessee into North Carolina's Cataloochee Valley. Outraged by the killing, burning, and looting Kirk's raiders wreaked in Cataloochee, North Carolina Confederates, Cherokees, and farmers chased Kirk and his men back over the mountains.

But Kirk captured some Cherokees and used them as guides over rugged Indian Gap Trail. One of the Cherokees, who either would not or could not go any farther, was shot and left for dead near this spot. Confederates found the man, tried to help him, but he died. They buried him in a shallow grave in the flat area alongside Road Prong. Later, wild animals clawed out his remains and passersby saw the man's bleaching bones.

Indian Grave Flats, a clearing that also once held a homesite, is now thick with rhododendron. Just upstream—audible as well as visible—is Trickling Falls, where Road Prong tumbles prettily down stepped ledges of rock overhung by rhododendron.

0.4 Standing Rock Ford. The one challenging ford of Road Prong, Standing Rock Ford requires agile rock-hopping and some caution. Even so, wet feet are likely. On the other side, a 12-foot-high anvil of rock stands sentinel alongside the trail and gives the ford its name. Berry bushes, striped maple, and trillium line the rocky trail, which in wet weather may stream with an inch or two of water.

0.8 Talking Falls. The falls spray out in a noisy fan as the waters of Road Prong are forced between two large boulders. Along the trail grow Michaux's saxifrage, nettles, purple-fringed orchids, and colonies of umbrella leaf. It must not have seemed so attractive to the 19th-century South Carolinian who set out over Indian Gap against advice that a winter storm was approaching. The young man sought shelter under an overhanging rock near Talking Falls, and was found frozen to death there some days later. The trail continues upward, past fern and moss gardens that look like a sloping Garden of Eden.

1.2 A slight rise, a short descent, and the trail passes bluets and wood-sorrel. The scent of Fraser fir is a clue that the elevation is above 4,000 feet; in fact, about 4,600 feet. After four or five easy rock-hops over the stream, which has narrowed considerably, the trail passes a huge log pile, the result of Hurricane Opal in 1989.

Although the trail is less defined now than when it was the route over the Smokies, it was never a smooth road. Horace Kephart, who chronicled the lives of Smokies' mountaineers in *Our Southern Highlanders,* trekked from Smokemont over Indian Gap with a government agent sometime around 1905. The agent was after three moonshiners, a man and his sons. The moonshiners, or blockaders, had fled from North Carolina into the Sugarlands on the Tennessee side. Kephart wrote:

"Beyond was a steep and rocky trail, going down, down along a brawling torrent into the gloom of narrow gulfs that were choked with laurel and spruce and balsam. This was the beginning of the Sugarlands, a country of ill fame…known on our side of the mountains as Blockaders' Glory….

"The trail was what remained of a military road that had been made across the Smokies in the Civil War….We slipped and slid. The toes of our street shoes punished us. Rocks of all sizes everywhere. Any boulder less in size than a house we called a 'pebble.'"

2.0 The last half-mile through spruce-fir forest is fairly steep and rocky, but full of beauty, including flame azaleas and the fragrance of evergreens. Beauty was probably the last thing on Confederate General Zebulon Vance's mind. Earlier in the war, Colonel Thomas and his men had been driven from Tennessee by Union forces. Late in the war, the general had been ordered to make a show of strength by again penetrating Tennessee via Indian Gap.

In the cold of January 1864, soldiers took wheels and axles off their wagons to reassemble when they reached more level ground. They had to drag wagons and cannons down this road because even Colonel Thomas's prior work could not make Road Prong Trail less steep or much less rocky.

When Horace Kephart quoted writer James Lane Allen in *Our Southern Highlanders,* he might have had Road Prong Trail in mind:

"There are roads that make a man lose faith. It is known that the more pious companies of them, as they traveled along, would now and then give up in despair, sit down, raise a hymn, and have prayers before they could go further. Perhaps one of the provocations to homicide among the mountain people should be reckoned this road. I have seen two of the mildest of men, after riding over it for a few hours, lose their temper and begin to fight."

Today, the road is not an obstacle, but the goal, offering exercise, natural beauty, and a glimpse of history.

Senator Thomas Clingman.

2.4 Clingmans Dome Road. Road Prong Trail ends at a grassy meadow alongside Clingmans Dome Road. An interpretive sign shows what travel on the trail was like in the old days. Because roads over the mountains were so rough, it was often easier for horses to pull a sled over rocks and through creeks. Wagons were too likely to lose a wheel, and if a wheel broke…well, a sled was just less trouble on bad ground.

About 100 feet below Indian Gap stood a cabin, built around 1824. For more than 75 years, the cabin served as a meeting point for surveyors, cattle drovers, and others. Return by the same route to Chimney Tops parking lot.

INDEX OF PLACE NAMES AND PEOPLE

BIBLIOGRAPHY

Brewer, Carson. *Hiking in the Great Smokies*. Knoxville, TN: Newman/National, 1962; reprint, 1994.

Bush, Florence Cope. *Dorie: Woman of the Mountains*. Knoxville, TN: University of Tennessee Press, 1992; reprint, 1998.

Costner, Ella. *Song of Life in the Smokies*. Maryville, TN: The Brazos Press, 1971.

Davis, Hattie Caldwell. *Reflections of Cataloochee Valley and its Vanished People in the Great Smoky Mountains*. Maggie Valley, NC: by the author, 1999.

DeFoe, Don; Beth Giddens; and Steve Kemp, eds. *Hiking Trails of the Smokies*. Gatlinburg, TN: Great Smoky Mountains Association, 1994; revised, 1995.

Dunn, Durwood. *Cades Cove*. Knoxville, TN: University of Tennessee Press, 1988.

Dykeman, Wilma. *At Home In The Smokies*. Washington, DC: National Park Service, 1984.

Frome, Michael. *Strangers in High Places*. Knoxville, TN: University of Tennessee Press, 1966; reprint, 1980.

Kephart, Horace. *Our Southern Highlanders*. New York: The Macmillan Company, 1913; Knoxville, TN: University of Tennessee Press, 1984.

Oliver, Duane. *Hazel Creek From Then Till Now*. By the author, 1989.

Powers, Elizabeth, with Mark Hannah. *Cataloochee: Lost Settlement of the Smokies*. Charleston, SC: Powers-Hannah Publishers, 1982.

Sherrick, Everett. *Trails of Invitation*. Sevierville, TN: The Mountain Press, 1996.

Shields, A. Randolph. *The Cades Cove Story.* Gatlinburg, TN: Great
   Smoky Mountains Association, 1977; reprint, 1981.

Smith, Mary Bell. *In the Shadow of the White Rock.* Boone, NC:
   Minor's Publishing Company, 1979.

Trout, Ed. *Historic Buildings of the Smokies.* Gatlinburg, TN: Great
   Smoky Mountains Association, 1995.

Tyson, Lona Parton. *Reflections of the Pinnacle: Story of the Parton
   Roots.* Gatlinburg, TN: Crescent Printing Company, 1986.

Weals, Vic. *Last Train to Elkmont.* Knoxville, TN: Olden Press,
   1993.

Williams, Michael Ann. *Great Smoky Mountains Folklife.* Jackson,
   MS: University Press of Mississippi, 1995.

Wise, Kenneth. *Hiking Trails of the Great Smoky Mountains.*
   Knoxville, TN: University of Tennessee Press, 1996.

ABOUT THE AUTHOR

Michal Strutin has been involved with natural and cultural history from her time as an editor at *Outside* and *National Parks* magazines. Her books include *Discovering Natural Israel*, *Grist Mills of the Smokies*, two volumes of *Smithsonian Guides to Natural America*, and the award-winning *Places of Grace: the Natural Landscapes of the American Midwest*, with photographer Gary Irving. *Chaco: a Cultural Legacy* and *A Guide to Northern Plains Indians*, both written for the national parks, focus on cultural history.

Strutin has worked for *Rolling Stone* magazine and written for the *New York Times*, *Modern Maturity*, and many others. She is an avid gardener, and her love of the outdoors has taken her into backcountry areas across America and abroad. She lives with her husband near the Great Smoky Mountains in east Tennessee.